SANTA BARBARA
A GUIDE TO EL PUEBLO VIEJO

Revised and updated second edition

By
Rebecca Conard, Ph.D.,
Mary Louise Days,
Christopher H. Nelson, Ph.D.,
Richard E. Oglesby, Ph.D.

Introductions by
David Gebhard, Ph.D., first edition, and
Richard E. Oglesby, Ph.D., second edition

Published by The Santa Barbara Conservancy

The Graphic Communication Institute
California Polytechnic University, San Luis Obispo, California
2016

"Project: A Typical Block of State Street, West Side" – Allied Architects Association of Los Angeles, 1925

Copyright 2016
Published by The Santa Barbara Conservancy
Santa Barbara, California
SBConservancy.com

ISBN 978-1-889937-25-0

Publisher's Cataloging-in-Publication
(Provided by Quality Books, Inc.)

    Conard, Rebecca, author.
      Santa Barbara : a guide to El Pueblo Viejo / by
    Rebecca Conard, Mary Louise Days, Christopher H. Nelson,
    Richard E. Oglesby ; introductions by David Gebhard,
    first edition, and Richard E. Oglesby, second edition.
    -- Revised and updated second edition.
      pages cm
      Includes bibliographical references and index.
      ISBN 978-1-889937-25-0

      1. Architecture--California--Santa Barbara--
    Guidebooks. 2. Buildings--California--Santa Barbara--
    Guidebooks. 3. Santa Barbara (Calif.)--Buildings,
    structures, etc.--Guidebooks. 4. Street names--
    California--Santa Barbara--Guidebooks. 5. Santa Barbara
    (Calif.)--Guidebooks. 6. Guidebooks. I. Days, Mary
    Louise, author. II. Nelson, Christopher H., author.
    III. Oglesby, Richard Edward, 1931- author, writer of
    introduction. IV. Gebhard, David, writer of
    introduction. V. Title.

    NA735.S42C66 2016   720.9794'91
                   QBI16-900027

Indexing by Amron Gravett, Wild Clover Book Services
Printed in Korea by Four Colour Print Group, Louisville, Kentucky

Table of Contents

Credits

SANTA BARBARA
A GUIDE TO EL PUEBLO VIEJO
2016 Second Edition

Committee
Mary Louise Days, Steve Hausz, Michael H. Imwalle, David P. Jones,
Richard E. Oglesby, Ph.D., Judith D. Orias, Donald G. Sharpe

Photography
David P. Jones

Graphic Design, Production Management
Steve Hausz

Landscape Historian
Susan Chamberlin

Special Assistance
Donald Olson, Fermina Murray

Dedication

This second edition book is dedicated with affection and respect to the memory of Miss Pearl Chase, who, from 1920 to 1979, was instrumental in preserving and beautifying the El Pueblo Viejo area of Santa Barbara, and who inspired a community to recognize and protect its architectural and landscape heritage. It is also dedicated to the late Louise Boucher who was a tireless steward of this heritage and who worked to preserve the aesthetic character of our city. Mrs. Boucher and the late David Gebhard were deeply involved in preparation of the first edition of *Santa Barbara ~ A Guide to El Pueblo Viejo.*

Pearl Chase   *Louise Boucher*

Financial Assistance

Financial assistance for production of this publication was provided by the Rossi Family Foundation; Joe Rution; Susette Naylor; Reina del Mar Parlor No. 126, Native Daughters of the Golden West; William Wood; Jeannie de la Guerra Davis; Brooks and Stella Larson; Donald Olson and Nancy Franco; Orias Family; Richard E. Oglesby; Santa Barbara Trust for Historic Preservation; Allied Neighborhoods Association; Fermina Murray; Keith J. Mautino; Sheila Lodge; Mary Louise Days; Santa Barbara Parlor No.116, Native Sons of the Golden West; Reid and Robin Cederlof; Omega Financial Group, LLC; John and Michael Self; Lynn P. Kirst; Fred L. Sweeney; Volentine Family Foundation; City of Santa Barbara; Kent Hodgetts and Tanny Keeler; American Riviera Bank; The Towbes Foundation; LMA Architects; Sue Adams; Don and Kay Sharpe; Stephen C. Murray; Paul and Virginia Hernadi; Dick and Carol Nash; Richard and Mimi Gunner, Santa Barbara Inn; William R. LaVoie, Architect; Anna Marie Gott; Patricia Gott; The Pearl Chase Society; Architectural Foundation of Santa Barbara; Kellam de Forest; Michael and Terri Imwalle; Wm. Howard Wittausch, A.I.A.; NS Ceramic; Citizens Planning Association.

The Santa Barbara Conservancy is grateful for their generosity.

Acknowledgements

We wish to thank the following individuals and organizations for their generous assistance during the preparation of this second edition of *Santa Barbara ~ A Guide to El Pueblo Viejo*.

Santa Barbara Trust for Historic Preservation, the Presidio Research Center, David Jones, Kristina W. Foss, Michael Redmon and the Gledhill Library, Betsy R. Cramer, Fermina Murray, Ronald Nye, Ph.D., Susan Chamberlin, Richard Redmond, Stella Larson, Jaime Limon, Nicole Hernandez, Penelope Tinker, David Bolton, W. Howard Wittausch, Richard Six, several members of the City Planning Division counter staff and the Public Library reference section, Anne Petersen, Ph.D., Charles Varni, Ph.D., William LaVoie, D. Duffy Smith, Lawrence Thompson, Brian Cearnal, Luke Swetland, Charles N. Johnson and Gary Kurutz, Lynn T. Brittner, Mitzi Clayton, John R. Johnson, Ph.D., Ernestine De Soto, Pam Boehr, Bill Dedman, Cherie Chako, Virginia Guess, Ph.D., Peter Becker, Jocelyn Gibbs, Jill Sattler, Ricardo Sepulveda, Tanny Keeler, Julie and Adam Ross, Tom Schmidt, Bill Dewey, Jim Bartsch, Sue Adams, Fred L. Sweeney, Kathleen Brewster, Tara Rizzi, Robert Ooley, F.A.I.A., Shelley Bookspan, Ph.D., Milford Wayne Donaldson, F.A.I.A., Henry Lenny, Paul Casey, George Buell, Sue Gray, Jeff Shelton, Mark Shields, Wayne McCall, Susette Naylor, Nancy McAleer Golden, Bill's Copy Shop, Rachael Boyer, Laurie Hannah, Dominique Samario, Michael Hall Gray, Douglas Campbell, Mark Shields, Roy Regester, Oswald Da Ros, Tina Pedotti

An Explanatory Note to Users

The buildings and sites described in this guide are located in the City of Santa Barbara's El Pueblo Viejo ("the old town") Landmark District plus a limited geographical area outside the district boundaries. El Pueblo Viejo's irregular boundaries extend through the downtown and along the waterfront. It also includes the neighborhood of Mission Santa Barbara, Mission Historical Park, the 1891 stone bridge, and the Santa Barbara Museum of Natural History. Entries contained herein are arranged so as to divide this large district into smaller sections that can easily be covered on foot if the reader chooses to use the book as a walking tour guide.

Brief historical overviews introduce each of four areas: the Oceanfront, State Street Plaza, the Presidio and Pueblo, and the Mission. The State Street Plaza and Presidio and Pueblo represent the downtown section of El Pueblo Viejo, the latter further divided into two subsections: East of State and West of State.

For each entry, the historic name (usually the building name when built or name of an owner) appears after the street address. Later names are shown in parentheses. Names of the architect or designer, if known at the time of this writing, are given on the same line as the date of construction. Construction dates for listed buildings are given as determined from available source materials. Where it has not been possible to ascertain an exact date, the abbreviation "ca." is given in front of an approximate date.

If a building has been designated officially as a historic place, the appropriate designation(s) appear in abbreviated form at the end of the text.

NHL	National Historic Landmark
NR	National Register of Historic Places
NRD	National Register of Historic Places District
CHL	California Historic Landmark
SBL	City of Santa Barbara Landmark
SBSM	City of Santa Barbara Structure of Merit

Please note that many private residences have been included in this book. Their inclusion here does not give the viewer permission to trespass on private property. Retail businesses, museums, and public buildings are open to visitors at regularly established hours.

A Master Map of the city of Santa Barbara follows the introductions to the 1st and 2nd editions of the book. This map depicts the discontiguous boundary of El Pueblo Viejo Landmark District, as well as a key to the areas of the city covered in this book. Following the historic overview for each area is a numerical listing of the buildings and sites, and the map(s) for that area. All of the entries in the book (except for the very last) appear on the map(s) accompanying each section of the book, and each map has a key map indicating the area of the city represented. As the map areas may overlap, numbers for entries on adjacent maps are grayed, and there is an indication of the map number for the adjacent maps.

Introduction to Second Edition

Richard E. Oglesby

In his eloquent introduction to the original edition of *Santa Barbara ~ A Guide to El Pueblo Viejo*, the late Dr. David Gebhard carefully chronicled the tortuous path taken by the city toward development of a unified approach to the planning, composition and general architecture of Santa Barbara. While several other places went through a similar process, especially during the City Planning Movement of the early 20th Century, most of them failed while Santa Barbara went on to become, and remain, an extraordinary success story. Why that happened, Dr. Gebhard perceptively noted, and, if it were to endure, had to keep happening, was the vital activity of a group of private activists operating within the overall agreement on the part of the rest of the community. It all came together after the earthquake of 1925 offered the opportunity to put into practice the ideas that had been percolating for so long. Santa Barbara was the first city, for example, to create an Architectural Board of Review with the power to influence the course of development. It was already in existence in 1925 and helped ensure that the principles established during the City's rebuilding after the earthquake would endure. Santa Barbara went on to add other institutions affecting planning and historic preservation to give official voice to the general public, and to continually educate that public as to the virtues of relating the built environment to the physical situation of the city, and the worth of presenting a common appearance to the rest of the world. Embraced by the public, city government, and the planning, preservation and architectural communities, Santa Barbara created for itself an Hispanic architectural theme, and coupled it with such things as height limits on downtown structures, landscaping requirements, even to such details as paint colors to maintain the beautiful face it presents to the world. The city continued to embrace that notion down to the publication of the first edition of this book, an amazing accomplishment considering the revolutionary changes in population, technology and attitude that took place after 1925.

Dr. Gebhard would, I think, be enormously pleased to see that, more than a quarter-century after he wrote, the City of Santa Barbara continues to maintain its control over development within El Pueblo Viejo, with its institutions intact and its general architectural expression still the Hispanic motif. Not only does the Mission still stand as the most important architectural influence on the City, supplemented by the County Courthouse, once touted locally as "the most beautiful building in America," but they are gradually being reinforced by the ongoing efforts of the Santa Barbara Trust for Historic Preservation to reconstruct portions of the 1782 Presidio. That is not to say that the road to the 21st Century has been smooth. Some structures that appeared in the first edition have been lost over that span of time. The present editors have added other structures, both old and new, that enhance the city, and have even included buildings outside the boundaries of El Pueblo Viejo to indicate that the unique beauty that is Santa Barbara is not simply limited to the downtown area. Battles are still being fought continuously over all the original issues, density probably being the most contentious as population pressures and limited space militate toward taller and denser development. Especially noteworthy is the fact that some contemporary architects have not only embraced the Hispanic idiom, but have created innovative designs which not only carry on the theme, but adapt it to modern needs and requirements. Further, they have joined with the general population to show respect for the overall environment of the city, cradled as it is between the mountains and the sea, so that some of these large structures do not impose themselves on the setting. Rather, they fit unobtrusively into it, adding their individuality to the whole without dominating it, and providing a classic example of the built environment complementing the natural one.

Whether Santa Barbara is a shining example of what might be accomplished in other places, or is simply the unique combination of a wonderful natural setting recognized, embraced and complemented by a particular population acting on an unprecedented opportunity is for others to decide. Santa Barbara has incorporated its past into its present and, hopefully, through its established institutions, continuously engaged population and City General Plan, will carry the city's individual signature on into the future. In the meantime, this volume will introduce the reader to the various elements that have made the name Santa Barbara synonymous with gracious living and perhaps stimulate others to adapt the city's experience to their own situations.

Richard E. Oglesby, 2016

Introduction to First Edition

David Gebhard

"Beautiful buildings surrounded by ugliness partake of the ugliness and their beauty is impaired. So it is with all American cities where there is no architectural control," so noted Herbert Hoover in 1931.[1] Mr. Hoover, then President of the United States, was a frequent visitor to Santa Barbara and had often spoken with warmth, understanding and approval of the community's effort, not only to control its architecture, but to create a specific image by adhering to the architectural forms associated with its factual and mythical Hispanic past. Considering its relative remoteness, and smallness, it is surprising how important a position Santa Barbara has occupied within the history of twentieth century American planning and architecture.

It was, as Thomas W. MacKesey of the American Institute of Planners pointed out in 1939, the first community in America to set up a municipal Board of Architectural Review by law.[2] It was also among the earliest of the American cities to press for a uniform architectural expression; and finally it is one of the regrettably small number of American communities which has continually sought to control closely its planning and architecture for well over half a Century. While it would be admitted that those fifty-plus years of architectural controls in Santa Barbara have experienced blemishes and flaws, still it is a remarkable record when one takes into account not only the tremendous social and economic changes which have occurred in these decades, but also the appreciable shifts which have come about in planning and architecture.

We tend to look back to the 1920s exclusively in terms of its enthusiastic commitment to laissez-faireism, of Calvin Coolidge's "The business of America is business"; but the twenties was as well the decade during which the professional planning of American cities really began to take place.[3] Planning and architectural controls though could only be realized after the ground had been prepared so there was a consensus that a community should be carefully planned. Here too, the Santa Barbara experience looms large in the history of American planning. Many American communities have experienced intense but brief sallies into well thought out planning schemes, and even into the more difficult areas of architectural controls.

Most of these have ended up as an ideal, not as a realized fact; for most were never allowed to leave the printed pages of a planning document. And for those that did, their effective life has, in most instances, been all too brief.

Santa Barbara has frequently been cited as the one community which prepared the ground for planning, architectural controls, and preservation, and once these concepts had been initiated, concerted effort was made to continue the education processes so that there would (hopefully) always be a broad basis of support.[4] Santa Barbara's experience with planning and architectural control pointedly indicates that a consensus of support can seldom if ever be the result of governmental activities. No professional planner or elected public body can create, let alone maintain, such a unanimity of purpose. To establish a long-lasting continuity of community support for planning, the urge must come from the citizens themselves. Santa Barbara's decades of affirmative results in architectural control narrow down, as we should expect, to the biographies of a number of its dedicated citizens. But it would be a mistake to see the maintenance of community support for planning and architectural controls in Santa Barbara solely in terms of the activities of its few dedicated women and men. The crucial questions are: How has it been possible to carry on this effective continuity of community involvement and support for over half a century? Is there something in this process which could be applied to other American communities, or is this phenomenon so special to Santa Barbara that it would be difficult to realize elsewhere?

At least a suggestion of answers to these and other questions can be provided by seeing what Santa Barbara was seeking to accomplish through planning and architectural controls, to understand how this was accomplished, and finally to appraise its successes and failures.

The effort to preserve and enhance Santa Barbara's Hispanic tradition was not an exclusive invention of the 1920s. As early as 1874, the editor of the *Santa Barbara Daily Press* noted, "The old landmarks and the most charming characteristics of Santa Barbara are disappearing before the march of 'improvements,' and though our practical people cannot move mountains, nor change scenes, nor spoil climate, they are doing all they can to despoil the quaint beauty of the place and make it just [another] commonplace American town."[5] Though such concerns were voiced on and off in the years that followed, it was in the twenties that a concerted effort was made to halt the unbridled "improvements" that were despoiling the city's character.

The planner, Charles H. Cheney, who was early involved in the initial steps of planning and architectural control in Santa Barbara in the early 1920s, set down what was first needed: "Plan for individual character. Every city, county or region has something of its very own, of life and subtle character, individuality. This is most precious. Its presentation and enhancement is the prime duty of every planner."[6] To translate this ideal into a readable physical artifact was, of course, the next step. The design of cities, of gardens, and of buildings are realized through readable agreed-upon images. A special sense of place can be most readily recognized by the unusual features of its natural physical environment, and by the imagery utilized in its planning schemes, its landscape architecture, and in the design of its buildings. The way in which we manipulate the latter can, as we are all aware, enhance or destroy the former. Mountains and hills, rivers and bays may remain, but carelessness can minimize or obliterate their contributions to the sense of the uniqueness of place.

From the early 1890s on Southern Californians became increasingly concerned with the question of enhancing an environment which should be distinct from the rest of the United States. Caroline L. Overman indicates the self-consciousness of Californians when she wrote, "...that whatever architecture in the semi-arid region is destined to become, it will not be commonplace and it will not follow the fashion set by other portions of the country."[7] What was distinct about California, in addition to its climate and natural environment, was its Hispanic tradition, expressed especially through its nineteenth century adobe houses, its renowned mission churches, and its receptivity to luscious tropical and semi-tropical horticulture. Out of these ingredients evolved one of America's first major regional architectural styles, that of the Mission Revival.[8] This romantic sense of historic continuity was then the device which was openly used in California to suggest that this was a special geographic environment which fulfilled Cheney's dictum, that it has "...something of its own, of life and subtle character, individuality."

Bit by bit the Hispanic language of adobes and of the mission churches was enriched by landscape and architectural images inspired by Mexico, Spain, Moorish North Africa, and of the Mediterranean shores of France and Italy. With its strong Hispanic inheritance it should not be a surprise that the city of Santa Barbara fully participated in this regional desire to create a distinct geographic personality. For Santa Barbarans, though, the question was not only how the city might contribute to the regional quality of Southern California, but how the community itself could emerge with its own distinct personality. From the beginning it was seen that this goal could become reality only if it were initiated and sustained by private individuals and organizations, who would on the one hand educate the citizenry and on the other would work closely with the elected and appointed officials of local government. It was also seen from the beginning that this goal could only come about if planning, landscape architecture, and architecture were approached as a single unified problem. The city itself was to be the designed artifact. Streets, parks, gardens, and buildings were individual components whose task was to contribute to the cityscape. By 1931 Cheney could look back and comment, "Santa Barbara is another instance where cooperation of minds and efforts toward preserving the early Spanish style of architecture already possessed by the city, is giving beauty and individuality to a community that seemed just a few years ago destined to be just another ordinary city."[9]

Although Santa Barbara's historic borrowings of the twenties and later were as diverse and catholic as the rest of Southern California, still in the end there was a marked difference; for the dominant theme of its urban and suburban architecture was inspired by the vernacular buildings and gardens of Spain's rural environment and small towns, supplemented by similar examples from Mexico. This reliance upon simplicity of volumes and surfaces accounts not only for the initial success of the Spanish Colonial Revival in Santa Barbara during the 1920s, but it also explains why this historic interpretation was able to weather the ins and outs of architectural fashion, from the 1930s to the present. These "painterly" Hispanic buildings of Santa Barbara provided a connection between high and low art, and between the traditional and the then newly emerging Modem. Santa Barbara's abstract version of the Hispanic had a remarkable variety of advantages ranging from economy of cost to the importance of landscaping as a foil for these simple forms.

The earliest of Santa Barbara's efforts to establish a distinct image dates from 1909, when a group of its citizens formed the Civic League, and engaged the nationally known planner Charles Mulford Robinson.[10] At the beginning of his report Robinson pointed out that since "...there is no manufacturing section to be developed, and catered to, at whatever sacrifice to aesthetic charm...," that the community could concentrate on "...the enhancement of the city's attractiveness." While Robinson did not directly discuss architectural controls in his report, he did indicate that regulations should be adopted which would establish guidelines for design of commercial and residential streets, the accompanying landscaping, setbacks, etc. He was emphatic that public and private landscaping should be one of the principal devices to enhance the unique physical setting of this community.

It was the half dozen years after 1919 that planning and architecture in Santa Barbara reached fruition. The process was at the beginning a private one initiated in 1920 by the Santa Barbara Community Arts Association.[11] The individuals who organized and directed this private organization pursued a thoughtful, but low-keyed planned program. The three elements in this program were: to formulate specific proposals which could serve as the basis for legislative action by the City and the County; to bring about through education a solid consensus of its citizens; and finally to prevail upon the City and County governments to enact the needed legislation.[12] From the beginning it was realized that all three of these goals must be cultivated simultaneously, and that with the growth Santa Barbara was experiencing in the early 1920s it was imperative that planning and architectural controls be established as soon as possible. At the beginning Bernhard Hoffmann, Pearl Chase and their associates had "...been carefully educating the public to the need and values of architectural control, had set up an advisory committee of architects to pass on plans when voluntarily submitted, and had even persuaded the banks and lending agencies not to make loans except on plans approved by this committee..."[13] The Community Arts Association, through its Plans and Planting Committee, engaged Charles Cheney (Olmsted and Olmsted) to prepare the needed building and zoning ordinances; then to provide a plan for the crucial waterfront area of Santa Barbara; and finally to suggest the rationale and mechanisms needed to create architectural controls.[14]

Their choice of Charles Cheney was fortunate, for not only was he one of America's most respected professional city planners, he was a strong advocate of architectural controls as an essential planning device. Like other planners practicing in the 1920s, Cheney had to assume a realistic posture as to the legal basis for public architectural controls. While he was willing to mention begrudgingly the economic advantages for a community in adapting architectural controls, the substance of his argument rested on his belief that no city could be well planned without a mechanism to control its architecture. He continually returned to this theme in his writings. "Plan architectural control of all buildings, signs and physical appearances. The general architecture, mass, appearance of all buildings, private as well as public, is essentially a matter of public concern...Plan to maintain the 'town picture'....The city needs protection from disfigurement, and the preservation of old buildings, of natural beauty, and architectural monuments."[15]

Cheney's position was that laissez-faireism in architecture and planning must be replaced by community considerations. Though a professional planner, he did not feel that architectural controls should be administered by a governmental bureaucracy or by elected officials. Instead he envisaged that both the public planning and architectural processes would serve as a point of contact between the public and private sectors. Planning commissions and architectural boards of review should be composed of private citizens. Ideally, the membership of such bodies should strike a balance between those private citizens with direct expertise, i.e. architects, landscape architects, engineers and others, and those whose basic credentials were a sense of civic obligation. Like other planners, Cheney pointed out that these public review bodies would be able to fulfill their duty only if they saw themselves as a bridge between the past and the future.[16]

If we glance back into Santa Barbara's history, especially that of the late nineteenth and early twentieth centuries, it should not be a surprise that the Spanish/Mediterranean tradition of architecture was seized upon as the image which would provide a linkage between the past, present, and the future. The community had been one of the principal early Spanish towns of Alta California and, like Monterey, the town possessed several renowned and striking examples of early nineteenth century Spanish and Mexican architecture. The Mission Church overlooking the city and the adobe dwellings clustered around the former Presidio lent a sense of old world age which was unusual for an American community west of the Mississippi. Nineteenth century "Victorian" architecture ranging from the Italianate to the Eastlake and Queen Anne was looked upon in the teens and twenties as a subject of embarrassment. Coupled with this negative reaction to the late nineteenth century architecture was the dream that Southern California would emerge as a new Mediterranean coast of North America.

Immediately after the First World War Santa Barbara began its concerted effort to revamp its visual image, so that past and present would symbolically merge as one. Bertram G. Goodhue, who had designed the Panama-California Exposition of 1915 in San Diego in the Spanish Churrigueresque mode was engaged to plan an entire commercial streetscape in the Hispanic/Mediterranean mode in Santa Barbara. "These buildings will not follow ordinarily commercial lines, but will be set back of the street line and will have patios, corridors and covered walks."[17] Shortly afterwards, in 1919, a competition was held for the design of a new combined courthouse and city hall for Santa Barbara County, and for the City of Santa Barbara.[18] The program for the competition required that a Hispanic/Mediterranean design be provided. Both Edgar Mathews' winning design, and the second prize design by Mooser and Simpson fulfilled this dictum. In looking over these designs it is easy to see why Mathews' scheme was selected, for it best summed up Santa Barbara's desire to create a special Hispanic image for itself—an image which would provide a visual linkage between its own late eighteenth/early nineteenth century provincially charming architecture, and the vernacular traditions of Spain and Mexico.

Next to actually constructing buildings and groups of buildings to convey architectural and planning ideas, is the public exhibition of architectural drawings and models. Goodhue's scheme for an entire street and the courthouse competition were presented via the display of drawings. Those were followed by a wide variety of suggested "Spanish Improvements" for Santa Barbara, all conveyed by the exhibition of drawings. James Osborne Craig and George Washington Smith (with drawings by Lutah Maria Riggs) suggested how De La Guerra Plaza (1921-22) could be replanned so that the buildings of the past (in this case the De La Guerra Adobe and the (Yorba-Abadie Adobe) would be joined by a group of new Hispanic buildings, the total assemblage of which would create a distinct sense of the moment as well as of the past.[19] Smith (via drawings prepared by Lutah Maria Riggs) went on to indicate how other sections of the city including the beach front (1922) could be transformed into the Hispanic.

Between 1923 and 1925 the architects of Santa Barbara and the Community Drafting Room, together with the Allied Architectural Association of Los Angeles, demonstrated through the public exhibition of drawings, how individual blocks of State Street could be rebuilt within a unifying Hispanic architectural imagery.[20]

The step from concept to reality occurred first in the planning of the El Paseo complex. Here, in miniature, the architect James Osborne Craig (between 1921-22) created the Hispanic town which was the goal of the Community Arts Association.[21] El Paseo provided the perfect ingredients for such an exposé. The De La Guerra Adobe and eventually the Oreña Adobes down the street constituted the balance points of the past. The Street in Spain, the patio-oriented El Paseo Restaurant, the central courtyard, and the numerous passages and open spaces effectively demonstrated what could be accomplished through a unified Hispanic approach to planning, architectural landscape and architecture. El Paseo effectively brought the lesson home to a broad public in a way which could never have been accomplished through the gradual construction of individual buildings, or by the display of drawings, models, or the written word.

Other examples of how a homogeneous city would appear were put in place between 1922 and 1925. De La Guerra Plaza itself, as a part of the community's historic center, slowly began to assume an Hispanic flavor. A new City Hall was built (Lockard and Sauter, 1922-23) just north of

Looking west on Plaza de la Guerra; schematic drawing by Lutah Maria Riggs and George Washington Smith, 1922-23.

the low one-story Yorba-Abadie Adobe; the Daily News (now the News-Press) building (George Washington Smith, 1922) was sited to close off the southern end of the Plaza, and the Plans and Planting Committee of the Community Arts Association prevailed upon the owners of the property on the west side of the plaza to remodel at least minimally the De La Guerra Plaza sides of their buildings.

As in the El Paseo complex, a play was created between the past and the present. The Yorba-Abadie Adobe with its adjacent California pepper trees and the De La Guerra Adobe to the north added the needed note of historic reality. Further down De La Guerra Street to the east, Bernhard Hoffmann accomplished a similar relationship in the Meridian Studios (George Washington Smith, 1922) where the nineteenth-century Lugo (Meridian) Adobe terminated a small courtyard, embraced on two sides by a story-and-a-half artist's studio.

Thus from the beginning it was recognized that the Hispanic tradition which Santa Barbara was seeking could not be realized by a scattering of individual buildings. The character of the smaller Hispanic cities of Andalusian Spain and of the provincial regions of central and northern Mexico was a result of the spaces between buildings, of variations in the way the buildings were related to the street and to one another; and above all in the variety and importance of horticulture. The site plan for the Lobero Theater, one of the city's major landmarks of the twenties (George Washington Smith, 1922-24), created a narrow winding paseo to the west; and a pepper tree-shrouded low-walled courtyard to the north. The north side of Carrillo Street, between State and Anacapa Streets, illustrated not only how the new and old could be developed into a picturesque street scene, but also how several small-scaled paseos could help to break up the visual rigidity of the gridiron streetscape. Vegetation — palms, citrus trees, olives and California pepper trees, plus semi- tropical flowers, shrubs and a profusion of vines hinted that the buildings were in part intruders into an Andalusian or Mexican arcadia.

The story of Santa Barbara's 1925 earthquake and the rebuilding of the community's downtown within the Hispanic architectural tradition has been told many times.[22] But as Pearl Chase, one of the key personages the Community Arts Association, noted, the quick enactment of legislation to create the architectural controls to bring this Hispanic image about would never have been possible without the preparations made by this private association.[23] By 1925 a consensus had been formed, an Architectural Advisory Committee was already in existence, and legislation needed for an ordinance to establish an Architectural Board of Review had been drawn up. "It should be noted here," wrote Bernhard Hoffmann in 1925, "that for some time the community consciousness as to its proper architectural expression had been becoming more definite and informed."[24] The remarkably rapid rebuilding of downtown Santa Barbara after the earthquake was of great and long-lasting value for those who argued for architectural image. The sudden, instant homogeneity of the commercial core of the city was impressive. At what seemed, like the touch from a fairy's wand, a humdrum (it could be anywhere in the U.S.A.) city had become something special. The abstraction of this idea, realized through a few individual examples, through drawings and writings, had become a reality. Santa Barbara's hoped-for transformation, which had commenced with El Paseo, was now there for everyone to see. Articles in newspapers, and popular as well as professional magazines glowingly extolled the results and went on to observe that here at last was a community where the ideals of civic controls outweighed the visual anarchy characteristic of most of America's cities.[25]

That architectural controls in Santa Barbara ultimately rested not upon officially appointed bodies, but upon community consensus, was pointedly illustrated in the approach taken to the design of the new Santa Barbara County Courthouse. The scheme proposed by the San Francisco firm of William Mooser and Company was a variation on its earlier second prize design of 1919. Though this design was Hispanic, it was formal. A single building set in the middle of the block was decidedly out of scale with the Andalusian quality of the City. The County Board of Supervisors was prevailed upon to appoint a non-official architectural advisory body, which would advise the Mooser firm on the design of the building.[26] In a fashion traditional of Santa Barbara, this body consulted with members of the community's own architectural profession. Its earlier design was discarded and was replaced by an entirely different scheme designed by J. Wilmer Hersey. The new building was broken into four separate parts which were arranged in an informal "L" around a sunken courtyard; a courtyard which in its sunken portion symbolically designated the site of the nineteenth century courthouse. The scale and detailing of these four connected but visually separate buildings were no longer formal, overpowering and classical, but were now provincial and vernacular. Hints of public civic grandeur occurred here and there in individual elements—the great arched entrance (which leads one on only to a view of the hills and mountains beyond), the clock tower, and over-scaled balconies and loggias. What dominated the design, however, were the gleaming white stucco walls, posed behind extensive vegetation. The Courthouse, along with the stagehouse of the Lobero Theatre and the Fox Arlington Theatre (now the Arlington Center for the Performing Arts; Edwards and Plunkett, 1929-30) were impressive case studies of how larger volumes could be maneuvered so that they added to rather than destroyed the provincial Andalusian scale of Santa Barbara.

The slight surge of building activities experienced in Santa Barbara at the end of the 1930s was reasonably controllable, though the aggressive advocates of the "Modern" were beginning to question the validity of Santa Barbara's cultivated Hispanic tradition. This was particularly apparent in the many remodelings of retail store fronts in the downtown area which occurred both before and after the Second World War. In all but a few instances the Plans and Planning Committee was able to mellow the belligerent Modernism to the point where these new street level facades turned out to be mild background designs.

With the embracing of the Modern in the post-World-War-II years by a portion of the architectural profession as the one and only style, the visual homogeneity of Santa Barbara began to be compromised. But those who upheld traditionalism in Santa Barbara remained as determined and subtle in their battle with Modernism as they had been in these earlier efforts of the 1920s to Hispanize the city. In 1947 an official public Architectural Review Board was established by the City Council. In 1958 this board published a general statement of policy indicating the approach which it was taking towards architectural control. "The design of the buildings [in Santa Barbara] has been inspired chiefly by types developed under similar climatic conditions along the Mediterranean, in Mexico and in Southern California. The successful adaptation of these architectural forms, with ingenious variations to meet modern needs, using simple materials and soft colors, has resulted in the achievement of an architectural harmony that distinguishes Santa Barbara from other cities."[27]

The second area which demanded even more attention if Santa Barbara was to "...retain its charm and spirit..." had to do with planning considerations. The control of land use, of density and above all of building heights was rightly seen as a consideration which was as important as the design of individual buildings. If the city's low silhouette, devoid of high rise, could be maintained, then the sense of continuity of the Hispanic tradition would be assured. After the construction of the eight story Granada Building in 1922- 1924 (A. B. Rosenthal) an ordinance was adopted (in 1924) which prohibited any commercial structures over six stories high, or residential buildings over three stories. On June 26, 1930, the first "comprehensive" Zoning Ordinance was adopted by the City. In this ordinance commercial and industrial buildings were even more severely limited to four stories (sixty feet in height), and multiple residential units were restricted to three stories (forty-five feet in height).

During the years 1967 through 1969, numerous proposals were made for exceptions to these height restrictions. In 1968-69, when a determined effort was made to destroy the concept of height limitation through the proposed construction of two eight-story towers on the El Mirasol Hotel site, this was correctly seen by the Plans and Planting Committee and the Citizens Planning Association as a possible death blow to Santa Barbara's architectural tradition.

The proposal was fought with great intensity in the courts and through a charter amendment, with the result that height limitations were taken out of the arena of politics, and placed within the safety of the City Charter itself.[28]

When in the early 1960s a general plan had been drawn up for the City by Eisner-Stewart and Associates, the City's unique Hispanic image was directly set forth and enshrined in the document.[29]

Just prior to Eisner's general plan studies, a quiet event took place which would eventually provide the public controls needed to nudge Santa Barbara back into its Hispanic tradition. This was the creating in 1960 by the City Council of a small obscure public body designated as the Advisory Landmark Committee. Notwithstanding its name, the principal task of this committee was to act as an historical design review body for the El Pueblo Viejo District which comprised the central core of the City, the sixteen blocks in and around the site of the historic late eighteenth century Presidio. Gradually, more stringent Hispanic architectural controls were reinstated, and the original sixteen block El Pueblo Viejo District was expanded, eventually including portions of the City as far away as the Mission itself. Simon Eisner wrote of these new efforts for preservation and architectural continuity: "The 'El Pueblo Viejo' ordinance represents a start toward the full statement in legislative terms of the desire of Santa Barbara to preserve its reputation as one of the nation's most attractive historic cities."[30]

In the decade of the 1960s the Plans and Planting Committee and Santa Barbara Beautiful were joined by two additional private organizations. These were the Citizens Planning Association of Santa Barbara County (founded in 1960), and the Santa Barbara Trust for Historic Preservation (founded in 1963). The first of these organizations concentrated its principal attention on planning, and of the politics of planning. The Santa Barbara Trust for Historic Preservation dedicated its major efforts to the full scale rebuilding of Santa Barbara's 1782 Presidio.

By the mid-1970s it was recognized that a more publicly visible body was necessary to administer the architecture of the city's historic core. A new committee was established in 1977, designated as the Landmarks Committee [The Landmarks Committee was incorporated by a 1993 amendment into the city charter and renamed the Historic Landmarks Commission.] The boundaries of the El Pueblo Viejo District were redrawn to include all of the business core of the city and the principal streets giving access to the city from the freeway (Highway 101). In conjunction with these changes, the City's Architectural Board of Review adopted a policy for the edges of the El Pueblo Viejo District, so that new or remodeled structures adjacent to it would convey a sense of the Hispanic tradition.

The lesson which Santa Barbara provides is that the unique quality of its manmade environment rests upon a cultivated community concern and consensus. This common agreement or goal may be expressed through elected or appointed political bodies, but ultimately it remains as an affair outside of government itself. The Santa Barbara experience pointedly illustrates how elitism (the activity of the few) and democracy (popular consensus) can emerge as one. Santa Barbara's ideal was summed up in 1929 when Bernhard Hoffmann wrote, "The tempo of our age has been so speeded up with jazz, radio, the automobile and the aeroplane that now more than ever before, it is necessary so to build and plan and execute so that simplicity, sincerity and beauty may not be overlooked or ignored in the mad rush."[31]

David Gebhard, 1986

Notes

1. Quoted in Charles H. Cheney, "Architectural Controls," *The American Architect*, vol. 140, April, 1931, p. 23.

2. Thomas W. MacKesey, "Aesthetics and Zoning," *Journal of the American Institute of Planners*, vol. 5, no. 4, 1939, p. 98. Rollin L. McNitt, "Architectural Control Under the Police Power," *Community Builder*, vol. 1, January 1928, pp. 26-28.

3. Mel Scott, *American City Planning*, Berkeley: University of California Press, 1969, pp. 183-269.

4. David Gebhard, *Santa Barbara: The Creation of a New Spain in America*, University Art Museum, University of California, Santa Barbara, 1982. "Community Building in Santa Barbara," *Christian Science Monitor*, October 1, 1925. T. J. Franklin, "The Personality that is Santa Barbara," *Sunset*, vol. 57, July, 1926, pp. 42-43.

5. *Santa Barbara Daily Press*, January 3, 1874.

6. Charles H. Cheney, "Building for Permanency," *20th National Conference on City Planning, Dallas, Texas*, 1928, pp. 38-39.

7. Caroline L. Overman, "Modern Spanish Architecture in California," *The House Beautiful*, vol. 5, April, 1899, p. 33.

8. David Gebhard, "Architectural Imagery, The Mission and California," *Harvard Architectural Review*, vol. 1, Spring, 1980, pp. 137-145. Karen Weitze, *California's Mission Revival*, with a foreword by Harold Kirker, Los Angeles: Hennessey and Ingalls, 1983.

9. Charles H. Cheney, "California Cities Capitalize Natural Charm — A Symposium," *Western Architect*, vol. 40, March, 1931, pp. 11-12.

10. Charles Mulford Robinson. *The Report of Charles Mulford Robinson Regarding the Civic Affairs of Santa Barbara, California,* Santa Barbara: printed for the Civic League by the Independent, 1909.

11. M. Urmy Seares, "The Community Arts Association of Santa Barbara, California," *California Southland*, no. 60, vol. 6, December, 1928, pp. 12-13; 22; "Arts Association — Santa Barbara Plans and Planting Branch," California Southland, vol. 7, January, 1925, pp. 15-31. Edward Sajous, "How a Community Arts Association is Raising Architectural Standards," *American City*, vol. 29, July, 1923, p. 39.

12. Pearl Chase, "Bernhard Hoffmann — Community Builder," *Noticias*, vol. V, no. 2, Summer, 1959.

13. Charles H. Cheney, "Progress in Architectural Control," *Architect and Engineer*, vol. 90, August, 1927, p. 46.

14. "Charles H. Cheney will assist the Building Ordinance Committee of the Santa Barbara Chamber of Commerce in framing a new building code for the city," *Architect and Engineer*, vol. 75, November, 1923, p. 112. Olmsted and Olmsted, *Major Traffic Street Plan and Boulevard and Park System*, Santa Barbara: Plans and Planting Committee, 1924.

15. Charles H. Cheney, "Building for Permanency," *National Conference on City Planning*, Dallas, Texas, 1928, p. 39. Two later papers by Cheney on the subject are: "Architectural Control In America," Proceeding, *National Conference on Planning*, Chicago, 1940, pp. 125-129; "Architectural Control," *The Octagon*, February, 1940, pp. 18-19.

16. Charles H. Cheney, "Progress in Architectural Control," *Architect and Engineer*, vol. 90, August, 1927, pp. 45-46.

17. *Architect and Engineer*, vol. 58, September, 1919, p. 118.

18. "Competition for Santa Barbara County Court House and Memorial," *The Building Review*, vol. 18, November, 1919, pp. 85-87; 95.

19. Mary Osborne Craig, "The Heritage of All California," *California Southland*, No. 33, September, 1922, pp. 7-9. "When Santa Barbara's Dream of 'A Street in Spain' is called into being by Her Peoples" *Santa Barbara Daily News*, May 20, 1922, Special Photogravure Section; Irving F. Morrow,"A Step in California Architecture," *The Architect and Engineer*, vol. 70, August, 1922, pp. 46-103.

20. Irving F. Morrow, "New Santa Barbara," *The Architect and Engineer*, vol. 86, July, 1926, p. 46; illustration of drawings for State Street, *Pacific Coast Architect*, vol. 28, November, 1925, pp. 35-36.

21. Harris Allen, "The 'Street of Spain, ' Santa Barbara, California," *Pacific Coast Architect*, vol. 27, March, 1925, pp. 23-39. Henriette Boegkmann, "The Little Street of Spain," *International Studio*, vol. 81, June, 1925, pp. 184-188.

22. "Santa Barbara Earthquake Number," *Bulletin, Allied Architectural Association of Los Angeles*, vol. 1, no. 10, August 1, 1925; "The Santa Barbara, California, Earthquake," *The American Architect*, vol. 128, July 15, 1925, pp. 47-48; Winsor Soule, "Lessons of the Santa Barbara Earthquake," *The American Architect*, vol. 128, October 5, 1925, pp. 295-302; "What Earthquakes Cannot Destroy," *The Literary Digest*, vol. 86, August 1, 1925, pp. 29-30. Bernhard Hoffmann, "The Rebuilding of Santa Barbara," *Bulletin of the Seismological Society of America*, December, 1925, pp. 323-328. Pearl Chase, "Santa Barbara Resurgent,""The Reconstruction of State Street," (unpublished paper, Dept. History, University of California, Santa Barbara, 1970).

23. Pearl Chase, "Bernhard Hoffmann— Community Builder," *Noticias*, vol. V, no. 2, Summer, 1959, pp. 6-7.

24. Bernhard Hoffmann, "The Rebuilding of Santa Barbara," *Bulletin of the Seismological Society of America*, vol. 15, December, 1925, p. 325.

25. "Santa Barbara; The Case for a Unified Architecture," *Architectural Forum*, vol. 59, July, 1933. pp. 84-85. Edward F. Brown,"Does Beauty Pay?" *The American City Magazine*, vol. 30, February, 1924, pp. 165-166.

26. "The Santa Barbara County Courthouse," *California Southland*, no. 97, vol. 10, January, 1928, pp. 11-13.

27. *Policy for Architectural Control Adopted by the Architectural Board of Review of the City of Santa Barbara, California*, Santa Barbara, August, 1958.

28. The City Charter establishes a maximum height of sixty feet; commercial buildings are limited to four stories, and multiple residential buildings to three stories, according to zone.

29. Eisner-Stewart and Associates, *Santa Barbara, California: The General Plan*. South Pasadena: Eisner-Stewart and Associates, 1964, pp. ix, 9.

30. Ibid. p. 10.

31. Bernhard Hoffmann, "Architectural Aphorisms," *The Architect and Engineer*, vol. 96, March, 1929, p. 111.

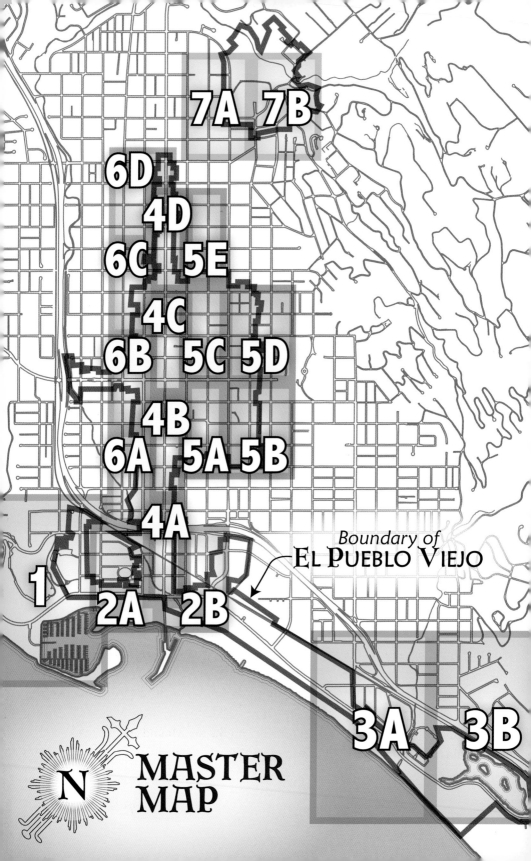

7A 7B

6D

4D

6C 5E

4C

6B 5C 5D

4B

6A 5A 5B

4A

Boundary of
EL PUEBLO VIEJO

1

2A 2B

3A 3B

N MASTER
MAP

Oceanfront

Prior to the arrival of Europeans on the Pacific Coast of North America, the area now known as Santa Barbara's oceanfront was, from time immemorial, the territory of the Barbareño Chumash, a sophisticated society of hunter-gatherers and fishermen who populated the territory. Producers of their remarkably seaworthy tomols, double-ended plank canoes, the Chumash enjoyed a thriving trade, fueled by a money economy, with other villages scattered along the mainland coast from Malibu to San Luis Obispo County as well as the offshore islands in the Santa Barbara channel. Although village sites shifted over time, the first European arrivals noted Syuxtun, the principal village, located approximately at the junction of West Cabrillo Boulevard and Chapala Street, where some 500 Chumash lived in conical, tule-thatched houses. There they shared a life of relative abundance, harvesting acorns from the oaks dotting the hills behind, shellfish from the estuary of what is now Mission Creek, larger fish from the channel, and small game from the surrounding countryside. Yet their entire way of life essentially, and almost immediately, disappeared when Europeans established themselves in the area, beginning with the Presidio in 1782 and the Mission in 1786. The Chumash were forcibly reestablished away from the oceanfront, housed in adobe shelters at the Mission, and turned away from traditional practices in favor of Catholicism and compelled to accept a European approach to life. The oceanfront then became a part of Mission lands.

When those lands were eventually broken up in the early 1830s, title to various portions of the coastal property passed into the hands of a variety of early day settlers, many of whom had dreams of development. But aside from a few major accomplishments, such as Stearns Wharf and the advent of the railroad, serious development did not occur until the beginning of the 20th century. That is not to say that the area was little used once Anglo-American settlement began. After Charles Nordhoff visited Santa Barbara in the winter of 1872 and then praised its "equable climate" in *California—A Book for Travelers and Settlers*, the oceanfront became a renowned health spa and recreational resort. Invalids, as they were called in Victorian-era parlance, flocked to the Santa Barbara coast, advertised widely as the "sanitorium of the Pacific," in hopes that the sulphur springs on Burton Mound and the sea air would cure their ailments. The Arlington Jockey Club, a group of wealthy, eastern-bred men, raced horses on the beach as well as at two tracks laid out in the East Beach area (see entry #40). A mule-drawn streetcar, established in 1876, carried residents and visitors to and from the bathhouses that dotted the area now known as West Beach. Crowds frequently gathered at the Agricultural Park to watch balloon ascensions, circuses, county fair events, and, of course, horse races. This popular spot would have had a resort hotel long before the Potter (1902; entry #11) except that the financiers known as the Seaside Hotel Company wisely decided not to risk building luxury accommodations so near the shoreline, which was subject to treacherous waves in stormy weather before the breakwater was constructed. The company members instead agreed on an inland location and proceeded to build the Arlington Hotel (1875; entry #95).

By the turn of the twentieth century, Santa Barbarans fully realized the inherent commercial as well as aesthetic values in nature's bounty. The decades since then have witnessed a series of confrontations and compromises between those who would exploit the area's full revenue potential as a tourist and fishing spot and those who have sought to enhance the area's natural beauty. The result has been gradual development balanced between competing commercial and aesthetic interests.

Initial preservation efforts came from the local business community, whose concern lay foremost with preserving what we now call "open space," not with preserving the cultural remnants of the past. The Chamber of Commerce, in particular, spearheaded efforts between 1899 and 1913 to raise money in order to buy oceanfront land. The Chamber was openly motivated by a desire to create a scenic waterfront that would continue to attract a wealthy tourist class. Many of those wealthy seasonal visitors so attracted to the area were likewise attracted to the business community's idea; and they continued land-syndicate purchases as well as other philanthropic civic projects throughout the 1920s and 1930s. These early twentieth century businessmen, although concerned with matters economic, nevertheless launched a preservation movement locally, the concerns of which have been broadly conceived to include the natural physical setting as well as the built environment.

As a result of privately initiated land acquisition projects, by 1920 the city owned several parcels of oceanfront land, although few efforts had been made to realize their potential as scenic areas. The East Boulevard Improvement

Association set about to change the situation in 1924, three years after the Ambassador (Potter) Hotel had burned. Upon learning that out-of-town developers were eyeing the East Beach area, the Association arose to stop these developers from building "undesirable amusement and cheap store programs" similar to those "being carried out on the old Ambassador Hotel grounds."

Working with the Chamber of Commerce, the Association engaged Charles Cheney of the firm Olmsted and Olmsted to plan an oceanfront parkway that would be Santa Barbara's counterpart to New York's Central Park and San Francisco's Golden Gate Park. These two groups then embarked on an ambitious plan to secure the rest of the beach property necessary to implement Cheney's plan, adopted by the city in late 1924. Although they made great strides toward their goal, by 1930 citizens at large seemed unwilling to pass the bond issues necessary to finance Cheney's plan through to completion.

During the late 1920s, moreover, another vision of Santa Barbara emerged to compete with the one established earlier. Its adherents envisioned the oceanfront not as a rural-like park, but as a bustling port of entry for freighters and passenger ships. The new, commercial-oriented image reflected some deeper changes in the character of the city. The heyday of wealthy part-time residents was on the wane. Tourists continued to come to Santa Barbara, but the automobile and middle-class affluence transformed the city from a winter retreat into a short-term vacation spot. The population, moreover, increased steadily until the early 1930s, when it stabilized at about 35, 000. With this transformation came the threat of losing the economic ballast of eastern capital. Eschewing the idea of an industrial-based local economy, Santa Barbara leaders turned their attention to developing a city which would appeal to this new tourist clientele.

The Great Depression, followed by World War II, intervened, however, to slow both the economy and development. Nevertheless, by the late 1930s, the city had acquired the extensive park system now dressing the oceanfront, thanks to the efforts of many seemingly tireless citizens. Private benefactions and New Deal relief funds allowed the city also to build, acquire, or improve several recreational facilities. Population growth resumed after the war, spurring considerable building activity in the oceanfront as well as throughout the city. Many West Beach motels were built in the late 1940s or 1950s, and the surrounding residential neighborhood developed fully in the post-war years. Since then, the oceanfront has supported a compatible mix of residential, commercial-industrial, and recreational use; and constant updating, remodeling, and new construction have kept the neighborhood viable. It is this continuing balance between protected open space and ever-changing mixed use that gives the oceanfront much of its distinctive character.

The first bathhouse ca. 1910.

The second public bathhouse (1915–1937, Russel Ray, architect) faced northeast along Cabrillo Boulevard from the original Plaza del Mar.

Oceanfront

No.	Property Address/Location	Property Name
1	821 Coronel Street	Hunt-Stambach House
2	412 West Montecito Street	Trussell-Winchester Adobe
3	414 West Montecito Street	Fernald House
4	Castillo Street between Yanonali and Mason Streets	Pershing Park/Carriage Museum
5	Castillo Street at West Cabrillo Boulevard	Plaza Del Mar-Band Shell
6	401 Shoreline Drive	Los Baños del Mar
7	West of Stearns Wharf	Breakwater and Harbor
8	113 Harbor Way	Naval Reserve Armory (Santa Barbara Maritime Museum)
9	Marina, West of the Breakwater	Santa Barbara Yacht Club Building
10	18 Bath Street	Casa del Mar Inn
11	100-200 Block of West Cabrillo Boulevard and West Mason Street	Ambassador Park/Burton Mound
12	202 and 122 West Cabrillo Boulevard	(Hotel Milo)
13	112 West Cabrillo Boulevard	Veterans Memorial Building
14	15 Chapala Street	(Villa Rosa Inn)
15	103-107 Natoma Avenue	(La Ronda Apartments)
16	114 Chapala Street	
17	118-120 Chapala Street	Hollander Buildings
18	203 Chapala Street	
19	West Montecito Street at Chapala Street	Moreton Bay Fig Tree
20	136 West Yanonali Street	Van Horn House
21	216-218 West Yanonali Street	
22	116-118 Bath Street	
23	232 Natoma Avenue	Eagle Inn
24	212-216 Natoma Avenue	Huntstable Houses
25	210-220 West Mason Street	Ambassador Bungalows
26	211 West Mason Street	(Hotel Milo)
27	226-232 West Mason Street	Mason Apartments
28	22 and 28 West Cabrillo Boulevard	(Harbor View Inn)
29	State Street at Cabrillo Boulevard	Stearns Wharf
30	1 Garden Street	Larco Fish Market (Santa Barbara Visitor Center)
31	East Beach and East Cabrillo Boulevard	Chase Palm Park

32A	Former Junction of Punta Gorda Street and Cabrillo Boulevard	Site of Southern Pacific Roundhouse
32B	633 East Cabrillo Boulevard at Calle Puerto Vallarta	Fess Parker's Hotel
33	East Cabrillo Boulevard between Calle Puerto Vallarta and Milpas Street	Cabrillo Ball Field
34	901 East Cabrillo Boulevard	(Santa Barbara Inn)
35	1118 East Cabrillo Boulevard	Cabrillo Pavilion
36	1121 East Cabrillo Boulevard	Hotel Mar Monte
37	1015-1023 Orilla del Mar	Los Patios
38	East Cabrillo Boulevard between Por la Mar Drive and Niños Drive	Dwight Murphy Field
39	1300 East Cabrillo Boulevard	A Child's Estate (Santa Barbara Zoo)
40	East Cabrillo Boulevard, East of A Child's Estate	Andrée Clark Bird Refuge
41	1407 East Cabrillo Boulevard	Bellosguardo - The Clark Estate
42	East Cabrillo Boulevard and Channel Drive	Watering Trough and Fountain
43	40 Los Patos Way	Former State of California Department of Motor Vehicles Building
44	1801 East Cabrillo Boulevard	Patio de las Aves
45	50 Los Patos Way	Johnson House

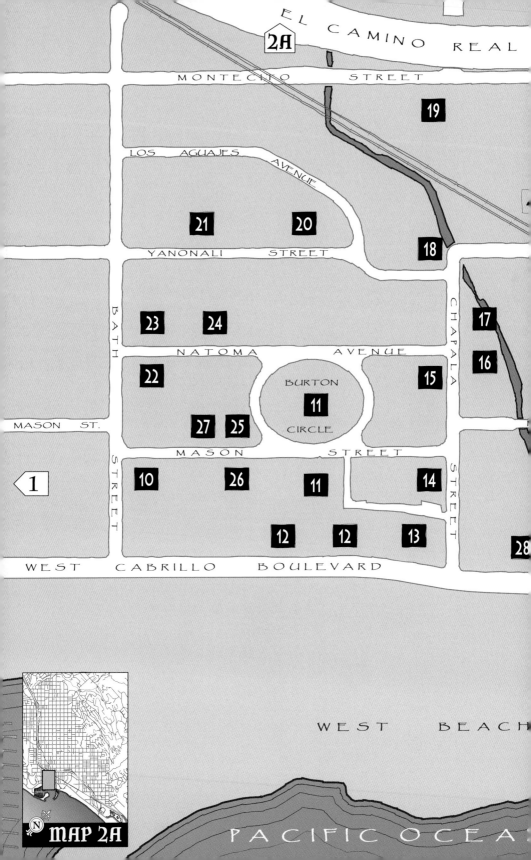

32A

32B

CALLE PUERTA VALLARTA

PUNTA GORDA STR

U.S. HIGHWAY 101

33

34

CABRILLO BOULEVARD

ORILLA DEL MAR

CORONA DEL MAR DRIVE

38

37

POR LA MAR DRIVE

NINOS DRIVE

POR L

36

35

EAST BEACH

POR LA MAR CIRCLE

DEL PARQUE DR

CABRILLO BOUL

CABRILLO BOULE

PACIFIC OCEAN

MAP 3A

ON STREET

S STREET

SALINAS STREET

OLD COAST HIGHWAY

OCEAN VIEW AVE

PARK PLACE

HARBOR VIEW DR

SCENIC DRIVE

OWN ROAD

EL CAMINO REAL

U.S. HIGHWAY 101

OLD COAST HIGHWAY

39

ANDREE CLARK BIRD REFUGE

40

41

CABRILLO BOULEVARD

LOS ATOS WAY

45

43

44

42

CHANNEL DRIVE

N

MAP 3B

1.
821 Coronel Street
Hunt-Stambach House
ca. 1874; Peter J. Barber

This charming Italianate house, with its distinctive cupola, designed by Santa Barbara's first major architect, Peter J. Barber, has graced the city for 140 years, and has been moved so many times, actually to four separate addresses, that it has been called Santa Barbara's first mobile home. Lewis Doan and his moving company had the privilege of moving the structure twice. Originally built and owned by businessman and Civil War veteran, C. C. Hunt, the house stood on the corner of State and Anapamu Streets in the center of uptown Santa Barbara. It was purchased by Dr. Henry L. Stambach who, when threatened by a major development scheduled for the site, moved the residence to 15 West Victoria Street in 1890, where it became both his home and office. There it remained until 1955, when again the house was threatened by development. Concerned citizens, loathe to see the unique edifice destroyed, prevailed upon the Assistance League of Santa Barbara to obtain the house and move it to 401 West Montecito Street, where it remained for a decade. In 1965 the land under it was sold to the Mobil Oil Corporation, which proposed demolition of the house in favor of a service station. Again concerned citizens intervened, and found a buyer for the house in the person of John Alexander, who had the building moved to its present location. They included Edwin Gledhill, Elmer Whittaker, Mary Louise Days, Walker Tompkins, and Judy Orias. The Hunt-Stambach House stands in tribute to Santa Barbara's care for its history and architecture. **SBL**

2.
412 West Montecito Street
Trussell-Winchester Adobe
1854

Reflective, perhaps, of Captain Horatio Gates Trussell's eastern background, this clapboard and shuttered adobe suggests the single-story Monterey Greek Revival style. A seafarer, Captain Trussell took much of the timber

used in constructing the adobe from the ship "Winfield Scott," wrecked on Anacapa Island in 1853. In 1881, Miss Sarah Winchester, a local schoolteacher, purchased the adobe, and the Winchester family occupied it for several decades. A City Landmark, the adobe is owned by the Santa Barbara Historical Museum, and is not open to the public. **CHL,SBL**

3.
414 West Montecito Street
Fernald House
1862; attributed to Roswell Forbush
1880; remodeled and enlarged; Thomas Nixon

Eclectic in its overall design, this 19th century dwelling is a combination of Gothic Revival with Eastlake, Queen Anne, and even Craftsman details. First located at 422 Santa Barbara Street, the house and its surroundings occupied nearly an entire city block. The family of Judge Charles and Hannah Hobbs Fernald lived there continuously for over 80 years. In 1959 the Santa Barbara Historical Society acquired the house and moved it to its present location behind the Trussell-Winchester adobe. It, too, is a City Landmark, but is presently open to the public by appointment only. The gardens of both are contemporary historic interpretations. **SBL**

Thomas Schmidt @ SBVintagePhoto.com

4.
Castillo Street between Yanonali and Mason Streets

Pershing Park

ca. 5 acres, acquired by the City in 1926-1927

A news item from August 5, 1939, boasts that: "They booted calves out of the chutes at Pershing Park yesterday. Los Vaqueros whirled the kinks out of their riatas. It was the day of stock horse competition that is becoming the highlight of the Old Spanish Days celebration." In addition to housing the Old Spanish Days rodeo, Pershing Park was also the venue for the National Horse and Flower Show for many years beginning in 1919. The park continued to host various horse shows and races until 1958, when the arena was demolished. This was also the site of barns that housed the streetcars which were in city-wide use throughout the early 1920s. The park, in addition, has been used as an athletic field from pre-World War I days to the present. In the 19th century, the area was the Sexton Nursery's growing grounds.

During the 1960s and early 1970s the park's physical environment changed considerably as aging structures were removed, lighted athletic fields were added, and the Old Spanish Days Carriage Museum was constructed. The museum, now known as the Carriage and Western Art Museum of Santa Barbara, located at the north end of the park at 129 Castillo Street, houses a variety of pre-automobile vehicles, and is well worth a visit.

5.
Castillo Street at West Cabrillo Boulevard

Plaza del Mar

Portion of 7.5 acres; acquired by the City in 1899,1900,1934

1919 bandshell; Chamber of Commerce

When Cabrillo Boulevard was pushed through the old beachfront plaza in 1934, it severed the connection with the parkland to the north from the beach area around Los Baños del Mar. This focused the attention of park-goers on the concrete bandstand, constructed in 1919 and well used by local citizens and organizations. It was designated a City Landmark in 1990.

The park includes several interesting plantings, including Moreton Bay (Ficus macrophylla) and Rusty Leaf (Ficus rubiginosa) Fig trees, as well as several rare Eucalyptus not common in Santa Barbara. Dr. A. B. Doremus, longtime volunteer park superintendent, was in charge of the original planting and had hoped to establish a grove of Montezuma Bald Cypress (Taxodium mucronatum), the famous "Council Tree of Mexico," Unfortunately, only one survived. **SBL**

6.
401 Shoreline Drive
Los Baños del Mar
Portion of 7.5 acres; acquired by the City in 1899, 1900, 1934
1938 pool; Associated Architects

Originally this area constituted a single beachfront plaza surrounding a municipal swimming pool. Since the 1870s, in fact, Santa Barbarans and tourists have been coming to this spot to swim, stroll, picnic, and generally relax. As early as 1873 privately owned bathhouses accommodated ocean bathers, but in 1891 the city designated part of the area as a "public garden."

By the turn of the 20th century the plaza had been improved with lawns, beaches, palm trees, and walkways. The first Los Baños del Mar, built in 1901, contained, in addition to its heated indoor salt water pool, such amenities as a bowling alley, billiard parlor, roof deck, and outdoor bandstand. The bathhouse burned in 1913 and was replaced two years later by a new facility built by the Edison Electric Company, whose streetcar line terminated at the plaza. When the 1925 earthquake damaged the second pool and building, they were temporarily closed. After several years of lobbying in Washington, D.C. for

First Bath House ca. 1910

depression-era work relief projects, the City was awarded PWA funds in 1937 to assist in the construction of the present Los Baños del Mar. Deterioration caused the facility to close around 1990. The City land-marked Los Baños in 1992, prepa-ratory to a massive rehabilitation of the facility, which reopened to visitors in 1996. As home to Olympic champion swimmers, among others, Los Baños del Mar serves the modern public even as it recalls an earlier era of beach recreation.   **SBL**

7.
West of Stearns Wharf
Breakwater and Harbor 1927-1930

Santa Barbara's man-made harbor owes its environmentally fragile existence to decades of dream-ers, the philanthropy of Max C. Fleischmann, and the generosity of American taxpayers. Thwarted by an inability to bring large ships close to shore, development minded Santa Barbarans, as early as 1850, petitioned the federal govern-ment for funds to create a harbor. Repeated petitions were rejected by Washington, and it was not until the 1920s that local citizens appeared willing to finance such an expensive undertaking. Harbor proponents, however, disagreed on the site; some advocating dredging out the Goleta slough, others proposed dredging the estero that is now the Andrée Clark Bird Refuge, and still others promoted constructing a break-water to the west of Stearns Wharf. The 1925 earthquake temporarily diverted attention away from the municipal harbor project, but in 1926 Fleischmann, heir to the Fleischmann Yeast fortune, offered the city $200,000 if the city would match that amount so that the project could move forward. Construction of the riprap breakwater proved more costly than estimated, however, and Fleischmann later donated another large sum to help see the project through to completion. It certainly helped that Fleischmann needed a safe harbor for his 218 foot long yacht, the *Haida*, in Santa Barbara.

Thomas Schmidt @ SBVintagePhoto.com

Unfortunately, no one foresaw entirely the immense impact this artificial barrier would have on natural wave action and littoral sand drift. For several years after the breakwater was completed, sand accumulated at the entrance of the new harbor, while beaches further down the coast gradually eroded because the coastal current no longer brought replenishing sand. The federal government, which had for so long rejected requests for funds to build a new harbor, now came to the rescue. After the breakwater created the harbor, the city qualified for federal funds under the Rivers and Harbors Act. Since 1935, several modifications to the breakwater and a constant dredging operation run by the Army Corps of Engineers have helped keep the sand accumulation problem within manageable limits. Severe storms have occasionally damaged both the breakwater and Stearns Wharf, but, problems notwithstanding, the Santa Barbara harbor provides small seagoing vessels an official port of refuge in a strategic location, and a safe haven for Santa Barbara's thriving fishing industry.

8.
113 Harbor Way
Naval Reserve Armory
(Santa Barbara Maritime Museum)
1941; Winsor Soule; WPA supervising engineer: L. J. Seckels

During World War II, Santa Barbara's harbor was virtually closed to recreational use. Military patrol vessels had priority use from 1941 to 1945, and the U.S. Navy provided maintenance and logistical support. The Naval

ca. 1945

Reserve Armory was quickly constructed in order to accommodate these emergency operations, with major financial assistance coming from the Works Projects Administration. Aesthetics were not sacrificed to necessity, however, as the Hispanic image is still in evidence, with a federal touch, but still in keeping with the dominant theme in Santa Barbara architecture.

In 1942, the Navy built its own wharf and the armory building officially became the Small Craft Training Center, Santa Barbara. Decommissioned in 1945, it was renamed the U.S. Naval Reserve Armory and the first maritime museum, the Santa Barbara Naval and Maritime Museum, was established there in 1982 by Lt. Commander Douglas Stouffer. In 1992, the government sold the entire property to the City of Santa Barbara for $2.4 million, not a bad deal for the government, which had originally obtained it from the City for $1 in 1939. The property was officially transferred to the City in 1995, a year after a group of interested citizens met to plan a maritime museum for the building. The notion met with enthusiasm not just from the ocean oriented community but the city as well, and Santa Barbara's excellent Maritime Museum opened in 2000. It is open to the public and remains a popular attraction for tourists and locals alike. **SBL**

9.
Marina, West of the Breakwater
Santa Barbara Yacht Club Building
1966; Cooke-Frost-Greer and Schmandt, design architects;
Richard Bliss Nelson, supervising architect; later design by James Zimmerman

When this clubhouse was christened in December 1966, it marked the end of nearly three decades of transiency for the Santa Barbara Yacht Club.

Organized in 1877, the club built its first meeting place at the foot of Stearns Wharf. After a devastating storm destroyed the building in the mid-1920s, members rebuilt their clubhouse in 1929 on the City owned wharf. Financial difficulties and internal strife, however, plagued the club for the next several years, and in 1938 the

City finally invited the club to leave the wharf. From then until the early 1950s the club met in members' homes or in rented quarters. In 1951 the club remodeled the old Union Oil Company office building in the harbor area, which it utilized until 1966, when the new edifice was constructed. A sweeping ocean view was most certainly the essential quality to be incorporated into the design, as the building proper sits behind two wrap-around decks, providing an unimpeded view of local regattas. Set high on pilings, it has thus far weathered the occasional storms that have attacked the coast.

10.
18 Bath Street
Casa del Mar Inn
1945
1952 additions and remodel; Owen King

One of several intimately scaled Hispanic style guest lodges in West Beach, the Twin Palms, as it was first known, began as a private dwelling. By 1952 two guest rooms had been added. In that same year, an extensive addition and some redesigning by Owen King, transformed the building into a substantial motel to lodge ever-increasing numbers of tourists. Both the original house and the later addition were built by well-known local contractor Charles Urton.

11.
100-200 Block of West Cabrillo Boulevard and West Mason Street

Ambassador Park/Burton Mound
.53 acres; acquired by the City in 1924
1902 Potter Hotel; John Austin

The double row of Phoenix canariensis palm trees which border this small bit of open space reputedly framed the promenade that led to the entrance of the luxury Potter Hotel, which was built in 1902 atop Santa Barbara's most important archaeological site, Burton Mound.

Early written accounts reveal that this man-made mound was an important Chumash village, Syuxtun (meaning "where the two trails run), and burial site. At one time the mound rose some 30 feet above sea level and measured 600 feet long and 500 feet wide. An 1883 account described the mound as "one grand catacomb … covered with immense quantities of sea shells."

In the late 18th and early 19th Centuries the site was considered part of the Mission lands. Title to the property went through many hands in the 19th century, including those of fur trader and early settler, Lewis T. Burton. Among other things, Burton was elected Santa Barbara's first American mayor in 1850. Although he was neither the first nor the last to own the land, the archaeological site came to bear his name. A large, single floor adobe, measuring 80 feet by 20 feet with a veranda on three sides, was located on the mound throughout much of the 19th century. It also became known as the Burton Adobe, although it was probably built in the 1830s by Joseph Chapman and later enlarged by Thomas Robbins, owners who preceded Burton.

Milo M. Potter disturbed the prehistoric site considerably when he built his hotel in 1902. The Potter was one of several opulent resorts dotting the Pacific coastline in the early 20th century. Los Angeles architect John

Austin designed the Islamic-influenced Mission Revival Hotel. Its amenities included a telephone in every one of its several hundred rooms, and dinner was served on Limoges china of a custom design bearing the hotel's crest, a Mission bell. Potter sold the hotel shortly before World War I, and its name was changed to the Belvedere. Again sold in 1919, it was renamed the Ambassador, hence the name of the park and nearby residential area. In 1921, a fire completely destroyed the hotel, ravaging the several-story building in less than two hours.

Although many mourned the loss of the hotel, its passing also provided archaeologists an opportunity to excavate the site in 1923. The surrounding area was subdivided for residential use in 1924. The small park plot was deeded to the City of Santa Barbara for use as a public area. The mound itself remained vacant for another three decades. Ambassador Park remains a delightful respite from the unremitting row of motels and restaurants along Santa Barbara's waterfront.

Burton Mound is a California Historical Landmark, and there is a state plaque in the park. **CHL, SBL**

12.
202 West Cabrillo and 122 West Cabrillo Boulevard
Hotel Milo
1951; Owen King

Defining Ambassador Park's western and eastern boundaries are these early 1950s versions of the Spanish Colonial Revival style. As with most examples of this period, the motels combine post-World War II Modern with some Hispanic elements. King's successful designs both enhance and are enhanced by the park's quiet coziness. Now joined under one ownership, which appropriated the first  name of the Potter Hotel's builder for its own, with the property at 211 West Mason Street (See entry #26), there is a unity in architecture surrounding Ambassador Park.

13.
112 West Cabrillo Boulevard
Veterans Memorial Building
1927; Soule and Murphy

In the early 1920s, a group of Santa Barbara architects proposed designs for several buildings along Cabrillo Boulevard in the West Beach area. This particular structure, standing atop a portion of the ancient Chumash village of Amolomol, was the only one to be built. Done in the Spanish Colonial Revival style, the Veterans building's most prominent feature is the pedestrian loggia, something the architects envisioned for buildings throughout Santa Barbara's business district.

Constructed by the well-known local contractors, Snook & Kenyon, the building was first known as the Ambassador Ballroom and later as the Vista del Mar Ballroom. The name was changed to Veterans Memorial Hall in 1935, but remained in use as a dance hall for many years thereafter. During World War II, when the U.S. Army maintained a rehabilitation center in the oceanfront area, the building was an important recreation spot. It is now owned and maintained by the County of Santa Barbara, serving as a veterans service office and meeting place for veterans organizations. **SBL**

14.
15 Chapala Street
(Villa Rosa Inn)
1930-1931; George M. Thomas Studio

This complex, originally named Belvedere Apartments, forms an extensive streetscape of Spanish Colonial Revival architecture. Although the building sits close to the street, the fully landscaped surroundings suggest a garden setting, an image depicted in many drawings of Santa Barbara architecture during the 1920s and 1930s. It was during that period that Santa Barbara made a successful effort to plant trees throughout the community which was, originally, nearly devoid of large vegetation.

15.
103-107 Natoma Avenue
(La Ronda Apartments)
1930; E. Keith Lockard

Built about the same time as the nearby Belvedere Apartments at 15 Chapala Street (See entry # 14), the landscape architecture of this Hispanic complex also suggests a garden setting. The architect, E. Keith Lockard, was one of Santa Barbara's major practitioners of the Spanish Colonial Revival style of the

1920s, and his positive contribution to the city's ambience is noteworthy. The property also hosts a large specimen of Cork Oak (Quercus suber).

16.
114 Chapala Street
1907; Augustus B. Higginson

The eclectic design of this building includes elements of Mission Revival and Craftsman styles, both of which were popular in the first decades of the 20th century. Its proximity to the Potter Hotel no doubt influenced its original use: from 1908 to 1916 the lower floor housed various fine art galleries and, in 1912, the building was called the Potter Art Gallery. The noted muralist and portrait painter, Albert Herter, had his studio here at one time, and from 1926 to the mid-1940s Carolyn and Edwin Gledhill, well-known local portrait photographers, had their studios here. This handsome structure has maintained its vitality for well over a century.

17.
118 and 120 Chapala Street
Hollander Buildings
1911 and 1912

Without its rooftop sun deck and garden, 118 Chapala Street is a rare Santa Barbara example of stripped classicism design, popular in World War I architecture. Built by local contractor, J. C. F. Miller for Frederick E. Junior, the building was first used as a ladies fine clothing store, L.P. Hollander and Company, whose clientele no doubt included guests at the

Potter Hotel. The building was later converted into a single-family residence and, in the mid-1920s, remodeled into two apartments. Its neighbor at 120 Chapala Street, similar in design, was built about a year later, at which time L.P. Hollander and Company switched locations. The shop remained here until the hotel burned in 1921; after that it was converted into a private residence as the neighborhood shifted toward residential and away from commercial use. **SBSM (120)**

18.

203 Chapala Street

ca. 1924

1940 remodel and additions; Edwards and Plunkett

1974 office additions; Gilbert Garcia

2009 remodel; Brian Cearnal

2016; Cearnal Collective, LLP

The original building on this site, a small-scale Spanish Colonial Revival style commercial building erected ca. 1924, represented the neighborhood commercial development that occurred after the Potter Hotel was destroyed by fire. It served a  variety of enterprises until 1940, when the building was remodeled for the Seven-Up Bottling Company by the architectural firm of Edwards and Plunkett. The original Spanish Colonial Revival style was retained, though the front façade was redesigned to include a tower. The latter was taken down a number of years ago. In 2016 the entire structure was demolished, soil conditions making a remodel impractical. In its stead a new 2- and 3-story building housing seven residential units is being constructed. In keeping with Santa Barbara's reverence for the past, the architects are replicating the original front portion of the old 7-Up building's façade , including the tower. The new construction will include windows salvaged from the original, and will be held to historical accuracy under the watchful eye of local historian Alexandra Cole.

19.
101 West Montecito Street at Chapala Street
Moreton Bay Fig Tree
.38 acres; acquired by the City in 1976

This majestic Moreton Bay Fig Tree (Ficus macrophylla), one of Santa Barbara's major tourist attractions, is rumored to have come from its indigenous Australia by ship. It was planted about 1874 near State and Montecito Streets and transplanted, in 1877, to its present location by Charles and Alonzo Crabb. Nearly a century later, in 1970, the City designated it a "tree of notable historic interest," and, in November 1976, the Southern Pacific Transportation Company deeded to the City of Santa Barbara the small parcel of land upon which it sits. Designated a City Landmark in January of 1982, the Moreton Bay Fig Tree hopefully will continue to offer its welcome shade for years to come. **SBL**

20.
136 West Yanonali Street
Van Horn House
1924

Although the design of this house is within the Spanish Colonial Revival tradition, the composition is remarkably formal, almost monumental. The original owner was J. A. Van Horn, the proprietor of an auto accessory shop on lower State

Street. As a small business owner, he was typical of the middle income residents who gave the Ambassador Tract neighborhood its distinctive identity, which lasted for several decades. Interestingly, the Ambassador Tract embraced the movement toward an Hispanic motif in Santa Barbara even before the 1925 earthquake offered the opportunity to remake the town.

The house was constructed by Way and Morgan, builders of a number of Ambassador Tract houses. Other relics of the Potter Hotel era in this block are the several species of Southern Hemisphere Conifers (Araucaria sp.), which remain from the hotel gardens.

21.
216-218 West Yanonali Street
Letsch Duplex

1937

Even this outstanding example of Streamline Moderne includes Hispanic elements, indicating that the Spanish Colonial Revival tradition was thoroughly integrated into Santa Barbara architecture in the 1930s. The architect, whose identity is unknown, successfully designed the duplex to suggest a single-family house. By 1940, shortly after the building was constructed for the original owner, Beulah Letsch, the West Beach area had become a recognizable community of mixed commercial and residential use, locally referred to as the Ambassador Tract.

The beautiful Floss Silk trees on the street date from 1960 and were planted under the direction of City Arborist, Will Beittel. Also present is a notable specimen of Montezuma Bald Cypress (Taxodium mucronatum) planted around 1900 by Dr. A. B. Doremus in front of 224 West Yanonali Street.

22.
116-118 Bath Street
1920; possibly John Austin

Built after the completion of the Potter Hotel proper, this annex reportedly was used to house the entourages of visiting royalty and other high officials. Wealthy families who brought with them tutors and governesses for their children also used this structure. Located some distance from the main building, the annex escaped the disastrous 1921 fire which leveled the hotel. It, and the double row of palm trees that line Ambassador Park, are the only remains of this once great resort hotel. The annex was later converted to apartments.

23.
232 Natoma Avenue
Eagle Inn
1929; A. H. Seiferle

This large Spanish Colonial Revival building, known for many years as the Natoma Apartments, was constructed by owner-builder C. Cicero, who also built the La Ronda Apartments at 103-105 Natoma Avenue. The cast stone ornamentation, in this case a stunning eagle, a common feature of the style, was used rather sparsely in Santa Barbara during the 1920s. Pointed arch doorways, reflective of Moorish architecture, are also rare in the city. Construction of this apartment building in the late 1920s signaled the beginning of attractively designed, high density residential buildings in the area. It is now a boutique hotel.

24.
212 and 216 Natoma Avenue
Hunstable Houses
1936 (212), 1939 (216); E. E. Hunstable

The Spanish Colonial Revival tradition continued with great vigor into the 1930s, although there was a tendency for the Hispanic imagery to become increasingly abstract, as is evident in these similarly designed duplexes. Here the emerging Modern and Moderne styles are integrated into the older tradition. Extant design sketches indicate that the owner-builder, Edward E. Hunstable, a salesman by occupation, also designed the buildings.

25.
210-220 West Mason Street
Ambassador Bungalows
1924-1925

After the famed Potter Hotel burned in 1921, the area returned, for a few short years, to an open field dotted with scattered houses. This bungalow court was among the first single and multiple family residences that began to appear in the area in the mid-1920s. Here the image of the middle-class family residence is reduced to the smallest possible size, yet the gardenlike setting fits in perfectly with the Santa Barbara image.

26.
211 West Mason Street
(Hotel Milo)
1936-1937; Alex D'Alfonso

Comfortably nestled on a quiet side street, this lovely Spanish style favorite of the visiting public was designed and built by Alex D'Alfonso. It was first used as an apartment building, but later, because of its proximity to the beachfront, was converted into a hotel to serve the vacationing public. It is now part of the sprawling Hotel Milo complex (See entry #12) connecting it directly to Cabrillo Boulevard.

27.
226-232 West Mason Street
Mason Apartments
1946; Howell and Arendt

In contrast to the prevailing Spanish Colonial Revival architecture of the oceanfront area, and especially to the Ambassador Court which sits adjacent to it, this complex presents a near perfect example of the pre-World War II Bay Tradition, which continued on through the late 1940s and 1950s.

28.
22 and 28 West Cabrillo Boulevard
(Harbor View Inn)
1947-1949; R. H. Pitman
1983-1984; Lenvik & Minor Architects;
Cunningham Design, Inc., landscape architecture

The original section of this motel was built shortly after the end of World War II. Its two-story design, with an arcaded lower floor and a wooden balcony above, illustrated the vigor of the Santa Barbara Hispanic tradition, even during a period when the Modern was close to universal in acceptance. The newer section is a carefully thought-out design which is sensitively related to the original, and makes for an imposing Hispanic structure.

29.
State Street at Cabrillo Boulevard
Stearns Wharf
1872

Thomas Schmidt @ SBVimagePhoto.com

The same entrepreneurs who hoped, in 1850, to see a harbor on Santa Barbara's shores, also endeavored to develop port facilities to accommodate commercial and passenger ships. It was not until two decades later, however, in 1871, that the City authorized John P. Stearns to build a wharf to fulfill that vision. Completed in September of 1872, this waterfront addition not only encouraged tourism – thousands disembarked here in the heyday of passenger steamers – but changed the course of the city's development, as real estate values soared, and cargo-carrying ships deposited precious lumber to sustain the Victorian construction boom.

Stearns quickly found, though, that operating a wharf was not all fun and profit. Wooden pilings, for example, seldom lasted more than five or six years before having to be replaced, and storms, like a pair of Sou'easters that battered the wharf over the winter of 1877-78, tearing out large sections of the structure and leaving the warehouse at the outer end only reachable by boat, proved to be major expenses. A more serious threat to Stearns' business on the wharf was the impending arrival of the Southern Pacific Railroad in Santa Barbara. When the tracks arrived in 1887, Stearns reorganized himself as the Stearns Wharf Company, and asked permission of the city to link the wharf to the Southern Pacific. Permission granted, Stearns then constructed a 1,450 foot railroad wye to carry tracks onto the wharf. As the new structure was completed, a local observer enthused, "The new railroad wharf has been built and the tracks of the Southern Pacific now run out to water deep enough to float the largest ship. The old wharf has been strengthened and Santa Barbara today can boast of the largest wharf on the Pacific Ocean from Sitka to Cape Horn." Perhaps, but the spur was abandoned a decade later, and the wharf's dogleg is the only remaining evidence of the old railroad wye.

Thomas Schmidt @ SBVintagePhoto.com

The wharf's utility began to change with the advent of motoring tourists after World War I and the demise of the Potter Hotel in 1921. Commercial usage continued, of course, but when the old Yacht Club building was converted into the Harbor Restaurant in 1941, the wharf itself became a tourist attraction and its function changed from "wharf" to "pier." By the mid-1950s, Stearns Wharf housed many of the establishments that some present visitors may remember – gift shops, a boat rental, a bait and tackle shop, a sport fishing concern, the Galley and Moby Dick coffee shops, and the legendary Harbor Restaurant, which was severely damaged in a 1973 fire. The wharf was closed to the public shortly after that, and remained off limits until 1979, when the City began extensive repairs and reconstruction. But serious difficulties continued. In February of 1983 a hundred-year storm tore into the harbor, with damage to the wharf estimated at over half a million dollars. In 1986 there was another fire, this time on the shoreward finger, and, in 1987 another storm caused severe damage. In November of 1998, fire broke out near the Moby Dick restaurant and destroyed much of the outer section of the wharf. Again it was rebuilt, and is now said to be the single most popular tourist destination in Santa Barbara.

Gilbert Barry designed the wharf reconstruction master plan as well as the buildings erected in 1980-1981, and a 1984 coffee shop addition. James J. Zimmerman designed the new Harbor Restaurant. In style, they are reminiscent of Colonial New England. Edwards-Pitman designed the structure on the dogleg of the wharf; the Santa Barbara Museum of Natural History Sea Center. Sharpe, Mahan and Associates designed the steel-wall kiosk at the wharf entrance.

Each time the City has been faced with major repairs or reconstruction, it has opted to stay with the original concept, utilizing timber pilings and planked surface, and permitting public fishing from the structure, all of which retains a sense of history that only adds to the ambience of Santa Barbara.

In 1988, the grand presidents of the Native Sons of the Golden West and the Native Daughters of the Golden West unveiled a historical marker.

30.
1 Garden Street
Larco Fish Market
(Santa Barbara Visitor Center)
1911; Peter Poole

This tiny sandstone building was originally constructed at 214 State Street by stonemason Peter Poole as a market for one of Santa Barbara's most prominent early-day fish dealers. Andrea Larco migrated here from San Francisco in 1876, and, within a decade, he and his son, Sebastian, were leaders among the prospering fishermen who regularly shipped lobster to San Francisco in addition to supplying the local market with the catch of the day. Larco moved to 214 State Street in about 1905 from his previous location at 122 State Street. Between 1918 and 1931, several processing and storage facilities were added. The Larco market operated out of this stone structure from the time it was built, 1911, to 1943, when the site was sold to Farallone Fisheries. In 1982 the vacant structure was reopened as a fresh fish market before being converted to a restaurant in 1983.

In 1987, when Caltrans' proposed freeway widening project was to get under way, and the building stood to be demolished in the process, the state agency offered to move the structure free of charge to an appropriate site. Architect William Mahan led an effort to relocate the building to the corner of Cabrillo Boulevard and Santa Barbara Street and install it on a City parking lot to serve as a visitor center. The campaign was successful, the move was accomplished in 1988, and once again Santa Barbara's sense of the past led to the preservation of a charming memento of a moment in time. **SBSM**

31.
East Cabrillo Boulevard at East Beach
Chase Palm Park
Acquired by the City; 1891-1931

The genesis of this scenic boulevard and oceanfront promenade dates to 1891, when voters approved a $70,000 bond issue to finance the construction of the western section. Architect Peter J. Barber, mayor at the time, is said to have planned the palm-tree-lined drive after seeing such boulevards in Geneva during an 1887 trip.

Acquisition of the parkway between the boulevard and the ocean began in 1903, when a City ordinance authorized the condemnation of privately owned land. In the decades that followed, public-spirited wealthy citizens gradually purchased much of the condemned beachfront property. The East Boulevard Improvement Association was formed in 1924 for this express purpose. Its members, consisting primarily of local businessmen, planning advocates, and philanthropists, were fearful that "cheap amusements" would be built on the oceanfront by less refined, though no less entrepreneurial, developers. The Association engaged Charles Cheney, of Olmsted and Olmsted, to draw up plans for an expansive oceanfront park, plans which inspired it to purchase and hold land for that purpose. After voters approved park bond issues in 1925 and 1927, the Association sold its parcels to the City at cost plus interest. The last parcel to be acquired was the old lumber yard at the foot of Stearns Wharf, purchased by the City for $200,000 in 1931, after voters approved an additional bond issue, which was hotly contested because of the Great Depression. In 1926-1927, when Cabrillo Boulevard was reconstructed and slightly rerouted, the park strip buffer between Garden

Street and Por la Mar Drive was planted to screen from view the adjacent railroad and industrial area to the north.

"Chase" was added to the Palm Park name in 1978 to honor Harold S. Chase and his sister, Pearl, who were instrumental in its acquisition. A plaque, located at the foot of Santa Barbara Street and dedicated in November of 1982, memorializes the Chases for their leadership in Santa Barbara community development and conservation efforts.

In 1998, after a decade of planning, including input from potential visitors, particularly children, what they would like to see in a new park, Chase Palm Park Annex, across the boulevard from the original park, opened to the public as a "ten acre mini-fantasyland." A group had studied all of the suggestions, selected a number of the best ones, and hired architect George Girvin to put them all together in a coherent unit. Five million dollars, and an uncountable number of volunteer hours of labor later, the new park, with its marvelous carousel, spouting whale, running creeks, squirting fish, shipwreck, and more, instantly became an essential part of the waterfront. Its imaginative landscaping and wandering paths provide a peaceful respite from the clamor of the adjacent boulevard lined with Mexican Fan Palms.

32A.
Former Junction of Punta Gorda Street and Cabrillo Boulevard
Site of Southern Pacific Roundhouse
1926; A Mr. Christie of the Southern Pacific Railroad Company, in consultation
with the Community Drafting Room; E. C. Nichols, assistant engineer;
G. W. Corrigan, division engineer.

When an earlier brick roundhouse on this site, one which served Southern Pacific Railroad equipment, was severely damaged by the 1925 earthquake, the Plans and Planting Committee of the city's Community Arts Association urged representatives of the railroad to design a new facility in keeping with the Spanish Colonial Revival style. Legend has it that Pearl Chase, a member of the committee, displayed to Southern Pacific representatives a postcard depicting a bullring in Seville, Spain, as a suitable design idea.

In fact, the rebuilt roundhouse bore a striking resemblance to its legendary origin. From 1926 to 1961 the roundhouse served steam locomotives of the Southern Pacific. When the railroad converted to diesel equipment, the roundhouse was substantially altered and leased out as a warehouse. It was demolished in September, 1982, to make way for Fess Parker's convention center-hotel complex.

32B.
East Cabrillo Boulevard at Calle Puerto Vallarta
Fess Parker's Hotel
1985; Edwards-Pitman; Hoffman Associates, landscape architecture

In the late 1970s, and even earlier, various proposals were made for the location of a major hotel facing East Beach. One of those proposals evolved into the present design, which carries on the Hispanic architecture and landscape traditions of Santa Barbara. The Cabrillo Boulevard side of the complex is dominated by a large outdoor rotunda, a symbolic recreation of the circular form of the demolished Southern Pacific Railroad roundhouse. Toward the north and the mountains is the enclosed auto court with an entrance that successfully looks back toward both the turn-of-the-century Mission Revival style and to the Spanish Colonial Revival style of the 1970s. The separate wings of the building and the principal courtyard with its pool relate the hotel to that of the 1927 Biltmore Hotel in nearby Montecito.

A plaque commemorating the roundhouses was dedicated by the Native Sons of the Golden West on May 16, 1998.

33.
East Cabrillo Boulevard between Calle Puerto Vallarta and Milpas Street
Cabrillo Ball Field
5 Acres; acquired by the City, 1925-1927

This small park was acquired in five pieces after a 1925 ordinance designated that the property be used as a public park. The land included part of an area known as Shore Acres, a subdivision containing some substantial bungalows which were relocated in 1927. Voter-approved bond funds were used to buy the property from the East Beach Improvement Association, which had purchased and held the property for the city in the interim. The park, later improved with a baseball diamond, was used extensively by recuperating servicemen during World War II, and still serves as a ball field. At the westerly end of the property, near Fess Parker's Hotel, stands a modern sculpture, Herbert Bayer's "Chromatic Gate," in colorful contrast to its surroundings.

34.
901 East Cabrillo Boulevard
(Santa Barbara Inn)
2016; William R. LaVoie

The original Santa Barbara Inn, constructed on this site in 1957, was built in an undistinguished minimalist modern design appropriate to a motel/hotel of that period, but perhaps because it was so far from the center of Santa Barbara, not attuned to the style of architecture defining the city. Subsequently the boundaries of El Pueblo Viejo were expanded and the Cabrillo corridor was included within it. Thus when a major remodel of the complex was proposed, an opportunity to change the Inn's design into something more suitable to the city's Hispanic past was offered. Architect William R. LaVoie responded to the challenge, designing a structure which suggests that it was constructed over a period of time and incorporates an eclectic mix of styles including Spanish Romanesque, Moorish, Renaissance and Baroque which, overall, present an urban Hispanic impression perfectly appropriate to Santa Barbara.

35.
1118 East Cabrillo Boulevard
Cabrillo Pavilion
1926; Roland Sauter and E. Keith Lockard
1988 remodel; James F. Carberry

When the old Plaza del Mar bathhouse was closed in 1925 as a result of earthquake damage, David and Martha Platt Gray (he was the vice-president of the Ford Motor Company) offered the city $100,000 to build a new pavilion and bathhouse at the opposite end of the oceanfront on the condition that the city would furnish it. The city failed to do so, so the Grays built and furnished it on their own, and then gave the building to the city in 1927. The visible fruits of their persistence did not go unnoticed. "It was after the completion of the breakwater and the Gray Pavilion," according to former mayor, Patrick Maher, "that the people really began to see the possibilities for developing the waterfront and harbor into the recreational area it is today."

During World War II, Army Redistribution Headquarters and medical stations were located on the top floor, while the first floor bathhouse remained open for public use. Throughout the mid-1950s, the Mar Monte Hotel, across the boulevard, leased the complex from the city and used it as a convention center. It is now an event and rental facility and bathhouse operated by the City Parks and Recreation Department. **SBSM**

36.
1121 East Cabrillo Boulevard
Hotel Mar Monte
1927-1930; Walker and Eisen, Los Angeles
1935 remodel; Walker and Eisen
1956 swimming pool area; Richard B. Taylor
1977 remodel and additions; Richard Bliss Nelson
1982-1983; Sharpe, Mahan and Associates

Thomas Schmidt @ SBVintagePhoto.com

Construction on what was then called the Vista Mar Monte began shortly after the Cabrillo Pavilion was completed. When it opened in 1931, after three years of building at a cost of 5 million dollars, Santa Barbara had a new resort hotel to replace the Potter and the Arlington. The architecture of the new beachfront hotel conformed to the Spanish Colonial Revival image. While the previous two "Grand Hotels" accommodated patrician lifestyles from 1875 to 1925, the Mar Monte attracted famed Hollywood stars and other celebrities during the 1930s and 1940s. During World War II, the Mar Monte, as well as the nearby Biltmore and Miramar Hotels, was used exclusively for 18 months as part of the Army Redistribution Center. Here Pacific combat veterans relaxed before being relocated. Recent changes in ownership among several major hotel chains, together with the alterations they have made, result in the ability of the present Mar Monte to accommodate an ever increasing number of short-term visitors, and house them in an oceanfront location.

37.
1015-1023 Orilla del Mar
Los Patios
1930; William Mooser and Company

Los Patios was one of the first multiple residential buildings to appear in East Beach. Original owner Sam E. Kramer engaged the firm of William Mooser Company of San Francisco to design this many-angled Hispanic structure for use as an apartment building. It was converted to a motel in 1952 and later reconverted back to apartments.

The large arched opening leading to a courtyard is the design centerpiece of this apartment complex and echoes the magnificent arch of the Santa Barbara Courthouse (See entry #157), also designed by Mooser. Indeed, the arch became the San Francisco based company's signature approach to Hispanic imagery and is repeated in several of its buildings in other parts of the state. **SBSM**

38.
East Cabrillo Boulevard between Por la Mar Drive and Niños Drive
Dwight Murphy Field
10.5 acres; acquired by the City in 1925

The City of Santa Barbara purchased this acreage, as it did much of the oceanfront park land, from the East Boulevard Improvement Association. Always popular with soccer players, the park was first known as the Municipal Soccer Field. Depression-era federal funds were utilized to improve the field further, and, in 1933, it was dedicated and renamed in honor of Dwight Murphy, internationally known Palomino horse breeder, who presided over the City's Park Commission from 1927 to 1931. He was also a highly honored civic benefactor and philanthropist.

39.
1300 East Cabrillo Boulevard
A Child's Estate
(Santa Barbara Zoo)
16 acres; acquired by the City in 1953

The name of this popular spot reflects its history as much as its present-day use. Like Burton Mound, this place was once the site of a Chumash village dating back 5,000 to 7,000 years. The estate is best remembered, however, for Vega Mar (meadow by the sea), a rambling Mission Revival mansion featuring a very tall central tower, which easterner John Beale, a retired tea and coffee merchant, built on the knoll in 1897. When Beale died in 1914, his widow, Lillian, married John Howard Child, and Vega Mar became the Child Estate. Mrs. Child gained local notoriety in the 1930s when she allowed depression-era transients to build a hobo village on the property. In 1947, she gave the estate to the Santa Barbara Foundation which, after her death, turned the property over to the City of Santa Barbara. During the 1950s the mansion was used as a caretaker's residence and later a fraternity house. Allowed to fall into complete disrepair, it was utilized by the City Fire Department as a training exercise and was burned to the ground in 1959. In 1961 the Child Estate Foundation was formed, leased the property from the City, and, with the help of the Junior Chamber of Commerce, spearheaded a volunteer effort to develop the estate into a park and zoological garden, including a children's zoo. The project was hugely successful, and the Santa Barbara Zoo is now one of the finest in the region, attracting visitors from all over Southern California.

40.
East Cabrillo Boulevard, East of A Child's Estate
Andrée Clark Bird Refuge
42.42 acres; acquired by the City in 1909

Originally a tidal marsh, or estero, the bird refuge is one of man's more successful efforts to recreate nature within the 18th century English landscape garden tradition. In the 1870s, Bradley Race Track ringed the Salt Pond, as it was first known, and horses raced and trained there when the track was dry. Bradley's remained a favorite gathering place for racing enthusiasts until 1886, when competitors, known collectively as the Santa Barbara Land

Thomas Schmidt @ SBVintagePhoto.com

and Improvement Company, built the Estero Race Track and Agricultural Park slightly west of here, roughly in the area that lies between Santa Barbara and Salsipuedes Streets. In the early 20th century, when citizens turned their attention and efforts toward securing oceanfront land for public use, 60 people donated $100 each in order to purchase the old Salt Pond. They later sold the land to the City. Many of these subscribers envisioned that the city would turn the marsh into a municipal harbor, but that dream never became a reality. In 1928, Huguette M. Clark donated $50,000 as a memorial to her deceased sister, Andrée, so that the pond could be dredged to create a shallow, freshwater lake surrounded by walkways and bridle paths. Despite recurring problems with algae blooms and water levels, the Refuge has remained the attraction that Miss Clark hoped it would be.

41.
1407 East Cabrillo Boulevard
Bellosguardo – The Clark Estate
1903; Francis W. Wilson
1932-1936; Reginald Johnson

Built on a bluff, with a magnificent ocean view, the original Bellosguardo (beautiful lookout) was the dream of Oklahoma oilman, William Graham. Family difficulties, eventually resulting in a divorce, caused Lee Eleanor Graham to sell her mansion to the notorious United States Senator, William Clark, whose substantial fortune was derived from his railroad and mining interests. Clark died shortly after the purchase, but his widow stayed on. In the midst of the Great Depression of the 1930s, she decided to tear down the old house and build a new one. Noted architect Reginald Johnson and local builder, O. J. Kenyon, are responsible for the stunning stone 18th Century French country mansion which is the result. Subsequently, Mrs. Clark was given high praise for providing jobs for local unemployed workers during desperate times. With the recent passing of Senator Clark's last remaining child, Huguette, Bellosguardo is now in the hands of a foundation that was created in her will. **SBL**

42.
East Cabrillo Boulevard and Channel Drive
Watering Trough and Fountain
1911; Francis W. Wilson

This beautiful stone drinking fountain "for man and beast," of classical Beaux Arts design, was donated to the City by Dr. Charles Caldwell Park, a local physician, as a memorial to his two deceased sons. The Parks were a prominent Montecito family, and Dr. Park also served as president of Santa Barbara Associated Charities. The fountain is no longer connected to a water supply, but has been designated a City Landmark, and remains a wonderful echo of the past.   **SBL**

43.
40 Los Patos Way
Former State of California Department of Motor Vehicles Building
1936; Chester Carjola

The thick walls and deeply recessed windows of this wood-frame and stucco building create a feeling of the Hispanic-adobe tradition. Built in 1936 for the California Highway Patrol, the structure was originally located at 928 Rancheria Street (later U.S. 101). It was used by the Department of Motor Vehicles until 1961, when it was moved to its present site and utilized as a commercial building.

44.
1801 East Cabrillo Boulevard
Patio de las Aves
1984; James J. Zimmerman; Cunningham Design, Inc., landscape architecture

A large one and two-story complex of businesses and offices which carefully reflects the Monterey aspect of Santa Barbara's architectural tradition, these several buildings are arranged around a central court with a notable fountain by Marge Dunlap. They replace an earlier Spanish Colonial Revival Standard Oil service station designed in the mid-1920s by Edwards, Plunkett and Howell. The gardens are an early example of drought-tolerant planting design.

45.
50 Los Patos Way
Johnson House
ca. 1872

This story-and-a-half French Second Empire building is the larger section of a dwelling originally located at 812 De la Vina Street. The other, smaller section, is now situated at 810 De la Vina Street, where it has been put to commercial use. The original owner, W. H. Johnson, a sea captain, built the house out of redwood lumber presumably unloaded at the newly completed Stearns Wharf. The mansard roof is covered with slate. In 1962, when the house was condemned to make room for a parking lot, the owner moved this portion to its present location, restored and added to it, and converted the building to commercial use.

State Street Plaza

One of Santa Barbara's most striking and unusual features is the way the city's streets are laid out on the basis of a roughly northeast-southwest diagonal rather than the rigid north-south system incorporated into national land policy by Thomas Jefferson in the 1780s and prevalent virtually everywhere in the United States west of the Appalachians. This quirk is a result of local geography and of the area's original settlers, the Chumash, who followed the constraints of the land. In Santa Barbara's case it is two fault zones that have determined the geography—the Mesa zone to the west and the Mission Ridge zone to the north and east. The area between these two, the present City of Santa Barbara, was filled in by erosion, creating an alluvial basin. The main Chumash trail basically bisected this basin, running from the village of Syuxtun at the mouth of Mission Creek past a smaller village near the Presidio area northwest to the village at Mission Canyon. Thus geography, and the use of the land that it imposes, early determined the general location of what would later become Santa Barbara's main thoroughfare.

When the Spanish settlers arrived in 1782, they were almost as dependent on the land and its resources as were the Chumash. The land determined the location of the Presidio, later the Mission, and of course the harbor. Linking these three was the old Chumash trail. With minor variations it became the main path for the Spanish and subsequent Mexican settlement. Along its length, adobe dwellings were constructed, including Casa de la Guerra (entry #119) near the center of the alluvial basin, the Orella adobe (entry #81) on the northern fringe of the pueblo and, in the 1830s, the two-story Monterey-style adobe of Alpheus Thompson (entry #67). This last represented the brief fusion of Hispanic culture (as represented by the masonry adobe tradition) with the rising Anglo-American culture (here exemplified by the use of wood and a central plan) not only along State Street but more generally in Santa Barbara and California as well.

With the United States' victory over Mexico in 1848 came the victory also of Anglo-American ideas over Hispanic traditions. The most readily apparent of these new ideas, at least in city planning, was the imposition of a right-angled grid system upon the land, buildings, and ownership patterns. Rigid Yankee logic usually imposed this grid system regardless of local conditions; in Santa Barbara, however, the grid was adjusted to the

In 1887, part of the east side of the 800 block of State Street looked like this.

contours of the land and harbor and basically oriented on the axis of the former trail from the oceanfront to the Mission. This was the first step in eliminating the previous picturesque irregularity and replacing it with a system more efficient for transportation, property ownership and development.

The grid, however, existed only on plat maps until State Street was built and aligned in the 1860s and 1870s. In 1875 a streetcar line was constructed linking the oceanfront with the Arlington Hotel and bisecting the growing commercial district on lower State Street. North and south, two- and three-story false-front wooden buildings were erected (see Pierce Block entry #58 and the Orella Building entry #61), covered sidewalks were constructed, and the street paved. As commerce increased, larger buildings were put up by the now dominant Yankee entrepreneurs. These include, from south to north, the Fithian Building (entry #59), the Upper Clock Building (entry #75), W. W. Hollister's Santa Barbara College (entry #86), and the Lower Hawley Building (entry #88). Although these buildings were designed in a variety of imported eastern architectural styles—the French Second Empire being the most popular—they all shared the Anglo-American concern for general symmetry, right-angledness, and basic modular construction; that is, they reflected vertically what the street grid represented horizontally. Because of this, by the early twentieth century State Street, in its rigid commercial logic, resembled any American small town Main Street.

Although there were earlier attempts to Hispanicize State Street, it was not until 1925 and the earthquake that the opportunity arose to remake Santa Barbara's main thoroughfare. The destruction was so extensive that plans were drawn up to reconstruct virtually the entire street in a consistent Hispanic or Spanish Colonial Revival style. Even the name of the street was briefly changed from State to Estado, although this, unlike the Hispanic architectural mode, never caught on. Of course, the logic of the grid continued to dominate the town and especially State Street, but attempts were made to break from it even if only minimally. Instead of a uniform facade line abutting the sidewalk, it was recommended that some buildings be set back to create patios (Copper Coffee Pot, entry #81) and that others have projecting pedestrian arcades (entry #73).

Here is how it looked in 1926.

The Depression and World War II severely restricted new construction and, after the war, architectural fashion and the Santa Barbara economy dramatically changed. Architects employed elements of the Spanish Colonial Revival idiom, but in most cases new buildings and alterations to existing buildings were in the International Style of architecture. The other factor that influenced State Street in the 1950s and 1960s was the enormous expansion in automobile traffic. This had a particularly large impact on the 400-700 blocks of the street. There, car-related businesses proliferated, some which had been established as early as the 1910s. They brought with them a decline in more people-oriented businesses and an increase in visual and even social chaos. By the late 1960s State Street faced the same potential for urban decay prevalent throughout the country.

In an attempt to combat this, the city in 1969 transformed six blocks of State Street into a beautifully landscaped Hispanic drive-through plaza. Robert Ingle Hoyt was architect and Julio Juan Veyna was landscape architect. In 1982 the plaza was extended another block south. Richard B. Taylor was the architect and landscape architect. Contemporaneously, architects, through the encouragement of the Landmarks Committee, again began to rediscover the city's Hispanic tradition. Many commercial buildings have been restored to their earlier architectural style (St. Vincent's School, entry #219) or remodeled along Spanish Colonial Revival lines (Hitchcock Building, entry #88) and new construction on State Street, as elsewhere in downtown El Pueblo Viejo, is being carried out within the city's Hispanic tradition.

State Street Plaza

No.	Property Address/Location	Property Name
46	35 State Street	Hotel Californian
47	136 State Street	
48	209 State Street	Southern Pacific Railroad Station (Amtrak)
49	217 State Street	Hotel Neal (Reagan Ranch Center)
50	316-330 State Street	Auto Showroom and Seaside Oil Company
51	409 State Street	Faith Mission
52	415-419 State Street	
53	424 State Street	
54	428-434 State Street	
55	502-510 State Street	
56	515 State Street	
57	533 State Street	Neal Callahan Building
58	607-621 State Street	Pierce Block
59	625-635 State Street	Fithian Building
60	715-719 State Street	Alexander Building
61	718 State Street	Orella Building
62	721-723 State Street	Parma Building
63	722-724 State Street	Storke Placita
64	746 State Street	La Placita Building
65	801 State Street	Las Tiendas Building
66	808-818 State Street	El Paseo
67	805-807 State Street	Thompson Adobe Site
68	829-833 State Street	Howard-Canfield Building
69	903-911 State Street	Bothin Building
70	913 State Street	
71	921-925 State Street	
72	922 State Street	Nardo Building
73	928 State Street	
74	930 State Street	
75	936 State Street	
76	1000 State Street	
77	1001 State Street	
78	1008-1010 State Street	

79	1012 State Street	Chase Building
80	1025 State Street	
81	1029 State Street	Janssens/Orella Adobe
		Copper Coffee Pot Restaurant
82	1035 State Street	
83	1036 State Street	Elks Club Building
84	1110 State Street	La Arcada
85	1124 State Street	
86	1129 State Street	San Marcos Building
87	1130 State Street	Santa Barbara Museum of Art
88	1200-1204 State Street	Lower Hawley Building/Hitchcock Building
89	1214 State Street	Granada Theater
90	1227-1235 State Street	Upper Hawley Building in Victoria Court
91	1230-1232 State Street	
92	1301,1303,1303A State Street	Christian Science Reading Room
93	1311 State Street	
94	1315 State Street	
95	1317 State Street	Fox Arlington Theater
96	1321 State Street	Sheetz Building
97	1325 and 1327 State Street	(Opal Restaurant)
98	1329, 1331, and 1333 State Street	
99	1335 and 1345 State Street	
100	1330 State Street	
101	1400 State Street	Welch-Ryce-Haider Mortuary
102	1415 State Street	
103	1421 State Street	Santa Barbara Medical Clinic
104	1424 State Street	Brinks Grocery/Jordano's Market
105	1500 State Street	Trinity Episcopal Church
106	1513-1515 State Street	Moore Building
107	1525 State Street	
108	1628 State Street	Avery Garden Court
109	1734-1736 State Street	Van Dyke House

State Street Plaza

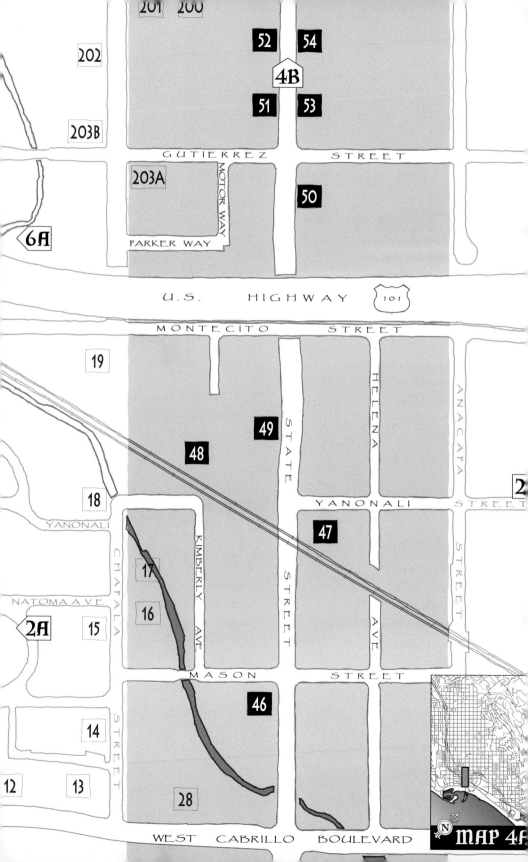

201 200

202

52 54

4B

203B 51 53

GUTIERREZ   STREET

203A
                MOTOR WAY

6A   50

PARKER WAY

U.S.   HIGHWAY 101

MONTECITO   STREET

19

49

48

HELENA   AVE

ANACAPA   STREET

18   YANONALI   STREET

2

YANONALI   47

17   KIMBERLY AVE

CHAPALA   STREET

16

NATOMA AVE

2A 15

STATE   STREET

STATE   STREET

MASON   STREET

14   46

12 13   28

WEST   CABRILLO   BOULEVARD

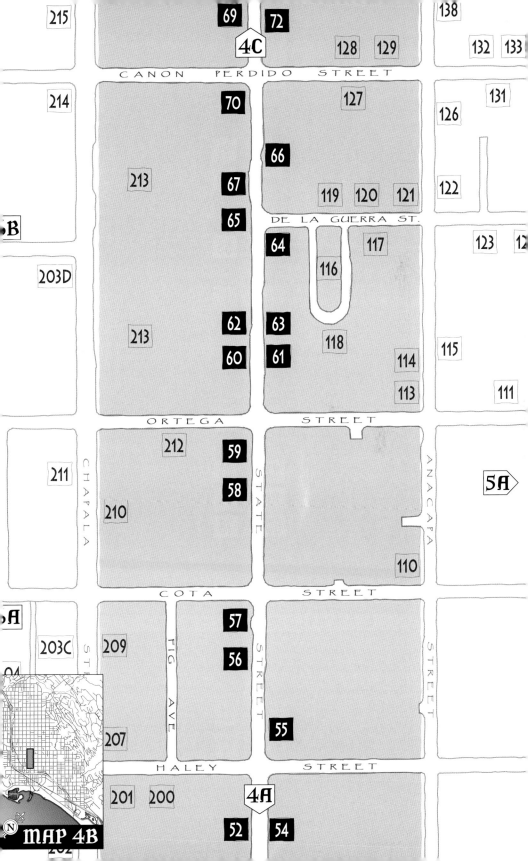

215

69

72

4C

138

128   129

132   133

CANON   PERDIDO   STREET

214

70

127

131

126

66

213

67

65

119   120   121

122

B

DE LA GUERRA ST.

203D

64

117

116

123   12

62

63

118

213

60

61

114

115

113

111

ORTEGA   STREET

212

59

5A

CHAPALA

211

58

STATE

210

ANACAPA

110

COTA   STREET

A

57

203C

209

56

FIG AVE

207

55

STREET

STREET

HALEY   STREET

201   200

4A

N

MAP 4B

52   54

202

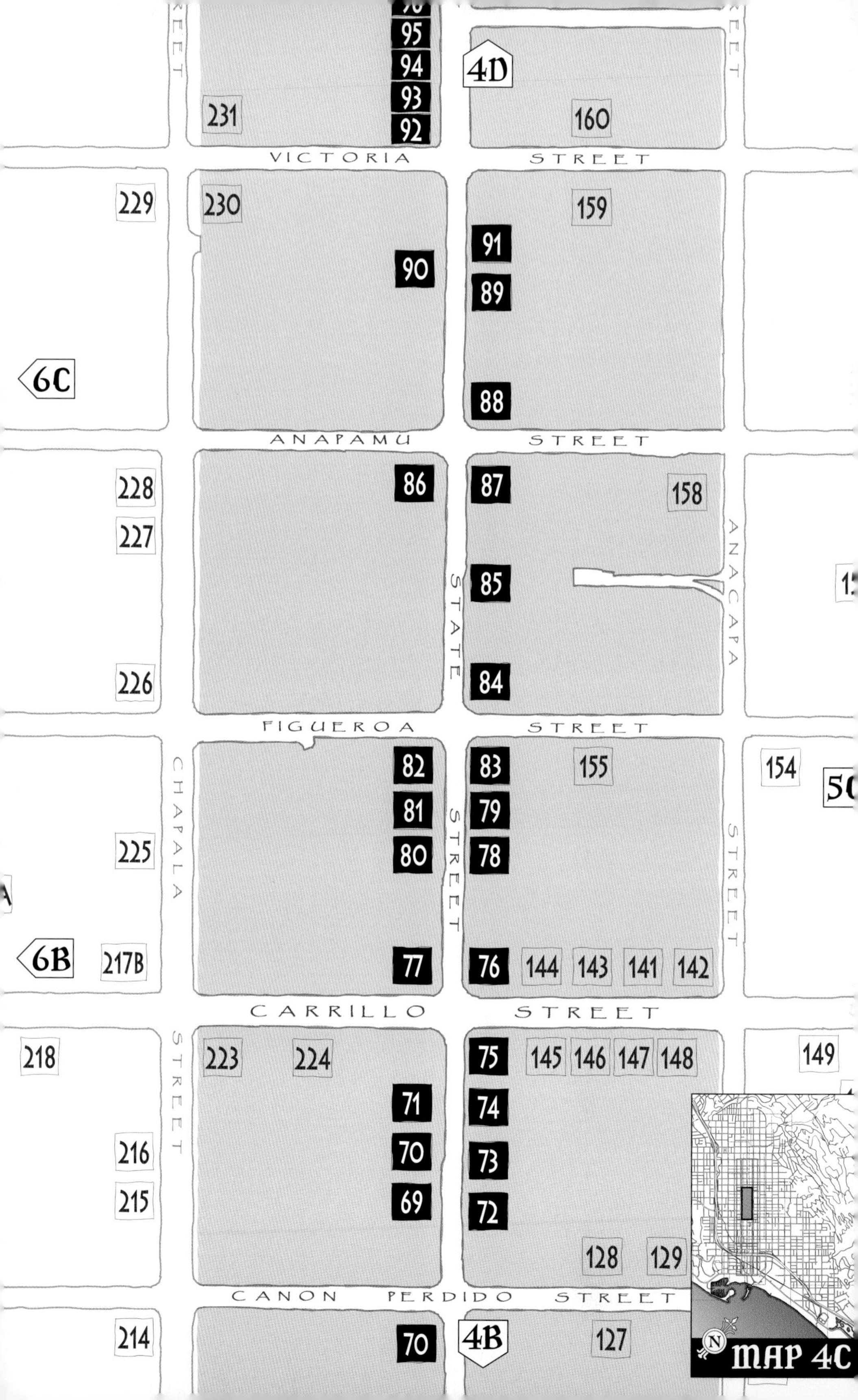

231

95
94
93
92

4D

160

229

230

159

90

91

89

88

6C

86

87

158

85

84

82

83

155

81

79

80

78

225

77

76

144 143 141 142

6B 217B

75

145 146 147 148

149

218

223 224

216

71

74

215

70

73

69

72

128 129

214

70

4B

127

MAP 4C

ANACAPA STREET

STATE STREET

CHAPALA STREET

VICTORIA STREET

ANAPAMU STREET

FIGUEROA STREET

CARRILLO STREET

CANON PERDIDO STREET

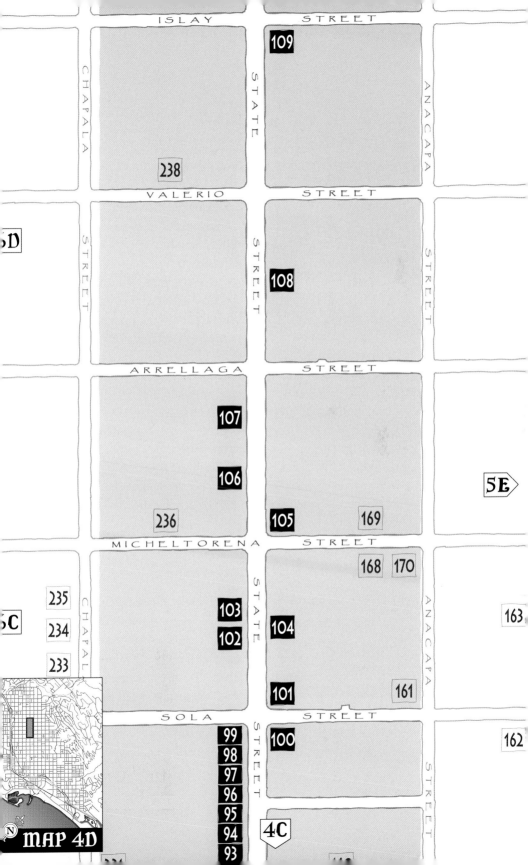

46.
35 State Street
Hotel Californian
1925; F. S. Ward
1926; Architectural Advisory Committee

This building was originally completed just four days before the infamous earthquake of June 1925. The hotel owners were forced to curtail operations when the outside walls crumbled, exposing a honeycomb of rooms. It reopened several months later after $50,000 worth of repairs were made. The façade, the only original part that remains, is a handsome example of 1920s Spanish Colonial Revival architecture, especially its arcade, a feature echoed by the building at 136 State Street.

Across Mason Street and a few steps north of the hotel once stood the building where brothers Allen and Malcolm Loughead first built their F-1, a ten passenger airplane. The Lougheads operated their Santa Barbara factory at 101 State Street from 1916 to 1921, after which they took the operation south to Burbank and renamed it the Lockheed Aviation Company. The building itself was irreparably damaged by fire in 1979, and a Native Sons of the Golden West plaque now commemorates the site.

47.
136 State Street
1926; Soule, Murphy and Hastings

The firm of Soule, Murphy and Hastings designed this Hispanic building in keeping with the 1920s plans for arcaded shops in the commercial district. This store building was originally used as a display room and warehouse for the Crane Company plumbing fixtures and supplies operation. In 1944, the City Council granted the United States Coast Guard's petition to use the building as a "pistol range." It has seen a variety of retail uses since.

48.
209 State Street
Southern Pacific Railroad Station
(Amtrak)
1905; Francis W. Wilson
1998-1999 restoration; Milford Wayne Donaldson, FAIA

After the Southern Pacific Railroad completed the Coast Line in 1901, making it possible for passengers to travel uninterrupted from Los Angeles to San Francisco, rail excursions became popular. The increased rail traffic, however, necessitated larger facilities in Santa Barbara. When the railroad realigned the local tracks in 1905, it also built a new passenger depot, the fourth to be constructed in the city since 1887, when the railroad first arrived. A local architect, Francis W. Wilson, active here from the 1890s to the early years of the 20th century, was engaged to do the new building. The Mission Revival style was selected so that the depot would "conform in general style to the Mission Architecture so appropriate and so popular in Southern California." The station was sited to allow passengers and their escorts easy arrival and departure by way of State or Chapala Streets. For over five decades an attractive lawn area, known as Depot Park, lined the access driveway between the depot and State Street.

In 1998 the state's most noted restoration architect, Milford Wayne Donaldson, was chosen to perform his craft on the depot, with the result that the Santa Barbara railroad station stands resplendent as a magnificent Mission Revival style example, as it did in the beginning. The depot had already been declared a City Landmark in 1980, and it remains as one of a very few such railroad stations remaining in California. The landscape was also restored in 1998-1999 by David Black, who, working from old photos, recreated the park opposite the tracks as well as the rock-edged pathway that led from the depot to the Chapala Street entrance of the old Potter Hotel. Thus the Southern Pacific Railroad Depot remains an ideal introduction to the city for rail travelers.

The Native Daughters and Native Sons of the Golden West dedicated a commemorative plaque in December 1999.   **NR, SBL**

49.
217 State Street
Hotel Neal
(Reagan Ranch Center)
1905-1906; J. W. Bagley
1926; Sauter and Lockard
1979; Contract Design Limited
2006 remodel; Hochhauser Blatter

No sooner had the Southern Pacific Depot been finished than developer and hotel man, Neal Callahan, built a Mission Revival style hotel to serve the increasing number of rail passengers and visitors to the city. The restaurant located on the ground floor was, in fact, first called the Southern Pacific Eating House. Substantial repairs were made to the building following the 1925 earthquake, but its general motif remained unchanged. By Santa Barbara standards, the Neal was a modest hotel; as late as 1935 the single room rate was $1.00 per night, while the much newer and larger Hotel Californian at 35 State Street charged $2.00, and the luxurious Mar Monte at 1121 East Cabrillo Boulevard, on the beach, charged $3.50-$6.50 per room. In 1980 the hotel was remodeled into a restaurant, emulating its neighbor at 225 State Street, originally a commercial laundry building (1909), which had morphed into a restaurant in 1977. In the 2006 remodel, the interior was entirely redone for the Reagan Ranch Center, which now occupies the building. Hopefully, the Hotel Neal building will continue to grace the Santa Barbara scene well in to the future.

50.
316-330 State Street

Auto Showroom and Seaside Oil Company Building
1911; 1913; J. Corbley Pool
1917; Russel Ray (attributed)
1926 alterations; Lionel Pries
1937 addition; Carleton M. Winslow and R. H. Pitman

Henry Bothin of Montecito and San Francisco had this group of buildings constructed for the El Camino Car Company. The original nondescript auto showroom buildings were severely damaged during the 1925 earthquake, and it was Lionel Pries who provided the romantic brick and stucco Moorish arcaded street front. Seaside Oil Company, a local corporation, established its headquarters at 330 State Street in 1937 and remained there for 35 years. Winslow and Pitman added the three-arched loggia and its tower to the north in 1937. Though small in size, this two-layered tower, with its thin lantern, is one of the really handsome tower designs in the city. A mildly streamlined Moderne service station adjoined the tower to the north until the early 1970s. Wings for Douglas Dauntless dive bombers were manufactured at 322 State Street during World War II. The Bothin Helping Fund, the direct descendant of the original builder, and the organization that did so much for Santa Barbara after the earthquake, made the northwesterly section of the main building available to Work, Inc., a non-profit training program for handicapped persons, in 1974. Restaurants and retail shops now inhabit the complex. **NR, SBSM**

Thomas Schmidt @ SBVintagePhoto.com

51.
409 State Street
Faith Mission
1888-1889; Peter J. Barber (attributed)

When this building first opened as the Faith Mission, its function was described as "reclaiming young men from their erring ways and pointing out to them the right path to follow to enable them to become good Christians and worthy members of society." By 1931 the structure had been converted into a hotel, The Savoy, and during World War II was used by servicemen. Architecturally the building is a significant example of Italianate/Eastlake styles. The broadly projecting and heavily detailed cornices at the roof line and over its door and window openings give the façade a three dimensional, almost sculptural appearance. They are formed of galvanized metal wired to the brick wall, and provide added interest to the general look of State Street. **NR, SBL**

52.
415-419 State Street
1892, 1897
1926; Sauter and Lockard

The original building on this site was constructed in 1892 to house the Pierce Furniture Company, a firm that had begun operations at another address in 1883. It was in keeping with the rapid development of lower State Street as the American business community moved to Santa Barbara, and in 1897, a second building was built and attached to the first structure. The store's façade was seriously damaged in the 1925 earthquake, and the owners, F. F. and

Sallie Pierce, engaged the prominent firm of Sauter and Lockard to reface and rehabilitate their building. The architects adopted the popular Spanish Colonial Revival style, meshing perfectly with the other rebuilding taking place along Santa Barbara's main commercial street. The Pierces remained in business at this address until the mid-1940s, when the Kincade Furniture Company took over, maintaining the tradition of a furniture store on the site until it, too, closed in 1977. The building remains both a viable commercial structure and a prominent contributor to the Hispanic feel of Santa Barbara.

53.
424 State Street
1915; J. Corbley Pool
1925; repairs, L. H. Pries
1938; alterations, Chester Carjola
1974; Edwards-Pitman
2009; Henry Lenny

This large brick structure was occupied by automotive-related uses for many years. It was built by H. E. Bothin in 1915 for the Western Garage and the Western Machine and Foundry Company. The building suffered a serious fire in 1917. The foundry also had a location at 530-536 Anacapa Street. Bothin Helping Fund owned the State Street property when earthquake repairs and alterations were carried out in 1925 and 1926 for the foundry company. A plaster shield above the entrance expresses a stylized W and M in its motif. By 1945 Marvin Light sold Goodyear Tires here. Pep Boys auto supplies occupied the property for many years. It is now a general retail establishment.

The building's two-story façade is a handsome example of a simplified Spanish Revival commercial building. Four bays with arched windows grace the ground floor, two on either side of the arched entry. At the second story four small wrought iron balconies denote four sets of French doors.

54.
428-434 State Street
1884
1925; William A. Edwards

The locally prominent De la Guerra family owned this property for approximately one hundred years. The City's earliest maps show it in Francisco de la Guerra's name, and later records indicate that his grandnieces owned it until the 1940s. By 1884 a two-story brick building had been constructed on the site, housing shops on the first floor and a hotel on the second. The 1925 earthquake severely damaged the second story, so the Hotel Grand section was removed and architect William A. Edwards remodeled the front of the ground floor into a balanced four-bay structure with Moorish arches in the center section. Restaurants and shops continue to occupy the premises. **SBSM**

55.
502-510 State Street
1925-26; Wm. A. Edwards, architect and J. J. Plunkett, associate
1932 alterations; Edwards and Plunkett

Thomas Schmidt @ SBVintagePhoto.com

Known as the Medico-Dental Building in its early years, this Spanish Revival style structure was built for Mrs. West Bates. Cafes and shops rented the first floor while doctors' offices occupied the second floor. Mrs. Joseph A. Andrews, who developed Plaza Rubio, owned the structure at the time of the 1932 alterations. By 1940 the El Camino Hotel was located in the building and the Salvation Army became a major occupant in the 1950s. It stands as a welcome example of a post-earthquake "Spanish Californian" structure on an important corner.

56.
515 State Street
1926-1927; William Poole

On or near this site was the *Santa Barbara Herald Weekly* building in the 1880s. Its competitor, the *Morning Press*, was located next door. Later used as a meat market, the edifice was heavily damaged in the 1925 earthquake. A new structure, the present building, was erected in the almost mandated Spanish Colonial Revival style in 1926-1927. Architecturally the alternation between the three large arched window openings and the smaller infill arches not only adds interest, but contributes to the Hispanic ambience of State Street.

57.
527-535 State Street
Neal Callahan Building
1926-1927; Roland F. Sauter and E. Keith Lockard

The site of this large building has been occupied by hotels since 1856. In that year, the two-story American House opened for business. In 1870 the hotel burned to the ground and was rebuilt two years later as the Occidental Hotel. Located at the hub of the Anglo-American business district at the time, the Occidental was the largest hotel in the city and boasted a telegraph office, barber salon, billiard hall, saloon, and "two fine privies" to the rear. Later it became the Mascarel Hotel, and, at the time of the 1925 earthquake, was the Hotel Barbara. Critically damaged by the earthquake, the Hotel Barbara was demolished. The present structure was built in 1926-1927 by Neal Callahan, a pioneer hotel man who had come to Santa Barbara in 1894. To avoid a repeat of the 1925 disaster, Callahan built his hotel to be earthquake proof, with 13 inch reinforced concrete walls. The architectural style employed by Sauter and Lockard was, of course, Spanish Colonial Revival, in keeping with the "new" Santa Barbara. The plateresque detailing about the entrance is particularly impressive, as is the fact that a hotel still graces the building.

58.
607-621 State Street
Pierce Block
Ca. 1874, 886
1925; Fitzhugh and Teal

Charles Pierce built the city's first lumberyard on the site of this building in about 1871. His office and residence were at 611 State Street, adjacent to the Post Office building at 609 State, which he also owned. These buildings were expanded over the next several decades until they stretched from 607-621 State Street.

Architecturally, they were in the then-fashionable false-front commercial style. After the 1925 earthquake, the stores were joined and remodeled in the Spanish Colonial style. The long façade seen here was typical of much of the Hispanic architecture of the period.

59.
625-635 State Street
Fithian Building
1895-1896; Thomas Nixon
1925; Sauter and Lockard

When originally constructed by Civil War hero Major Joel Fithian in 1895-96, this building was a three-and-a-half story French Second Empire structure with a high clock tower. Located at one of the city's busiest intersections, it contained stores on the first floor, offices on the second, and a meeting hall on the third. Often called the "Lower Clock" building to distinguish it from Mortimer Cook's building farther up State Street, it incorporated Benigno Gutierrez's brick drug store which was, until it went out of business in 1979, California's oldest pharmacy. The

Fithian Building suffered considerable damage in the 1925 earthquake, and the third story and clock tower were removed. The present Spanish Renaissance style appearance of this important building dates from Sauter and Lockard's remodeling of 1925 for its then owner, Dr. C. C. Park. The building remains a vital part of downtown Santa Barbara.

Native Daughters of the Golden West commemorated the drug store's centennial with a plaque in 1955. The store had been housed in an earlier building on this corner. **SBSM**

60.
715-719 State Street
Alexander Building
1896
1925; Architectural Advisory Committee
1934; Edwards and Plunkett

This is another example of a late 19th century building which now reads as a Hispanic design. It was damaged in the 1925 earthquake and was repaired with some changes which brought it closer to the Spanish tradition as espoused by the Architectural Advisory Committee. The present arcaded design of the building is the result of the Edwards and Plunkett 1934 remodeling. Some additional changes were made to the front entrance and the adjoining storefront windows in 1976. There is an attractive painted design under the roof eaves, often unnoticed by the casual passerby. **SBL**

61.
718 State Street
Orella Building
ca. 1875
1925; Soule, Murphy and Hastings

Beneath the Spanish Colonial Revival exterior of this building is one of State Street's oldest structures. Built in the 1870s, the Orella Building, like so many of its neighbors, was transformed to its present appearance following the 1925 earthquake. The arched first story and the shed tiled roof are typical of the approved architecture of the period and meld in nicely with the overall appearance of State Street.

62.
721-723 State Street
Parma Building
ca. 1880
1920

This building, a fixture on early State Street had been, before 1920, the site of the Portola Theater and a confectionery store. The Parma brothers' remodeling in that year created a grocery store, thus continuing the fruit and variety business G. B. Parma established in 1872. Originally, the prominent architectural feature consisted of an arcade "running lengthwise through the building with stores on each side and in the center," as one contemporary chronicler noted. The façade and the rear portion have since been altered, but the arches in front add their accent to this part of State Street. The soffit under the front eave has a painted design similar to the Alexander Building next door.

63.
722-724 State Street
Storke Placita

1973

1988; Henry Lenny

From at least the 1870s until 1925 this property was commercially developed. It remained an unreconstructed vacant lot for several years after the earthquake until purchased by Thomas M. Storke, founder and editor of the Santa Barbara News-Press, to provide access to his News-Press building from State Street. It was offered to the city in 1972, a year after Storke's death. An adjacent three foot section of the land had served as a public alley since 1868. It was popularly known as "Caesar's Alley," in remembrance of Caesar Lataillade, a City Councilman who once boasted that he could deliver every Spanish-speaking voter in Santa Barbara to the candidate of his choice.

In honor of the City's bicentennial in April, 1982, the government of Spain presented Santa Barbara with a bronze statue of King Carlos III, who had directed that the Presidio be established two hundred years before, and it was placed in the plaza. The statue's presence proved offensive to a segment of the local population, which expressed its displeasure by periodically defacing what was, at the time, Santa Barbara's only expression of public art. It was eventually removed from the plaza and now resides, perhaps more appropriately, in El Presidio de Santa Barbara State Historic Park. A compass rose now decorates the plaza, with its points indicating Santa Barbara's numerous Sister Cities.

64.
746 State Street
La Placita Building
1903-1904; Francis W. Wilson
1925-1926; Lionel Pries
1992: Brian Cearnal

Although originally constructed in 1903-1904 by the Santa Barbara Improvement Company, the building did not achieve its present appearance until after the 1925 earthquake. Less than a month after that disaster, the Bothin Helping Fund of San Francisco announced it would spend $300,000 to rebuild 12 large buildings in Santa Barbara, all of which would conform to the Spanish Colonial Revival style of architecture adopted by the city. The La Placita Building was considered one of the most important reconstructions "as its completion will remove the last vestige of 'Main Street' architecture from City Hall Plaza." It rests on the site of the two-story Leyva (Leiba) Adobe which predated 1851 and was demolished in 1903. This adobe home and store building protruded into the original line of East De la Guerra Street and is a reason why the present street is offset for two blocks.

The extensive remodel and addition of a third story in 1992 maintains the original style of the building, and is a complement to the neighborhood.

65.
801 State Street
Las Tiendas Building
1925; A. C. Sanders

This Spanish Style building was constructed in early 1925 on the site of the old Central Bank Building, and remains one of Santa Barbara's pre-earthquake Hispanic style structures. Although the first floor on State Street has been remodeled, the side façade, which used to face De la Guerra Street before the construction of the Paseo Nuevo mall, still shows the original arched first story and open balconied second story, though some of the openings have been altered. **SBSM**

66.
808-818 State Street
El Paseo
(Entrances on De la Guerra, Anacapa, and Canon Perdido Streets)
1922-24; James Osborne Craig, Mary Craig
1928-1929; Carleton M. Winslow

The construction of El Paseo was the first major step in converting Santa Barbara's architecture from American Main Street to Hispanic Pueblo. The people most responsible for much of the transformation were Bernhard and Irene Hoffmann, a wealthy eastern couple, who, with the help of a number of important locals, were to become two of the city's most influential citizens during the 1920s. They worked with architect James Osborne Craig and, after Craig's death, his wife, Mary Craig, to create this charming

ca. 1932

complex with its famed Street in Spain, central fountained courtyard (later remodeled), open air patio, restaurant, and quaint passageways, all of which surround and partially encompass the historic De la Guerra Adobe. The then current enthusiasm for Hispanic architecture was reflected in one reporter's praise: "What a place the Paseo de la Guerra is to be! It fairly exudes the spirit and charm of an old world plaza." Ever since, it has been a delight for both residents and visitors alike. The arcaded Anacapa Street façade, with its own small courtyard, was added in 1928-1929 by Carleton M. Winslow, and in the mid-1960s Lutah Maria Riggs closely advised on a remodel of the State Street entrance, especially in the context of the adjacent five-story building's construction.

In 1971, the complex was gifted to the Santa Barbara Trust for Historic Preservation by its then owner, Irene Suski Fendon, as a means of perpetuating its unique character. In 1989 the Trust sold the complex to a group of investors, but, in the process, assured the ultimate preservation of both El Paseo and the Casa de la Guerra. The Trust retained the Casa out of the sale, reserving it for future restoration, and also obtained a façade easement over El Paseo, keeping control over any possible future changes in its historic appearance. The easement also controls various artistically important interiors. El Paseo remains a monument to Hispanic architecture and a vital part of downtown Santa Barbara. **NR, SBL**

67.
805-807 State Street
Thompson Adobe Site
1834-1836

At 805-807 State Street, about midway between the two entrances to the Paseo Nuevo shopping center, still in the midst of Santa Barbara's business district, the Yankee trader, Alpheus

Thompson built, in 1834, an impressive two-story adobe house for his Californio bride, Francisca Carrillo. The building, with its second-story porch, was the first example in California of what would become known as the Monterey Style, as exemplified up north by Thomas Oliver Larkin's 1835 adobe in the capital city of Monterey. From December 7, 1846 to January 3, 1847, Lieutenant John Charles Fremont and his invading battalion stayed at the Thompson House, and it is generally believed that it was on this site that the first American flag was raised in Santa Barbara. The adobe was later utilized as the San Carlos Hotel. This important landmark of early Anglo-American California history was, regrettably, torn down in 1913.

There are Native Sons and Native Daughters of the Golden West plaques at an entrance to the mall to commemorate the adobe's history.

68.
829-833 State Street
Howard-Canfield Building
1903; John Parkinson

This building was originally built during the heyday of stone construction in Santa Barbara, in a mildly Beaux Arts classical mode, with projecting cornice, balustrade and pedimented entrance. It lost those distinctive design elements in 1950, during an attempt to "modernize" the structure. From its beginnings, the Howard-Canfield Building has housed several distinguished Santa Barbara businesses. Diehl's Grocery store, the city's most luxurious dry goods establishment, occupied the corner until the 1930s. Trenwith's clothing store, one of Santa Barbara's oldest retail establishments, was located here from 1904 until it closed in 1981. Despite its age, the Howard-Canfield Building remains one of Santa Barbara's most noteworthy retail and office locations.

69.
903-911 State Street
Bothin Building
1902; W. H. Aiken and J. V. Elliott
1926; Lionel Pries

The original building on this site, a three-story brick edifice in a vaguely classical style, was constructed for W. H. Aiken in 1902. Like all brick structures in the downtown area, it was heavily damaged in the 1925 earthquake. As it did elsewhere in the city, the Bothin Helping Fund financed its reconstruction and, in the process, created a significant two-story structure. Embracing the local notion of creating an Hispanic themed architecture for the city, the Fund, which retained ownership of the building, developed one of the really distinguished examples of the Spanish Colonial Revival in Santa Barbara. The distinctive first-story series of arches, and the recessed second-story loggia did much to set the tone for this portion of State Street.

70.
913 State Street
ca. 1885
1919; J. Corbley Pool

This is one of the few buildings on State Street not in the Spanish Colonial Revival style. It is a quaint doll-house-like structure with a partial mansard roof and pitched dormers, and provides a pleasing contrast to the rest of the street. From the beginning, it has housed a variety of retail shops.

For many years, it was the location of Michel Levy Shoes. Mr. Levy commissioned the 1919 alterations.

71.
921-925 State Street
1914; J. Corbley Pool
1925; H. L. Wass

The present building was constructed for the widow and the stepdaughter of author Robert Louis Stevenson in 1914. The arcaded façade with central bullseye motif dates from the post-earthquake remodeling in 1925. For more than half a century it housed a Santa Barbara landmark, Osborne's Book Store, and now is home to several retail shops.

72.
922 State Street
Nardo Building 1887
1925; Stanley Edwards, Architectural Advisory Committee

Although the first story of this building has been altered, the second story is relatively intact with a projecting wooden balcony in the Monterey Revival style of architecture. This is one of the buildings in which the short-lived, though vitally important, Architectural Advisory Committee, which did so much to standardize downtown architecture in the Spanish Colonial Revival motif, influenced the remodel design. The building continues to house retail outlets in the midst of the city's prime business district. **SBL**

73.
928 State Street
ca. 1885; 1890
1925; Soule, Murphy and Hastings

When the 1925 earthquake struck Santa Barbara, damaging or destroying many buildings on State Street, architects and planners reiterated an earlier proposal that, in the rebuilding, the "east side of State Street should be arcaded to protect the pedestrian and the glass display windows from the late afternoon sun." This building, erected as two separate structures and remodeled into one, is significant in that it was one of the few to apply the arcade concept. The others that did not were castigated in the literature of the period as having the "zealous conviction that business, to be effective, must be disagreeable."

The Rogers Furniture Company, founded by E. F. Rogers, member of a pioneering merchandising family which came to Santa Barbara in 1874, occupied this location from 1904 to 1968. The building continues to serve as a retail outlet.

74.
930 State Street
1927; Edwards, Plunkett and Howell

This elegantly designed building gets its distinction through the continuation of the recessed arcade motif of its neighbor to the south. The sound proportions, minimal decoration and Doric columned arcade make this a classic example of Santa Barbara's "High Renaissance" phase of the Spanish Colonial Revival of the 1920s. It was built by Salisbury Field and Company for Logan and Bryan, bond brokers.

75.
936 State Street
1963; Melvin A. Rojko and Glenn Marchbanks, Jr.

This building, constructed in the 1870s, is on the site of pioneer banker Mortimer Cook's iconic three-story French Second Empire "Upper Clock Building." It was for many years the major landmark of this part of State Street and initiated the northward drift of the commercial center of Santa Barbara toward Carrillo Street. Architecturally, the present building is of interest in that it represents the continuity of the Spanish Colonial Revival in Santa Barbara when it had almost disappeared in the late 1950s and early 1960s.

76.
1000 State Street
1919-1921; Myron Hunt

This basilica-like bank building occupies a prominent location in downtown Santa Barbara. Prior to the present structure, one of the earliest gasoline stations in the city occupied this site. Originally the County Bank Building, it was praised at the time of its construction as a design "unique and singularly beautiful in material, lines, and coloring." Particularly noteworthy are the two Corinthian columns flanking the central arched entrance which are repeated in the interior. The architectural terra cotta, both before and after the 1925 earthquake, was manufactured by Gladding, McBean, and Co. This building not only survived the 1925 earthquake but retains its fundamental function as a bank.

77.
1001 State Street
1960; Arendt, Mosher and Grant
1997 remodel; Cearnal Architects, Inc.

The Eisenberg family owned this important business corner for many years, and their Eisenberg Shop and the Hitchcock Dry Goods store were on the site at the time of the 1925 earthquake. Retail shops continued to occupy the location until 1960 when the Crocker-Anglo National Bank (later Crocker National Bank) was constructed in accord with modern design style. By 1990 J. C. Penney Company had moved into the building from its previous location in the 1100 block, only to be followed by Wells-Fargo Bank. The building was given a major remodel to a Spanish Colonial Revival style in 1997. Saks clothing store became the occupant beneath the eye-catching arcade fronting State Street.

78.
1008-1010 State Street
1924; Soule, Murphy and Hastings
1988; Edwards-Pitman

The original two-story Hispanic Renaissance building which stood on this site was demolished in 1986, and replaced with the present three-story structure. The firm of Edwards-Pitman, sensitive to the architecture of the original building, and to the general theme of downtown construction, recreated the State Street façade, with its paired and balconied French doors on the second story and the large square first-story opening, thus maintaining the match to the adjacent Chase Building and fitting in seamlessly with the rest of State Street.

79.
1012 State Street
Chase Building
1917; J. Corbley Pool
1926; Soule, Murphy and Hastings

The Chase Building fairly exudes history because of its association with the Chase family, whose members were important benefactors to Santa Barbara, and promoters of its Spanish and Mexican heritage. Hezekiah G. Chase founded the family real estate business elsewhere on State Street, but moved to this address in 1917. Hezekiah, his son Harold Stuart Chase, and daughter Pearl Chase, were all prime movers in the Spanish Renaissance of the 1920s, and laid the groundwork for the complete rebuilding of downtown Santa Barbara after the 1925 earthquake. The family name can still be seen above the entrance, and is perpetuated by the present tenant. This structure is the surviving portion of the original Santa Barbara Abstract Company building developed by E. Salisbury Field at 1012-1016 State Street.

80.
1025 State Street
1916; William Poole
1983; Lisa Bregante

This one-story brick building was originally built for Josefa Erro, a member of the prominent Orella family, for many years the owners of a large portion of this block. It began as a grocery store before morphing into the Goldfish Café in the 1920s. Later it became a dry goods store and an Oriental arts shop. In 1983 the building was sensitively remodeled in accordance with El Pueblo Viejo district guidelines, and fits nicely into the general ambience of State Street.

81.
1029 State Street
Janssens/Orella Adobe
Copper Coffee Pot Restaurant
ca. 1859
1927; Edwards, Plunkett and Howell

With its charming outdoor patio, this inviting building is of both architectural and historic interest. Encased in the south wall of the present building is a remnant of the original 19th century adobe. This adobe dwelling was constructed by Augustin Janssens, the owner of the La Purisima Rancho in the Santa Ynez Valley. The Orella family purchased the property in 1872 and incorporated a portion of the original adobe in the 1927 structure, as well as the use of some of the original red tiles for the roof. A restaurant, the Copper Coffee Pot, occupied the building for a number of years and became something of a Santa Barbara institution and gathering place, a function dating back to its construction. The present tenant carries on the tradition.

Orella descendants placed a tile plaque on the building in 1990. **NR, SBL**

82.
1035 State Street
1930; Edwards and Plunkett
1957 addition; Howell and Arendt

This building, with its basilica plan and arched entrance, is similar to the County Bank building a block to the south. Although its exterior is less decorated than the County Bank building, the interior of 1035 State Street boasts Corinthian columns, a central nave, and side aisles reminiscent of early Christian churches. Note the relief image of Saint Barbara on the addition's façade.

83.
1036 State Street
Elks Club Building
1926; Parkinson and Parkinson

Originally constructed for the Santa Barbara Elks Club, this building initially housed retail store space on the ground floor, with the lodge hall above. Since then it has been used for several purposes, notably a large Montgomery Ward department store which boasted Santa Barbara's first escalator. The arcade on both State Street and East Figueroa Street continues the common Spanish Colonial Revival motif found all along State Street.

84.
1110 State Street
La Arcada
1926; John Cooper; Myron Hunt, consulting architect

La Arcada Court was constructed adjacent to the site of the mid-19th century Our Lady of Sorrows Church. This large church was of adobe and brick construction and, not surprisingly, its brick towers fell when the building was destroyed in the 1925 earthquake. It had been the downtown Catholic church, successor to the original Presidio chapel.

La Arcada's two-story Hispanic complex is organized around a T-shaped paseo system which connects State Street to the west, Figueroa Street to the south, and the Art Museum/Public Library courtyard and paseo north to Anapamu Street. An open-air restaurant is used as the focus where the two axes join. The State Street front of the building is arcaded on the ground floor and occupied by retail stores and restaurants, while within the paseos there are enclosed bridges on the second floor to connect the office space units. At the northeast corner of State and Figueroa Streets (site of the church), the architectural firm of Ketzel and Goodman in 1983 successfully remodeled a separate corner building so that it carries on the theme of the La Arcada building. The late owner of La Arcada, Hugh Peterson, maintained the structure magnificently, and his addition of sidewalk sculptural art in the paseos, and beautiful antiques in the barber shop add immensely to the complex's appeal. La Arcada Court remains one of the architectural gems that celebrate the uniqueness of the city of Santa Barbara.

85.
1124 State Street
1924

This fascinating façade, with its triple arcade and free standing and engaged Corinthian columns, whose capitals accentuate the delicate classical style of the structure, is a fine example of the City of Santa Barbara preserving an important piece of the past. In the 1990s, the Santa Barbara Museum of Art embarked upon an expansion which included the removal of two buildings along State Street, one of which, built in 1924, included this façade. When the buildings were ultimately demolished, this façade was saved and moved to its present location where it continues to add interest to the architecture of State Street.

86.
1129-1133 State Street
San Marcos Building
1913-1914; J. Corbley Pool
1925-1926; Myron Hunt and H. C. Chambers

Originally this site hosted Santa Barbara benefactor Col. W. W. Hollister's Santa Barbara College (founded 1869), a two-and-a-half story Second Empire building with a three-and-a-half story curved mansard tower. This was the town's first secondary educational establishment, but it lasted only a few years. The building was then converted into a hotel, and it was here that Col. Hollister died in 1886. By 1913 this use, too, was outmoded, and a new, four-story office building was erected by John Hawley. On June 29, 1925, the great Santa Barbara earthquake struck. The L-shaped building was caught in its powerful vise; the west section pounded against the north and the corner portion collapsed, trapping in the rubble a dentist who had gone to work early. He was the first of 13 earthquake fatalities that morning. Rebuilding the structure took place quickly and efficiently. The top two floors were eliminated, and cast concrete Churrigueresque ornamentation was applied to the façade. Note the paseo leading to the delightful central courtyard and patio, where the building's frieze features medallions of historical figures. **SBL**

87.
1130 State Street

Santa Barbara Museum of Art
1914; Oscar Wenderoth, Francis W. Wilson
1941; David Adler, Chester Carjola
1981; Arendt, Mosher and Grant
1982; Warner and Gray
1992-1993; Edwards-Pitman
2016; Kupiec Architects

Originally a federal post office, this building was one of
several in California which,
though provided by the government, took into account
the character of the com-
munity. It was in an ornate
Italian Renaissance design
with a central arcaded court-
yard, exterior applied pilasters, and decorations. After the post office was moved
to its current location on Anacapa Street
in the 1930s (See entry #126), this building
was remodeled and turned into the Santa
Barbara Museum of Art. The 1941 remodeling, by Chicago architect David Adler, with
input from local architect Chester Carjola,

Thomas Schmidt @ SBVintagePhotos.com

produced a design far more Hispanic than the original structure. Internally,
the central patio was converted into a more delicate, almost Regency, space.

In 1961 the museum expanded with the construction of two new wings,
and in 1983 Paul Gray, of Warner and Gray, designed a new addition to
the southeastern portion of the building. This new addition provided an
entrance which faced out upon a courtyard connected to the block-long
paseo system, and looked out directly upon Library Avenue, with its view
of the Courthouse tower. The design of this wing continued the theme of
the previous remodels and expansions, and is as successful as that provided
originally by David Adler. A new marble entrance, carrying on the theme of
the State Street loggia of the museum, provided an invitation to a two-story interior space. The years 1992 and 1993 saw a further expansion of the

museum's space as Peter Edwards and John Pitman, both second generation Santa Barbara architects, carried on the earlier tradition while remodeling the front entrance. The adjacent buildings at 1120 and 1124 State Street were demolished to make way for a three-story addition, and utilized façade features from the removed structures to keep the State Street frontage, which included a gift shop on the first floor, in keeping with the rest of the street.

Adjacent to the museum is a memorial to Elizabeth and Lockwood de Forest, landscape architects who were responsible for much of the planting on the site. The thorny hedge along the State Street frontage is Kei-Apple (Dovyalis caffra) selected for its barrier quality.

At the time of this writing, the museum is undergoing an expansion and renovation.

88.
1200-1204 State Street
Lower Hawley Building
Hitchcock Building
1887
1926; José L. Curletti
1982; Donald E. Pedersen

Constructed by Walter Hawley, a San Francisco financier, for his carriage and hardware store, this building was erected at about the same time as his other building across the street and up the block (See entry #90). In many ways Hawley continued the development work of Col. W. W. Hollister, whose San Marcos Hotel building stood across the intersection. The Hawley-Hitchcock building originally had a projecting cornice with brackets and a corner turret. All of this was removed following the 1925 earthquake by the then owner, Mrs. Herbert R. Hitchcock, proprietor of a dry goods establishment. The structure was redesigned into the Spanish Colonial Revival style during a substantial remodeling in 1982, conforming it to Santa Barbara's overriding theme.

89.
1214 State Street
Granada Building Façade
1924; A. B. Rosenthal, Charles M. Urton, builder.

Although the eight story Granada Building stands out as an anomaly on the low skyline profile of Spanish Colonial Revival Santa Barbara, it has one extraordinary feature on the upper stories, now marked as a City Historic Landmark, the glazed terra cotta façade. The building, controversial even in 1924 for its height and deviation from what many Santa Barbarans envisioned as the future of the downtown, was nonetheless constructed. It survived the 1925 earthquake with only minor damage, but because of its out-of-character presence, the city passed a maximum height ordinance, limiting future commercial construction to sixty feet. The terra cotta cladding, together with a few other bows to the Spanish Colonial Revival style, were added to the building to assuage the critics, and apparently the effort was successful, as a local newspaper reported at the time, "The treatment which has been given the façade is an inspiring surprise and proves that a skyscraper, contrary to popular belief, may have a distinct personality," and "The facciata in rose and cream glazed terra cotta is gracefully intricate without losing the dignity that such a structure demands." The upper floors remain all of that, and more, beckoning the gaze of locals and tourists alike away from the theater front to the art form above. **SBL (façade)**

90.
1227-1235 State Street
Upper Hawley Building in Victoria Court
1887; Peter J. Barber
1946 remodel; Roy W. Cheesman
1978; Designworks

As with 1200 State Street, this building was the work of Santa Barbara pioneer businessman, Walter N. Hawley, who chose as his architect, Peter J. Barber, Santa Barbara's most famous 19th century designer. Barber's original design was a conflation of French Empire and Italianate styles, and featured a balustrade at the edge of the roof, as well as a central mansard tower. These were removed after the destruction of the 1925 earthquake, as the entire block was rebuilt and remodeled to conform to the Spanish Colonial Revival style. The 1930s saw more remodeling, especially when Sears, Roebuck and Company moved in. Later, in 1946, architect Roy W. Cheesman, who did so much to beautify this area, reconfigured the State Street entrance to the building.

The 1960s saw a general decline in business along the 1200 block of State Street, and when Sears left in 1968, local business interests came together to create "The State Street Drive Through Plaza" to reinvigorate the downtown area. Designed by architect Robert Ingle Hoyt and landscape architect Julio Juan Veyna, the "Drive Through Plaza" eliminated street parking, expanded the sidewalk area, and featured extensive landscaping, all to create "an enhanced pedestrian experience," which now extends down to the waterfront.

In 1978 a group of investors, seeking to further improve the business climate of this area of State Street, decided to combine the buildings at 1221, 1225, the Hawley Building at 1229-33, and the corner building at 1235 State Street into a single entity called Victoria Court. While retaining the State Street façades to maintain the Spanish Colonial Revival feel, the interiors, following a Mediterranean approach, were altered to feature clusters of shops connected by a paseo system which opened out onto surface parking lots to the rear of the complex. Victoria Court, with the Upper Hawley Building incorporated, remains one of the major shopping destinations on the 1200 block of State Street. **SBSM**

91.
1230-1232 State Street
1947; Roy W. Cheesman

Originally constructed after World War II by Reginald Kerry to house his restaurant, which became a Santa Barbara institution, this building is an excellent example of the handsome Spanish Colonial Revival structures designed by Roy Cheesman. There are two others on this block, 1220-1224 State Street and 1226-1228 State Street (both 1948). Now housing a variety of retail outlets, this building continues to maintain the dominant appearance of State Street.

92.
1301, 1303, 1303A State Street
Christian Science Reading Room
1950-1951; Kem Weber and Roy W. Cheesman

Internationally known designer Kem Weber and architect Roy Cheesman successfully combined contemporary Spanish red tile and stucco with Streamline Moderne curves and angles in this building so that it forms a unit with the other Hispanic buildings along this block. Unity, in fact, was their chief goal, according to a statement Weber made to their clients, the First Church of Christ, Scientist, Santa Barbara. "As designer and architect we have only one aim … and this is to get as complete a unity of the building and its materials as well as its execution." Toward that end, Weber designed the interior as well, which features a vaulted ceiling with exposed beams, clerestory windows, a garden room, black walnut paneled walls, and furniture designed by Herman Miller. A curved, cast concrete planter in front of the building was, regrettably, removed in 1981.

93.
1311 State Street
1931; Edwards and Plunkett
1936; Schwartz and Fell

The Monterey Colonial Revival style balcony of this shop enhances and amplifies the intimate scaling of the building at 1309 State Street. Gilchrist's jewelry store occupied the premises for a considerable period, and the structure continues to maintain its vitality as a commercial building.

94.
1315 State Street
1922 attributed; Arthur B. Benton
1926 addition; Edwards, Plunkett and Howell
1934 remodel; Hunt and Chambers

This Spanish Colonial Revival structure was originally built for the Arlington Hotel Company to house one of its shops. It was first leased by I. Magnin and Company, which continued in the space until 1947. In 1949 Lou Rose took over with another women's clothing store, and the building has remained an outlet for women's clothes to this day.

95.
1317 State Street
Fox Arlington Theater
1875 Arlington Hotel; Peter J. Barber
1910 Arlington Hotel; Arthur B. Benton
1930-1931; Edwards and Plunkett
1976 restoration; Arendt, Mosher, Grant, Pedersen and Phillips

The Fox Arlington Theater stands on the site of two elegant and world famous hotels, both of them named Arlington. The first hotel, a three-story Italianate wooden building, perished in a 1909 fire. The second, a hollow tile, concrete and brick four-story structure designed in Mission Revival style, was shattered in the 1925 earthquake. The small stuccoed brick arch located behind the theater near the corner of Sola and Chapala Streets dates to the second hotel. The arch, itself a City Structure of Merit, with its gate, formed part of a wall that enclosed an extensive garden and deer park which surrounded the hotel.

In the late 1920s, when word got around that Fox West Coast Theaters was considering a site for a new movie house, Joseph Plunkett, one of Santa Barbara's outspoken advocates for rebuilding the city in the Spanish idiom, requested a meeting with Fox officials. Legend has it that Plunkett borrowed a pencil from a Fox executive and sketched the initial design on the paper liner taken from a hotel dresser drawer, using the dresser itself for a drafting surface. He apparently

ca. 1920

After the 1925 earthquake.

made such an impression that Fox immediately commissioned Edwards and Plunkett to design the new theater.

With its magnificent spire towering above the city, the theater was to have been the center of a full block of small shops connected to a cross-axis paseo. Although the complete scheme was never realized because of the 1930s Depression, a paseo parallel to the theater façade connects Victoria and Sola Streets, and a graceful arched forecourt links the entrance to State Street, the latter an elegant reminder of what might have been. Inside the auditorium, a mock Spanish village runs along the walls, and an elliptically vaulted, "star studded" ceiling creates an illusory nighttime sky.

In 1976 the building was restored and converted into a performing arts center. For this it received the Historic Preservation award from Santa Barbara Beautiful, Inc., and in 1982 a plaque recounting the property's history was dedicated by the Native Daughters of the Golden West. The theater continues to maintain its vitality, and is home to the annual and highly successful Santa Barbara International Film Festival. For obvious reasons the Fox Arlington is considered to be one of the great monuments of the Spanish Colonial Revival in Santa Barbara. It was designated a City Landmark in 1975. **SBL, SBSM (arch)**

96.
1321 State Street
Sheetz Building
1926; A. C. Sanders
1931; Edwards and Plunkett
1935; Edwards and Plunkett
1995; Wm. Howard Wittausch

In 1926 architect A. C. Sanders designed this store building, constructed one year after the catastrophic earthquake that destroyed the Arlington Hotel. It was occupied by Albert Sheetz Confectioners. After the Arlington Theater was completed in 1931, the building was redone by Edwards and Plunkett to make it more compatible with the dominant feature on the block. The same firm made modifications once again in 1935 to provide a home for the Town House restaurant, which soon became one of Santa Barbara's legendary eateries. During the late 1930s  and World War II, however, the Town House deteriorated into a haunt for unemployed men and the wives of men in military service. That period was punctuated by the murder of the barkeep by a jealous customer. Shortly thereafter the Town House closed, and a variety of owners occupied the building until its purchase in the early 1960s by the Rose family. For several decades thereafter, the building housed two of Santa Barbara's most fashionable and well-remembered women's clothing stores, Village Fair and Post and Rail.

In 1995 Robert Morris purchased the property and had it redone into a mixed use facility, with living quarters upstairs. Architect Wm. Howard Wittausch did a masterful job of designing the building in accord with Santa Barbara architectural principles. He added the wrought iron balcony, the interior courtyard, the Moorish inspired arched loggia, the chimneys, and even a finial retrieved from a stockpile of Arlington remnants. That work earned him a commendation from the city of Santa Barbara design review boards. in 1999. The Sheetz Building holds an honored place in Santa Barbara's architectural history.

97.
1325 and 1327 State Street
(Opal Restaurant)
1946; Soule and Murphy

As part of the Arlington block of retail establishments, this simple building is tied into the rest of the storefronts by the roof finials, which replicate details found on the Fox Arlington Theater tower, and provide a touch of Santa Barbara's Hispanic architecture. Restaurants have occupied this space for many years.

98.
1329, 1331, and 1333 State Street
1940; Alex D'Alfonso

The simplified Spanish Colonial Revival design of this building, with its distinctive storefront windows suggesting Streamline Moderne, framed by black structural glass panels, blends nicely into the understated Hispanic streetscape along this block. It is located on the 1888-1892 site of the Arlington Hotel lawn tennis courts.

99.
1335 and 1345 State Street
1976; Stanley R. Riffle, Jr.

Although it is a fairly recent addition to the Fox Arlington block, this multi-level-roofed building, with its Monterey Colonial Revival balcony and its hexagonal tower, is a fitting capstone to the block's Hispanic architecture. The building won the New Small Business award from Santa Barbara Beautiful, Inc., in 1976 for its corner tower and two-story windows that "give a giant terrarium effect."

100.
1330 State Street
1980-1981; Holewinski and Blevins, in consultation with Edwards-Pitman

Similar in design to the financial institution at 1302 State Street, the Spanish character of this building is established by the sculptured stucco massing, the arched windows, a curvilinear exterior stairway, and the red tile roof.

The 1300-1900 blocks of State Street boast rows of Queen Palms (Syagrus romanzoffiana, formerly Arecastrum), a common Santa Barbara street tree first introduced to the area by nurseryman Kinton Stevens. Many of these were reportedly planted by Dr. A. B. Doremus in 1912.

101.
1400 State Street and 15 East Sola Street
Welch-Ryce-Haider Mortuary
1907; 1920
1956 additions and remodeling; Howell, Arendt, Mosher & Grant

In 1952, the Welsh-Ryce Corporation purchased the existing buildings on this site, a Gothic Revival church structure, formerly part of the Congregational Church, which dates to 1907; and a funeral parlor (originally built to house an auto repair shop) which dates to 1920. A Chapel and additional "slumber rooms" were added to these buildings in 1956. The architects chose a sedate Spanish Colonial Revival design for the remodel, perfectly in keeping with Santa Barbara's overall atmosphere. The principal feature of this complex is the very modest loggia which opens onto the parking lot.

102.
1415 State Street
1946-1947; Timothy L. Pflueger
1997 remodel; Lenvik & Minor Architects

The understated lines of this stylish Regency building, designed by one of San Francisco's leading architects, allows it to meld quietly into Santa Barbara's Hispanic streetscape. For many years it housed the upscale clothier, I. Magnin and Company, which catered to the needs of the city and its tourist visitors. With I. Magnin now only a distant memory, 1415 State Street maintains its dignity and viability by housing the United States Bankruptcy Court. The recent remodel was limited to the garage.

103.
1421 State Street
Santa Barbara Medical Clinic
1920, 1927, 1929-1930; Carleton M. Winslow
1978; Donald G. Sharpe

This elegant plateresque Spanish Colonial Revival building has been designated a Structure of Merit by the City of Santa Barbara because of the arcaded and ornamented two-story façade. The building's designer, Carleton M. Winslow, Sr., assisted Bertram G. Goodhue

in the design of the 1915 San Diego Panama-California Exposition which helped establish the Spanish Colonial Revival style in Southern California. Winslow designed this building five years later, and many of the details reflect the exposition's influence. Originally constructed to house physicians' offices, the building was extensively remodeled behind its façade in 1978 and converted into general offices. A plaster medallion at the top of the façade reads "SB" for the name of the clinic. **SBSM**

104.
1424 State Street
Brinks Grocery
Jordano Bros. Market
1933; Carleton M. Winslow
1972 alterations; Frank Homolka and Associates
1982-1983 additions; Frank Homolka and Associates

The original grocery store portion of this building is the northern section, with its gable tower. The market, which was almost, but not quite, Churrigueresque in design, was Santa Barbara's first supermarket, oriented to its south parking lot rather than the street. Designed by Carleton M. Winslow for Brinks Grocery, the 50' by 100' structure was erected by builder A. C. Jensen. From 1939 to 1957 the local grocery chain, Jordano Brothers, operated a market here.

Changes were made to the building in 1972 to accommodate a savings and loan organization, and the luxurious walled and fountained garden to the north, with its handsome Coral Trees (Erythrina caffra), was added at that time. The garden is an appropriate touch historically as well, since this was the site of the Verhelles' City Nursery during the first two decades of the 20th century. The 1982 wing more than doubled the original building. The low tower of the most recent wing conveys the atmosphere of the 1920s interpretation of the Spanish Colonial Revival.

105.
1500 State Street
Trinity Episcopal Church
1912; Philip Herbert Frohman and Harold Martin
Parish Hall
1925-1926; Soule, Murphy and Hastings

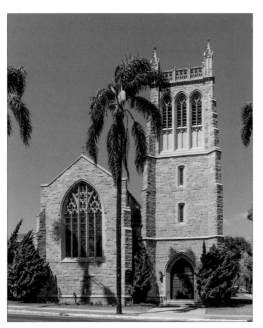

This stone veneer Gothic Revival church was the third church to be built by the Trinity Episcopal congregation, founded in 1866. After abandoning its first church when the Southern Pacific Railroad laid tracks at a noisome distance, and, after losing the second church, a rustic redwood building, to a fire in 1903, the congregation wisely chose to build its third church of native sandstone. Architect Philip Frohman, one of the designers of this English Perpendicular Gothic-influenced building, later gained recognition as the chief architect of the Washington, D. C., National Cathedral.

Church records reveal that a sizeable mortgage incurred to build this monumental fireproof structure was speedily retired. In 1919, "the mortgage was burned with pomp, circumstance, and much celebrating." The 1925 earthquake, however, tried the congregation's patience once more when the east and west gables caved in and the tower was nearly demolished. After a delay of about a year, while Mr. Frohman revised the plans to include earthquake-resistant steel reinforcements, the church was reconstructed at a cost which exceeded the original. It is not known if the congregation engaged in a revelrous mortgage-burning ceremony a second time. The building has undergone more structural retrofitting over the years to meet current earthquake standards. More recently, a labyrinth added to the courtyard on the west attracts contemplation. **SBSM**

106.
1513-1515 State Street
Moore Building
1906-1922; original buildings, most demolished since then.
1927 additions and remodel; Edwards, Plunkett and Howell
1933 and 1935 additions; Edwards and Plunkett

The village-like appearance of this Spanish Colonial Revival medical office complex is due to accretion as much as to the result of conscious planning. The original owner, Dr. Henry W. Moore, a dentist, built his residence and office here between 1906 and 1922. In the 1920s and 1930s, the Moore Estate three times engaged the well-known architects, Edwards, Plunkett and Howell, to make the major alterations and additions that give the complex its charming Hispanic look. The arcade, flagstone paseo, and interior courtyard, with its corner stairway and lush plantings, successfully open up the complex without diminishing its intimacy, a notable accomplishment by sensitive architects.

107.
1525 State Street
1985; Lawrence Thompson, Architects Inc.

The Plaza Linda Vista building can be called one of the first mixed use projects in downtown Santa Barbara. A handsome two- and three-story Spanish Revival structure, it includes six residences and 27,000 square feet of offices. It boasts ten landscaped patios at the ground level and numerous upper balconies with a Monterey Revival flavor. A dominant feature is the Plaza Mayor or courtyard reached from a paseo off the State Street frontage. The courtyard contains a fountain and is framed by Spanish-style architectural features. It has been used for civic events and celebrations. A portion of the complex also faces West Arrellaga Street. Plaza Linda Vista has received awards from Santa Barbara Beautiful. Sandstone planters abutting the street frontage were installed under the supervision of Gino Vendrasco, stone mason.

108.
1628 State Street
Avery Garden Court
1923; A. H. Avery

A well-known local contractor, A. H. Avery designed and built this courtyard complex in the 1920s, a decade in which many apartment buildings and bungalow courts were being constructed in Santa Barbara. This handsome Spanish Colonial Revival complex is an unusual example of this building type, in that it consists of a two-story central unit of 16 apartments flanked to the north and south by pairs of single-story duplexes. The designer-builder initially equipped each unit with a dumbwaiter so that tradesmen could deliver purchases without inconveniencing the occupants, and also with a conveyor that sent trash to a basement incinerator. The project was also known as Estado Court Apartments.

109.
1734-1736 State Street
Van Dyke House
1913-1914
1941 remodel; Edwards and Plunkett

This present day office building was originally the residence of rancher Sidney S. Van Dyke. Built in 1913-1914, the house remained in the Van Dyke family until about 1940, when ownership passed to Dr. Walter H. Pinkham, a dentist. Pinkham engaged Edwards and Plunkett to remodel the house for office use. The original style was no doubt Craftsman, as some Craftsman-like elements remain, but the alteration design is a sensitive blending of the older style and the Hispanic idiom, a typical example of the work of Edwards and Plunkett.

Presidio and Pueblo

By the time Jose Francisco Ortega, Felipe de Neve, and Fr. Junipero Serra founded the Santa Barbara Presidio on April 21, 1782, the Spanish empire had almost three centuries of frontier experience which they fully used in the plan and construction of the Presidio. They carefully selected the site with respect to the proximity of soil suitable for adobe bricks, trees for firewood and the wood portions of the building, stone, lime, fresh water, pasturage, an adequate harbor, and natives to Christianize. The structure's plan was based on similar forts built elsewhere in the Spanish empire. The resulting design, a square four hundred feet to the side enclosed in a nine-foot high defense wall with two diamond-shaped bastions located on the diagonal, theoretically would enable soldiers to protect the four sides of the fort with enfilading fire. Other standard features included a two-story high chapel opposite the main gate, and parallel rooms to the east and west with adjoining vegetable gardens for the soldiers and their families. The Comandante, priest, and officers enjoyed somewhat larger quarters adjacent to the chapel. The whole was an entirely planned structure, one the Spanish had perfected over several centuries of frontier military experience.

The Presidio, however, was actually more a garrisoned outpost than it was a military fort. The outer walls may have been of four-foot thick adobe, but it is doubtful whether they were ever meant to withstand a hostile attack. The Presidio's location protected it from attack by enemy ships, but also prevented it from being able to defend the harbor, except for a primitive redoubt overlooking the anchorage. The Presidio served as a permanent camp located in a remote and nearly inaccessible region. It provided housing for the governmental and military authority of the area. It showed the flag.

Unlike the Presidio, the pueblo of Santa Barbara appeared to be completely unplanned. As one early observer noted, houses were sited as if they had been blown out of a blunderbuss. Spain's "Royal Ordinances Concerning the Laying Out of New Towns" in the colonies of the Americas, promulgated in 1573, stated that the four corners of the plaza were to face the four points of the compass. The Presidio's plaza de armas was Santa Barbara's main plaza until the military abandoned the fortress. Shortly thereafter the streets were laid out at right angles to the newer plaza in front of Casa de la Guerra, not to the original civic plaza de armas.

The village consisted, by 1850, of approximately one hundred of these haphazardly located adobes. The heaviest concentration was around Casa de la Guerra (entry #119) some five hundred feet southwest of the Presidio. The earliest ex-muros adobe was probably Casa Arrellanes constructed about 1795 to the south of the fort (entry #178). There were no improved streets within the village, although a main path led south to the oceanfront and north to the Mission. To the south were located two fruit and vegetable gardens, although

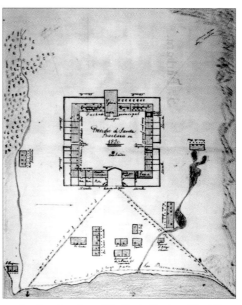

An 1820 drawing of the Santa Barbara Presidio showing uses of buildings, outlying adobe dwellings and the roads coming into the community.

these were probably later additions; the Mission provided food for the community before its secularization in 1833.

Architecturally, the town's adobes varied in size from the tiny one-room Buenaventura Pico adobe (entry #139) to the elaborate U-shaped De la Guerra mansion. This latter was hardly typical either in size or design, even though later during the Spanish Revival it would be cited as the prototypical architectural image of the colonial period. Very few other adobes followed this layout. Most were simple rectangles, one room wide, and varying in length from the twenty feet of the Pico adobe to the eighty-three feet of the Burton Mound adobe (entry #11). None had fireplaces or chimneys, very few had tile roofs. Instead, locally plentiful bitumen was used to waterproof structures. They were, all in all, rudimentary if picturesque structures not greatly superior in creature comforts to the tule dwellings of the Chumash.

Beginning in the 1830s with the arrival of the first Anglo-Americans, who brought with them commerce, civic orderliness, and much different standards of comfort, the pueblo began slowly to take on a quite different aspect. Increasingly, wood was substituted for adobe, streets for paths. Civil government functioned in distinct buildings, especially the first City Hall (entry

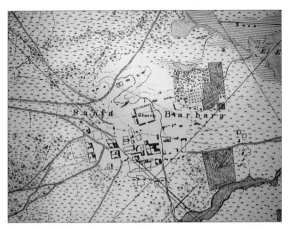

The 1852 United States Coast Survey map of Santa Barbara.

#117), and the Barber-designed County Courthouse (entry #157), replacing the former relative informality of Spanish and Mexican semi-military rule as represented by the rapidly decaying Presidio. Commerce flourished on State Street and residential areas flanked the business district to the east and west. The Presidio area, however, never became an important or fashionable Anglo-American residential district except near its northern fringe about Sola Street. While there were occasional isolated residences such as the 224 E. Figueroa Street house (entry #156), this area remained the Hispanic part of town focused, appropriately, on the remains of the Presidio. And although the descendants of the original settlers adopted many Anglo- American traits, especially in the architecture of their houses, they continued to maintain a basically cohesive Hispanic culture until after World War II when the downtown area underwent rapid commercialization.

At the heart of the Hispanic community and near the former Presidio were located Santa Barbara's Japanese and Chinese immigrant communities. These two groups settled in the East Canon Perdido Street area and nearby areas. They lived an almost entirely segregated existence with their own restaurants, joss houses (entry #128), groceries, and churches. As with the Hispanics, the Asian-Americans were almost entirely removed from the area by the dramatic changes which occurred during and following World War II.

The story of the Presidio area after the war is one of commercial expansion in which residences have been replaced by ever-larger office buildings. This continues to the present, notably on East Carrillo Street, one of the major axes of development in the downtown area (entry #150). Simultaneously, however, the old Presidio, where today's Santa Barbara began, is being gradually and painstakingly restored and reconstructed, more than two hundred and thirty years after its founding.

Presidio and Pueblo ~ East of State

No.	Property Address/Location	Property Name
110	27 East Cota Street	Lyon Moving and Storage Warehouse
111	117 East Ortega Street	Garretson House
112	600 Olive Street	Arnoldi's Café
113	705-707 Anacapa Street	
114	707 Anacapa Street	Gates Building
115	710 Anacapa Street	
116	De la Guerra Street between Anacapa and State Streets	De la Guerra Plaza
117	735 Anacapa Street	Santa Barbara City Hall
118	715 Anacapa Street	Santa Barbara News-Press Building
119	11-19 East De La Guerra Street	Casa de la Guerra
120	25 East De la Guerra Street	Oreña Store
121	27-29 East De la Guerra Street	Oreña Adobes
122	802-812 Anacapa Street	El Presidio Office Building
123	110 East De la Guerra Street	Santiago De la Guerra Adobe
124	112-116 East De Guerra Street	Lugo Adobe/Meridian Studios
125	136 East De la Guerra Street	Santa Barbara Historical Museum
126	836 Anacapa Street	United States Post Office
127	28A East Canon Perdido Street	Fortune Teller Cottage
128	21-27 East Canon Perdido Street	El Centro Building
129	33 East Canon Perdido Street	Lobero Theater
130	East Canon Perdido Street	El Presidio de Santa Barbara State Historic Park
131	122 East Canon Perdido Street	El Cuartel
132	123 East Canon Perdido Street	Cañedo Adobe
133	125 East Canon Perdido Street	Padre's Quarters
134	129 East Canon Perdido Street	Presidio Chapel
135	126 East Canon Perdido Street	Jimmy's Oriental Gardens
136	215 East Canon Perdido Street	Presidio Research Center
137	233 East Canon Perdido Street	
138	914-916 Anacapa Street	Cota-Knox House
139	920 Anacapa Street	Pico Adobe
140	924 Anacapa Street	Margaret Baylor Inn, Lobero Building

141	27 East Carrillo Street	Little Town Club
142	Approx. 21-35 East Carrillo Street	Aguirre Adobe Site
143	17-21 East Carrillo Street	Mihran Studio
144	11-15 East Carrillo Street	Hill-Carrillo Adobe
145	10 East Carrillo St	Gidney Building
146	12-14 East Carrillo Street	
147	16 East Carrillo Street	Masonic Temple
148	20 East Carrillo Street	El Castillo Building
149	100 and 114 East Carrillo Street	Recreation Center
150	222 East Carrillo Street	
151	1034 Santa Barbara Street	Folk Mote Music Company Building
152	1112 Santa Barbara Street	District Attorney's Office Building
153	1021 Anacapa Street	
154	1036 Anacapa Street	
155	10-18 East Figueroa Street	
156	224 East Figueroa Street	Brownsill House No. 1
157	1120 Anacapa Street	Santa Barbara County Courthouse
158	40 East Anapamu Street	Santa Barbara Public Library
159	24-28 East Victoria Street	Victoria Hotel and Shops
160	27 East Victoria Street	Normandy Hotel
161	21 East Sola Street	Our Lady of Sorrows Church
162	116 East Sola Street	
163	City blocks bounded by Anacapa, East Micheltorena, Garden, and East Sola Streets	Alameda Plaza
164	City Block bounded by East Micheltorena, Garden, East Arrellaga, and Santa Barbara Streets	Herter House site El Mirasol Hotel site (Alice Keck Park Memorial Garden)
165	220 East Sola Street	Alameda Court
166	1332 Santa Barbara Street	University Club
167	1301 Santa Barbara Street	
168	32 East Micheltorena Street	
169	33 East Micheltorena Street	Notre Dame School
170	1435 Anacapa Street	
171	1126 Santa Barbara Street	Schauer Building
172	914 Santa Barbara Street	Alhecama Center
173	914 Santa Barbara Street	Alhecama Theatre

174	915 Santa Barbara Street	Bonilla House
175	834 Santa Barbara Street	Moullet House
176	820 Santa Barbara Street	Rochin Adobe
177	814 Santa Barbara Street	Sloyd School Site
178	223 East De la Guerra Street	Site of the Arrellanes Adobe
179	724 Santa Barbara Street	
180	715 Santa Barbara Street	Covarrubias Adobe
181	228 East De la Guerra Street	Gonzales-Castro House
182	214 East De la Guerra Street	Ygnacio House
183	317 East De la Guerra Street	Senior Center of Santa Barbara
184	835 Laguna Street	Gonzales-Ramirez Adobe
185	322 East Canon Perdido Street	Pedotti House
186	312 East Canon Perdido Street	Vhay-Hyde House
187	301 East Canon Perdido Street	Grocery Store
188	820 Garden Street	Tiers-Peake-Schott House
189	908 Garden Street	Cordero Adobe
190	924 Garden Street	El Caserío
191	1027 Garden Street	
192	1028 Garden Street	Spiritualist Association Church of the Comforter
193	1116 Garden Street	Brownsill House No. 2
194	307 Lloyd Avenue	Holland Cottage
195	1122-1126 Garden Street	Maguire Bungalows
196	305 East Anapamu Street	First United Methodist Church
197	328 East Anapamu Street	Wood-Lockhart Cottage
198	1219 Laguna Street	Dutton Cottage
199	1236 Garden Street	

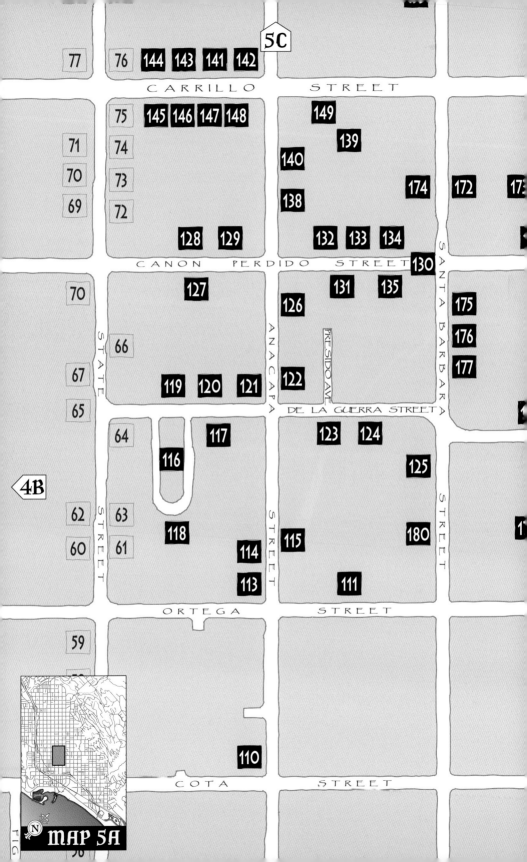

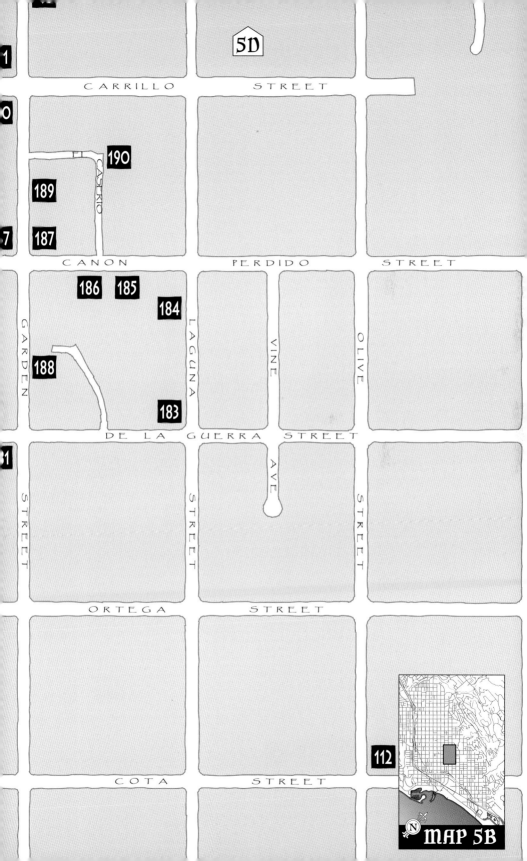

CARRILLO STREET

5D

190

189

CAS RIO

187

CANON

PERDIDO STREET

186 185

184

GARDEN

LAGUNA

VINE

OLIVE

188

183

DE LA GUERRA STREET

AVE

STREET

STREET

ORTEGA STREET

COTA STREET

112

N
MAP 5B

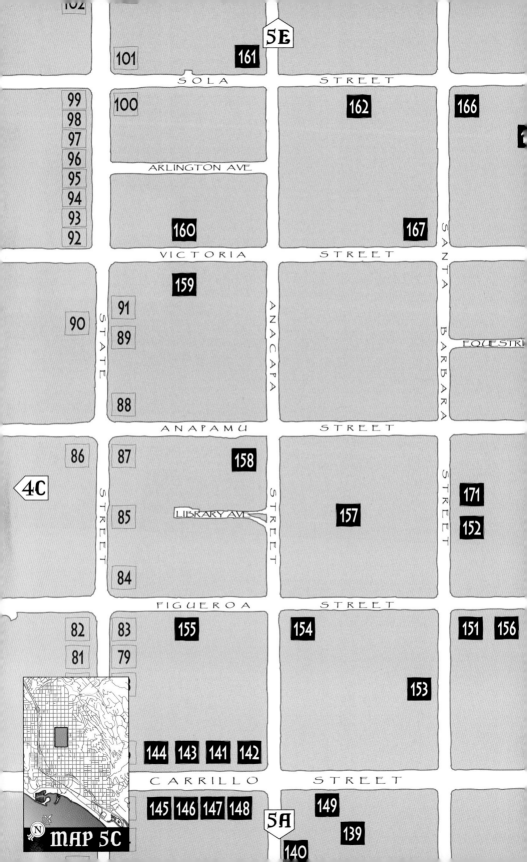

102

101

161

5E

SOLA STREET

99
98
97
96
95
94
93
92

100

162

166

ARLINGTON AVE

160

167

VICTORIA STREET

159

91

89

90

STATE

88

ANACAPA

SANTA BARBARA

EQUESTRI

ANAPAMU STREET

86

87

158

4C

85

LIBRARY AVE

STREET

157

STREET

171

152

84

STREET

FIGUEROA STREET

82

83

155

154

151 156

81

79

153

144 143 141 142

CARRILLO STREET

145 146 147 148

5A

149

139

MAP 5C

140

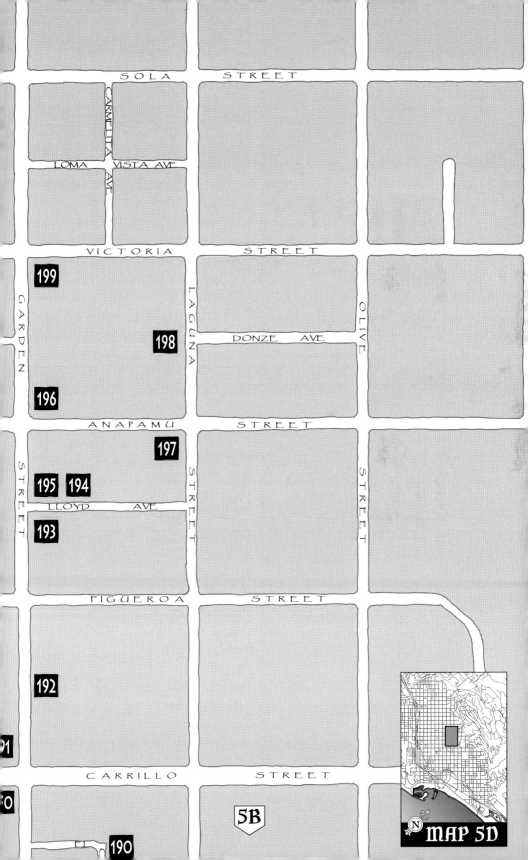

SOLA STREET

CARMELITA AVE

LOMA VISTA AVE

VICTORIA STREET

GARDEN STREET

LAGUNA STREET

OLIVE STREET

199

198

DONZE AVE

196

ANAPAMU STREET

197

195 194

LLOYD AVE

193

FIGUEROA STREET

192

91

CARRILLO STREET

5B

0

190

ISLAY STREET

STATE STREET

ANACAPA STREET

SANTA BARBARA STREET

109

VALERIO STREET

108

STREET

4D

ARRELLAGA STREET

107

106

169

105

MICHELTORENA STREET

168 170

104

163

5C

101

161

1

1

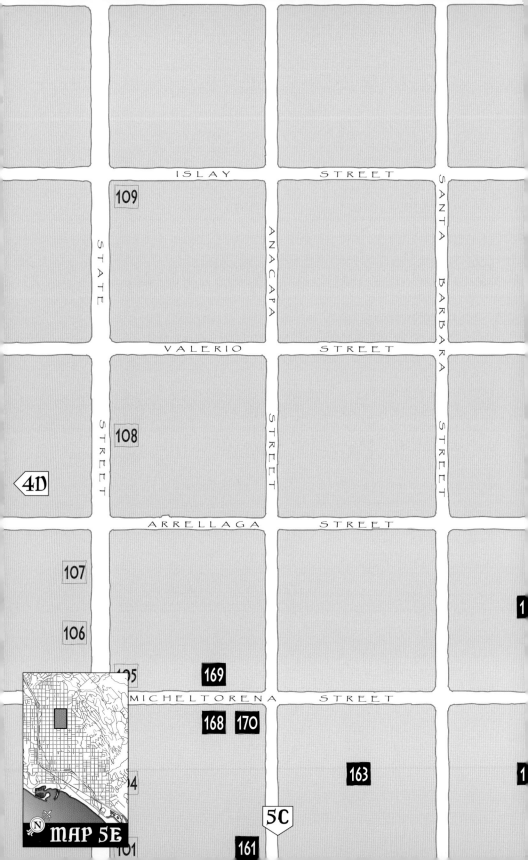

110.
27 East Cota Street
Lyon Moving and Storage Warehouse
1922

Missouri native Ray Lathim migrated to Santa Barbara in 1886 and, noting the rapid development of the city, founded the Lathim Express Company. His business thrived, and his son pushed it even further, being the first in Santa Barbara to utilize gas-engined trucks. As a result of his expanded business, Lathim joined with seven other moving and storage people to form the Lyon Moving and Storage Company, a worldwide association of movers, with offices in all 50 states and several foreign countries. Needing space in 1922, on land once owned by pioneer family member Josefa Bandini, and later by Santa Barbara developer Dixey Thompson, Lathim built a two-story, poured concrete warehouse. Two years later, he added a three-story, fireproof, steel reinforced concrete building to the first. Both structures withstood the earthquake of 1925

without damage. In 1926 Lathim completed a five-story addition, tying the whole together with classical arched openings, Spanish Colonial Revival style trim, metal grillwork and decorative plaster elements. These touches enabled a simple, though massive, warehouse to fit easily, almost unobtrusively, into the general theme of Santa Barbara architecture. Although the Lyon Company is now gone, the building is still remembered by that name.

111.
117 East Ortega Street
Garretson House
1891

In a neighborhood now almost entirely commercial, this house is a nearly unaltered survivor from the residential past of more than a century ago. Not only are the main features of the house intact – the fish scale decorated gable in the otherwise hipped roof, decorative porch columns, balustrade, bay window, and stained glass – the site has also retained its integrity with some original planting and the sandstone retaining wall still in place.

J. N. Garretson built his family home the same year he constructed his grocery store next door (now gone).

112.
600 Olive Street
Arnoldi's Café
1940; Joe Arnoldi

This iconic example of the stonemason's art was constructed in 1940 by master mason Joe Arnoldi, who had honed his craft in the Lake Como region of northern Italy. It was built to house the restaurant operated by Joe and his wife, Ilda, and almost immediately became a Santa Barbara icon. Although Joe and Ilda are gone, their restaurant remains a beloved piece of Santa Barbara history.

113.
701-705 Anacapa Street and 35-37 East Ortega Street
1925; Edwards, Plunkett and Howell

The present structure is near the site of the 19th century Magdalena Cota Adobe which once served as the County Courthouse and jail. The 1925 Spanish Colonial Revival building is unusual architecturally because of the pointed arch arcade along Anacapa Street, the corner tower, and the single pointed arch on East Ortega.

114.
707 Anacapa Street
Gates Building
ca. 1905

This tiny building is a late example of Santa Barbara's adobe tradition. Although constructed of wood, the building displays the scale and composition traditionally associated with adobe construction. The perimeter wall and garden fountain reflect Spanish landscaping concepts, making it a good fit in the Santa Barbara Hispanic motif. It is named for one of its owners. Note especially the large pepper tree and the palms in the garden. **SBSM**

115.
710 Anacapa Street
1887

Although significantly altered and surrounded by parking lots and commercial buildings, this quaint cottage exemplifies the middle-class residential character of this area over a century ago. The bargeboard in the gable ends and the steeply pitched roof establish its Carpenter-Gothic character. Note also the fine sandstone wall in front. **SBSM**

116.
De la Guerra Street between Anacapa and State Streets
De la Guerra Plaza
1855

Due to its location directly in front of the City's most important residence, the Casa de la Guerra, this plot of ground has been used as a public gathering space since the 1820s. In 1855, the City Council formally set it aside "forever" as a "Public Square and Promenade." Since "forever," in political terms, means only until the next vote on the subject, the plaza area was invaded by the erection of a typical American brick city hall and firehouse in 1874. The tall California Fan Palm (Washingtonia filifera) remains as one of two that flanked that building's rear entrance. With the growing appreciation of Santa Barbara's Hispanic heritage in the early 20th century, city hall was remodeled in a Mission Revival style. But, as it could not meet the needs of the burgeoning city, a new city hall was constructed in 1923 on the north edge of the plaza. The next year the old city hall was razed and the plaza returned to open space.

Over the years there have been many plans offered to change or enhance the plaza space, the last being an exhibition and symposium, organized by the owner of the Casa de la Guerra, the Santa Barbara Trust for Historic Preservation, entitled "Plaza de la Guerra Revisited." It brought together scholars, architects, historians, planners, and others to discuss the possibilities of the plaza, and offer plans for the future. It was an extraordinary affair, but at this writing De la Guerra Plaza remains a simple open space, but one which remains the ceremonial and civic center of Santa Barbara.

117.
735 Anacapa Street
Santa Barbara City Hall
1923; Sauter and Lockard

Constructed before the 1925 earthquake, Santa Barbara's City Hall is an early monument to the Spanish Colonial Revival movement in the city, and certainly was a stimulus for rebuilding the city in that motif. The removal of the previous city hall located on the plaza had been recommended as early

Thomas Schmidt @ SBVintagePhoto.com

The old City Hall, built in 1874.

The City Hall as remodeled in 1910.

as 1909, when it was described as the "incongruous red firehouse and city hall sticking into the Plaza like a sore thumb." The present building is distinguished by its graceful two-story arcade which faces onto the plaza (See entry #116). The architectural terra cotta decorating the exterior was manufactured by the renowned Gladding, McBean and Co. Note also the old California Pepper tree (Schinus molle) in front of the building. Both City Hall and the tree are City Landmarks.

Just south of City Hall was the site (now a parking lot) of the Yorba-Abadie Adobe. This adobe, which was built before 1826, was one of the most elaborately decorated homes in early Santa Barbara, having interior walls painted in a variety of colors and patterns. It became the home of the noted artist, Alexander Harmer, who had married Felicidad Abadie. The structure was badly damaged in the 1925 earthquake, and was eventually torn down to provide a few more parking spaces! A plaque commemorates its existence. **SBL**

118.
715 Anacapa Street
Santa Barbara News-Press Building
1922; George Washington Smith
1951; Edwards and Wade

Originally the *Daily News*, the News-Press building visually fixes the south side of De la Guerra Plaza as the north side is anchored by the iconic De la Guerra Adobe. It was designed by the distinguished architect, George Washington Smith, in a simple, almost classical style, but one which fit in with the growing movement toward a Spanish Colonial motif for the downtown area. The tower and east wing were added in 1951. The building is a monument to Thomas More Storke, the editor and publisher for more than 50 years of one of Southern California's oldest daily newspapers, the *Santa Barbara News-Press*, and recipient of the Pulitzer Prize. The architectural example set

by this building and the adjacent City Hall did much to encourage redesign of the plaza area following the 1925 earthquake. **SBL**

119.
11-19 East De la Guerra Street
Casa de la Guerra
1819-1827
1991; Milford Wayne Donaldson

ca. 1900

Of the four building blocks of early California– Presidios, Missions, Pueblos and Ranchos– all of which had their influences locally, the pueblo that grew up around the Presidio proved to be the foundation of modern Santa Barbara. The most prominent individual during that formative period was Don José de la Guerra, 5th Comandante of the Presidio, international trader and businessman, and patriarch of Santa Barbara's most notable family. It was he who built the magnificent U-shaped adobe mansion, certainly as impressive in its day as it is now, and used it not only as living quarters for his family, but also as the center of his enterprises. His home became the focus of local cultural activities, which achieved international attention with the wedding of one of his daughters to the American trader, Alfred Robinson, an event memorialized by Richard Henry Dana in his 1840 book, *Two Years Before the Mast*. From then on, the Casa courtyard became the home of city life, from Don José's entertainments of visiting dignitaries, to the Festival Arts events of the 1920s, to today's Old Spanish Days Fiesta. In the 1920s, the Casa de la Guerra was incorporated into El Paseo, and became the theme of the rest of the complex. In 1971 El Paseo was gifted to the Santa Barbara Trust for Historic Preservation, and when the latter sold El Paseo to a group of investors, it retained ownership of the Casa de la Guerra in 1989. In an extraordinary feat of meticulous restoration beginning in 1991, and lasting more than a decade, the Trust returned Casa de la Guerra to its original grandeur, and assured its permanent preservation. It is open on weekends to visitors, who can even view some of the original furnishings of the house. **NR, CHL, SBL**

120.
25 East De la Guerra
Oreña Store
ca. 1860

This building is one of the earliest brick commercial structures still standing in Santa Barbara. It was constructed about 1860 in the Italianate style by Gaspar Oreña, who also owned the adobes to the east (See entry #121). Used originally as a dry goods shop, it later served as a police courtroom, book shop, art goods store, and, from 1903 to 1913, as the *Daily News* office. Architecturally, the building, with its symmetrical arched façade, contrasts with the early California adobe tradition of the structures next door. It is an early example of the Anglo-Americanization of the town as expressed through its architecture. The exterior of this historic structure is protected by a conservation easement held by the Santa Barbara Trust for Historic Preservation. **NR, SBL**

121.
27-29 and 39 East De la Guerra Street
Oreña Adobes
1849
1858

The one-story adobe at 39 East De la Guerra Street was built in 1849 by José de la Guerra, fifth Comandante of the Santa Barbara Presidio. It was used at that time as a storehouse for merchandise brought in from ships visiting the harbor. It was later sold to Gaspar Oreña, who constructed the

Ed Borein at his studio

adjacent story-and-a-half adobe at 27-29 East De la Guerra Street. Although the Oreñas spent much time at one or another of their cattle ranches, most of their thirteen children were born here in the family's city residence. The adobes were restored in 1919-1920 under the direction of James Osborne Craig who, shortly afterwards, restored the Casa de la Guerra adobe and created the El Paseo complex surrounding it. Edward Borein, western artist, had his second Santa Barbara studio here at number 29 from 1923 to 1925. From 1921 to 1923 he had occupied a rear studio at the Yorba-Abadie Adobe in City Hall Plaza (Plaza De la Guerra) (See entry #117). In 1925 he relocated to studio 17 in El Paseo, remaining there until his death. While the roofs of the Oreña Adobes appear to be appropriate red tile, one of them is actually metal tile. These adobes are especially remarkable in that their present owners are descendants of the Oreña family. **SBL**

122.
802-812 Anacapa Street
El Presidio Office Building
1945-1946; Joseph J. Plunkett, Ralph T. Stevens, landscape architecture

This charming example of post-World War II Spanish Colonial Revival architecture is the final work of noted Santa Barbara designer, Joseph J. Plunkett, who did so much to create and promote the architectural Hispanicization of the city. With great sensitivity to Santa Barbara's history, Plunkett incorporated portions of two adobes, a Mexican-period guard house, and the Miranda Adobe at 806 Anacapa Street, home to José María Miranda, "El Maestro," architect at the time of

Thomas Schmidt @ SBVintagePhoto.com

Thomas Schmidt @ SBVintagePhoto.com

the padres, and tutor to the mission laborers who constructed the original Mission Santa Barbara. He remodeled the old Nardi Hotel (1906), which stood on the corner of De la Guerra Street. The most striking feature of the complex is the northwest corner room with its octagonal tower and dome with ironwork created by renowned artisan, Gunnar Thielst. The room was used as a wedding chapel for a number of years after its construction, and featured an altarpiece, a reproduction of a piece created in 1522 by Giovanni Della Robbia. This beautiful artwork is now at Mission Santa Barbara. At the rear of the building is Presidio Avenue, known as Santa Barbara's original city street, and once part of a path that ran from the waterfront to the Presidio and on to the Mission. In 1911 the street was officially declared a "public avenue and thoroughfare." Additional rental spaces were built across the avenue, next to the Post Office and facing a garden. Although the original owner of El Presidio Office Building, William Zimdin, later to be a founder of the City's renowned Direct Relief International, initially may have envisioned the main structure as a hotel, restaurant and shops, it has always been a multi-use edifice. With its open courtyard and fountain, it makes a fitting neighbor to the El Paseo complex across the street. **SBL (rear 35 feet), SBSM (remainder)**

123.
110 East De la Guerra Street
Santiago de la Guerra Adobe

ca. 1812

Though extensively altered, this single-story structure was reputedly built in 1812, making it one of the city's oldest remaining adobes. It was centrally located across from the Presidio's Mexican-era guardhouse (See entry #122), and adjacent to the Lugo Adobe (See entry #124). Santiago de la Guerra was the grandson of patriarch José de la Guerra, and nephew of the latter's son, Antonio María de la Guerra. He became a member of the "Lancers," a California cavalry unit formed by Antonio de la Guerra to fight with the Union forces in the American Civil War. The troop traveled as far as Arizona before news reached them that the war was over. **SBL**

124.
112-116 East De la Guerra Street
Lugo Adobe/Meridian Studios
ca. 1830
1922
1923; George Washington Smith
1925; Carleton M. Winslow, Sr.

The Meridian Studios consist of a grouping of five buildings of which the Lugo
Adobe, located to the rear, dates to the early 19th century. This adobe, like so many of
the period, was originally constructed by a
Presidio soldier. It passed through the hands
of a number of owners before Bernhard and

Irene Hoffmann, important city benefactors, purchased the property and remodeled the adobe in 1922. The following year the couple commissioned George
Washington Smith to design a master plan for the property, including a studio
building on the front of it. At this time, the Hoffmanns were also building El
Paseo a block to the west (See entry #66). In 1925 the complex was completed
with a two-story shop and second studio structure designed by Carleton M.
Winslow, Sr. Since its construction, the Meridian Studios have housed several
well-known artists and architects, including Winslow, Ettore Cadorin (the
sculptor of "Spirit of the Ocean" fountain at the Courthouse) (See entry #157),
painter Colin Campbell Cooper, architects Edwards and Plunkett, and, more
recently, the office of landscape architect Katie O'Reilly Rogers. Architecturally
the studios are distinguished by their pastel-colored stucco walls and the structures' diagonal siting to capture north light. This idea and the original landscape

design are attributed to landscape architect Lockwood de Forest, Jr. The tranquil courtyards are noted for their vines, including an ancient Wisteria in the main court and a Blood-Red Trumpet Vine (Distictis buccinatoria) on the iron fencing separating the complex from the street, thus creating a bit of old Spain, or Mexico, in downtown Santa Barbara. The unusual flowering street trees in this block of De la Guerra Street are Chinese Hibiscus (Hibiscus rosa-sinensis), which are gradually being replaced with Palo Verde trees (Cerecidium sp.) **SBL**

125.
136 East De la Guerra Street
Santa Barbara Historical Museum
1964-1965; Robert Ingle Hoyt
2012; Edwards-Pitman, Richard Redmond

Originally called the Santa Barbara Historical Society, this organization has been a force for the preservation of local history since formed as a voluntary association in 1932. After occupying a wing in Mission Santa Barbara for a number of years, the Society constructed its headquarters in the heart of El Pueblo Viejo in a Southwest style, which included Mediterranean-style landscaping in the front and the courtyard of the building to the rear. Recently a Spanish Colonial Revival style balcony was added to the De la Guerra front. Unfortunately, all that remains of the original landscape design by Elizabeth de Forest is the area around the entrance, including the boulder with its plaque. The courtyard has been remodeled several times, and contains a fountain and such notable plants as the Copa de Oro (Solandra maxima) vine and the creeping Rosemary cultivar called "Lockwood de Forest." A handsome plaque in the shape of the Great Seal of State was dedicated February 28, 1965 by the Native Sons of the Golden West and Native Daughters of the Golden West when the building opened.

126.
836 Anacapa Street
United States Post Office
1936-1937; Reginald D. Johnson; interior reliefs by William Atkinson

Prior to its present location, the post office occupied the building which now houses the Santa Barbara Museum of Art (See entry #87). When the old building proved insufficient to serve the growing town, Thomas M. Storke led an effort to convince the Federal Government to construct a new post office in appropriate Spanish style. The effort was successful, and Storke was allowed to select the architect of his choice, the prominent Reginald D. Johnson. The location of the new building was also purposely chosen to eliminate a structure in the middle of Santa Barbara's "red light" district

and initiate the rehabilitation of the area. The building's general massing and overall appearance fit into the Spanish Colonial Revival motif, certainly appropriate to its location in the vicinity of the Presidio.In the detailing, Johnson, looking to fuse the old and the new in an attempt to link Santa Barbara's past and future in the architecture of the building, used a number of decorative motifs derived from the then popular Streamline Moderne style. Such items as the chevron decorations, the Monel metal doors, and the eagle on the north façade, among others, exemplify that effort, making the post office a unique and important structure. The much admired bas-relief sculptures on the interior walls of the lobby were created by the artist William O. Atkinson, a native of Los Angeles. They depict the history of the transportation of the mail. It is on the National Register of Historic Places. At present it is serving as an elaborate postal sub-station, and its future use is in question.

During a festive, crowded dedication ceremony on May 8, 1937, the Native Sons of the Golden West unveiled a plaque set into the entry terrace. Architect Reginald Johnson gave an address. **NRHP, SBL**

127.
28A East Canon Perdido Street
Fortune Teller Cottage
1926; Carleton M. Winslow
1945; Joseph J. Plunkett

This oddly-sited little building was originally constructed for Bernhard Hoffmann as a parking shed for his El Paseo complex. It is probably a comment on the times that important architect, Carleton Winslow, and prominent Santa Barbara builders, Snook and Kenyon, were engaged to do such an apparently mundane project. In any case, the structure underwent several remodels over the years as needs changed. In 1945, Santa Barbara's most prominent advocate of the Spanish Colonial Revival style for the city, Joseph J. Plunkett, was retained to design a new entrance to the El Paseo parking lot. He came up with an arch over the driveway entrance, a new façade for the building, and a tower and roof for his fanciful creation, a striking appearance on that now almost empty block front, but one in keeping with the city's overall architectural theme. It is remembered by locals as the Fortune Teller Cottage because of the long tenancy of Madam Sonia Rosinka, Psychic and Palm Reader.

128.
21-27 East Canon Perdido Street
El Centro Building
1929; Edwards, Plunkett and Howell

Architecturally, this Spanish Colonial Revival building successfully blends with the Lobero Theater next door to the east. The building's balconies and the exterior brightly colored tile staircase are impressive aspects of the design. Historically, this block of Canon Perdido Street was the center for the activities of Santa Barbara's extensive Chinese population, and this particular site was the location of a tong-controlled Chinese joss house, a Chinese Masonic Temple, and substandard housing for Chinese laboring families. The original wooden building burned in a fire in the 1920s and was replaced by the present structure.

129.
33 East Canon Perdido Street
Lobero Theatre
1924; George Washington Smith, Lutah Maria Riggs

The Lobero Theatre is the oldest continuously operating theater facility in California. On this site in 1873, José Lobero, an Italian immigrant, opened Southern California's first opera house in a refurbished school building said to have been the largest adobe structure in the state. Although the exterior was relatively undistinguished, the interior was praised as "attractive and appropriate," and having an "air of quiet elegance." The opening night program consisted mainly of excerpts from Italian operas but was marred, as one reporter noted, "by outrageous and hideous catcalls, shrieks and noise of half-grown boys at the concert." In spite of this, the opera house prospered throughout much of the 19th century. By the early 1920s, however, the old structure had become dilapidated and the private Community Arts Association, after first considering renovation, decided ultimately to construct a new theater. The present building, with its graceful three-tiered design culminating in the 70 foot high stage house, was the work of prominent Santa Barbara architect, George Washington Smith, together with his associate, Lutah Maria Riggs. The Spanish style design, along with the contemporaneous City Hall and News-Press buildings, did much to propel the Hispanicization of Santa Barbara in the 1920s. In a bow to its long history, the adobe walls behind the Lobero were built from the bricks of the original theater.

Recently the entire area fronting Canon Perdido Street was remodeled, eliminating the brick walkway which led from street level to the theater's front entrance arcade, providing a new set of stairs up to a terrace at the arcade level, and removing the olive trees which shaded the lawn. Community protests forced the replanting of olive trees which had been specified by landscape architect Lockwood de Forest, Jr. There is a California historical landmark plaque at the site. **CHL, SBL**

Lobero Theatre 1924

130.
Portions of four city blocks surrounding the intersection of
Santa Barbara and East Canon Perdido Streets
El Presidio de Santa Barbara State Historic Park

Over the years since the Santa Barbara Trust for Historic Preservation first acquired and then donated El Cuartel (See entry #131) to the State of California, and the State Historic Park was created, the Trust, through a unique Operating Agreement, administers the Park for the California Department of Parks and Recreation. Beyond that, following the dream of eventually reconstructing the entire Presidio, the Trust continues to acquire the necessary properties within the footprint of the old fort, and to reconstruct elements as funding permits. The first segment to reappear was the Padre's Quarters, (See entry #133), adjacent to the Chapel on the south. Its spartan accommodations speak volumes about the life lived at the birth of modern California. Next door is the magnificent Chapel (See entry #134), reconstructed on the original foundations and, with the skill of architect Gilbert Sanchez, built as close to the original as modern safety regulations permit. The lavishly decorated interior, as bright and imposing as it was in the beginning, is due to the research and painting skills of the late Norman Neuerburg. The site of the Chapel is also interesting in that, in 1923, a Buddhist Temple was constructed over the original Chapel foundations. It served members of the local Asian community for a number of years before the congregation moved on and sold the property. The Trust eventually acquired the site, essential to the whole Presidio project.

Between the Chapel and Santa Barbara Street is a portion of the Comandante's quarters, with a set of stones embedded in the street indicating where portions of the buildings once stood. On the north side of Santa Barbara Street is a rebuilt section of the Northeast corner of the Presidio. It was completed in 1996, after extensive archaeological investigation, and architectural work by Milford Wayne Donaldson. This section consists of living quarters for the Alferez, a kitchen, and three residences for soldiers and their families, nine adobe rooms in all, together with yard walls and a stretch of the outer defense wall. The kitchen gardens are planted and maintained by students from the nearby Anacapa School.

To the south of the Cañedo Adobe (See entry #132) is the reconstruction of a portion of the Northwest side of the fort, with the rooms now being used as exhibit space, and the massive outer defense wall giving real definition to this portion of the park. Across Canon Perdido Street is the Park's latest acquisition, Jimmy's Oriental Gardens (See entry #135), in which the Park will eventually establish a museum to the Asian presence in the city.

The whole of El Presidio de Santa Barbara State Historic Park is a fascinating place, and is well worth an extended visit. **NRD**

131.
122 East Canon Perdido Street
El Cuartel

1788

El Cuartel is the oldest building in Santa Barbara, being a fragment of the Spanish Royal Presidio founded in 1782. Permanent buildings for soldiers' housing were begun a few years later under Felipe de Goicoechea, the second Comandante of the Presidio. For many years El Cuartel housed José Jesús Valenzuela, the gate keeper for the rapidly deteriorating fort during the Mexican Period of California history. In 1941, shortly after the adjacent post office was constructed, a number of public spirited citizens, led by Pearl Chase and her brother Harold, purchased El Cuartel, assuring its preservation. In 1964 a new group, naming itself the Santa Barbara Trust for Historic Preservation, purchased the property and presented it to the State of California. This formed the nucleus of what eventually became El Presidio de Santa Barbara State Historic Park, one of the first "urban" state parks in California. The Trust continues to operate the park for the State of California, and El Cuartel remains an integral part of this popular site. **NR, CHL, SBL**

132.
123 East Canon Perdido Street
Cañedo Adobe
1788

Initially built as one of the residential units for non-commissioned officers at the Spanish Presidio, this adobe was later granted to José María Cañedo during the period of Mexican rule. His son, and subsequent owners, occupied the house until 1923, when Elmer H. Whittaker of Montecito purchased the property. Whittaker remodeled the old adobe, adding onto the rear and rearranging the interior to make a home for himself and his wife Barbara. The front part of the adobe dates back to the original Spanish fort, with the exception of the four panel door and double-hung windows, both improvements from the early American period. Now included in El Presidio de Santa Barbara State Historic Park, the Cañedo Adobe is part of the ongoing restoration and reconstruction of the Presidio. It is joined to the rebuilt Padre's Quarters and will eventually be restored to its original condition. **NR, CHL, SBL**

133.
125 East Canon Perdido Street
Padre's Quarters
1788
1977-1981; Frank D. Robinson

The Padre's Quarters, abutting the Presidio Chapel on the west side, was the first portion of El Presidio de Santa Barbara State Historic Park to be reconstructed by the Santa Barbara Trust for Historic Preservation. The Trust

learned much about early construction methods and materials in an attempt to adhere as closely to the original as modern construction regulations would permit. Note the tule reeds underlaying the roof tiles, and the rawhide strips binding them to the rafters. This simple cell, with its spare furnishings, served both as living quarters and office for the itinerant priests who offered masses in the Chapel, and clearly reflects the vow of poverty taken by the Franciscan priests. **NR, CHL**

134.
129 East Canon Perdido Street
Presidio Chapel
1788
1982-1984; Gilbert Sanchez

The second portion of the Presidio to be reconstructed was the Presidio Chapel, then and now the most impressive of Presidio structures. Its two-story height posed greater construction problems than the Padre's Quarters next door, but the surprising strength of the adobe bricks enabled the Trust to build much closer to the original than expected. The corners are reinforced with concrete and steel, and cement bond beams strengthen the high walls to conform to modern earthquake regulations. The interior decorations, painstakingly painted by the late Dr. Norman Neuerberg, carefully mimic the originals, with the vivid colors reflecting the taste of the local Chumash people, who, along with the Soldados, provided the original labor for the erection of the Chapel. El Presidio de Santa Barbara State Historic Park, with all of its restoration, reconstruction and exhibits, is well worth an extended visit. There is a California Historical Landmark plaque in front of the chapel. **NR, CHL**

135.
126 East Canon Perdido Street
Jimmy's Oriental Gardens
1946; Roy Cheesman; Whittaker and Snook, builder.

This striking little building, with its obvious oriental influences and incongruous red tile roof, was built in 1946 to house the restaurant and bar of the original owner, Jimmy Chung. Catering to the downtown crowd

with good food and generous drinks, Jimmy Chung quickly built a strong business with devoted customers, while keeping alive the memory of the once thriving Asian community in the neighborhood. When Jimmy passed away in 1970, the business devolved upon his son, Tommy Chung, who enhanced the tradition by introducing a new menu. The Chungs, father and son, were devoted to family, and treated their patrons as members, endearing themselves to the community. Included in that extended community were members of the Santa Barbara Trust for Historic Preservation, developing the Presidio across the street, and when Tommy Chung decided to retire and sell his establishment, he made sure the Trust, with its stated goal of preserving the past, had an opportunity to purchase the property. To Tommy's delight, the Trust managed to do just that. Now, while keeping the building alive as a restaurant and bar, the Trust is developing plans for the use of the structure as a museum dedicated to the rich Asian heritage in Santa Barbara.

136.
215 East Canon Perdido Street
Presidio Research Center
1928; Soule and Murphy

This Spanish style building, with its projecting mirador, was once part of the Community Arts Association's Santa Barbara School of the Arts. It was the only substantial building constructed by the school, which eventually foundered in the financial crisis of the 1930s, and it served for several years as the home of studios for the local Adult Education program. It was later acquired by the Santa Barbara Trust for Historic Preservation which, with a substantial interior remodel, created a library and research center focusing on early California history. It is part of El Presidio de Santa Barbara State Historic Park. **SBSM**

137.
233 East Canon Perdido Street
1982-1984; Wahlquist, Lawrence, Richards, Inc., and Clayton Brooks

This is a recent version of the Monterey cantilevered balcony style, which, as it ages, will easily be mistaken for one of Santa Barbara's adobes of the late 1830s.

138.
914-916 Anacapa Street
Cota-Knox House
1871

A part of El Presidio State Historic Park, perhaps the oldest brick building still standing in downtown Santa Barbara, the single-floor, flat-roofed Cota-Knox house was constructed in 1871 as a residence for María Jesús Olivera de Cota by her son-in-law José Lobero. The new house was made necessary when Mrs. Cota's original adobe, which was located in the middle of the right-of-way of the newly developing Anacapa Street, was razed. Lobero, two years later, established his theater, the successor of which is still located across the street (See entry #128). A former Civil War surgeon, Dr. Samuel Budd Page Knox, purchased the home in 1878 and used the building as both his residence and office. He later added a wood-frame section to the building to house the pharmacy of his brother, Thomas. Dr. Knox, one of 12 physicians in Santa Barbara at the time, became well known by riding his high-wheel bicycle around the city.

Architecturally, the house, with its decorative brick construction and symmetrical façade, is an early example of the rapid Americanization of Santa Barbara in the 1870s. It became even more Americanized when Knox added a small Eastlake style porch to the front. The porch and the decorative brickwork were lost in the rebuilding after the earthquake of 1925. In 1954 the house was remodeled into an office building, and has, over time, suffered several of what one researcher called "incoherent additions." It was eventually purchased by the Santa Barbara Trust for Historic Preservation in 1976, and was designated a City Landmark in 1995. The Trust is presently pursuing plans to restore the house to its original appearance, including the charming Eastlake porch. **SBL**

139.
920 Anacapa Street
Pico Adobe
ca. 1825

This tiny gable-roof adobe has remained relatively unaltered due to its location in the middle of the block just outside the old Presidio walls. The family of a Presidio soldier, Santiago Pico, was the first owner. The original residence, a single room without fireplace, is a good example of a modest dwelling of the mid-nineteenth century. Buenaventura and Anita Cordero Pico resided here in the second half of the 1800s. This little jewel was gift-deeded to the Santa Barbara Trust for Historic Preservation in 1976, underwent some rehabilitation to make it habitable, and then was acquired by the State of California as part of El Presidio de Santa Barbara State Historic Park. A commemorative plaque was placed on the garden wall in 1982 by the Native Daughters of the Golden West. **SBL**

140.
924 Anacapa Street
Margaret Baylor Inn
Lobero Building
1926-1927; Julia Morgan

Presently called the Lobero Building, this structure is of interest both for its architect and its original use. Julia Morgan was the most important female architect of her time, as well as the first woman to attend the prestigious Ecole des Beaux Arts in Paris. She is, thus, an excellent example of the "liberated" women of the 1920s. It was precisely for them that this building was constructed, as a contemporary news account noted, "There is a proven need for a hotel in Santa Barbara for the use of business women." The hotel for women opened in March, 1927. Architecturally, the building's symmetry and classical details reflect Julia Morgan's Beaux Arts education. While the need for a

hotel exclusively for women quickly disappeared, the Lobero Building continues to contribute to the community. It served as a dormitory for University of California, Santa Barbara students in 1954 and 1955, and now operates as an office building. Julia Morgan posthumously received the AIA Gold Medal in 2014, the first woman to receive the honor.

141.
27 East Carrillo Street
Little Town Club
1885
1923-1924; George Washington Smith
1928; Edwards, Plunkett and Howell
1936-1937; Chester L. Carjola
1948; Harold John Vaile

In 1915, the local Little Town Club purchased this property, on which was located a one-story Italianate cottage that dated back to about 1885. The all-women club needed new quarters so its members, many of whom lived in Montecito, could con-

tinue to meet informally for lunch or to rest and visit one another while shopping in town. Various improvements were made to the building over the next few years but, by 1923, members considered the clubhouse inadequate for their needs. Rather than seeking out a new meeting place, the club engaged

1926

the masterful architect, George Washington Smith, to redesign the existing building and, with the help of expert contractors, Snook and Kenyon, he transformed the "little white cottage into a stucco building and an artistic charming club house." In 1928, Martha (Mrs. David Sr.) Gray donated money to add a two-story wing to the rear and western side. She chose the firm of Edwards, Plunkett and Howell to design the addition. When the existing dining hall was replaced, in 1948, by a one-story addition, the club dedicated the new hall to her. Chester Carjola designed the one-story dressing room addition to the rear (1936) as well as the library extension and front wall extension (1937). Despite the additions and alterations by several designers, this Santa Barbara style building, with its adjacent walled courtyard, originally the work of landscape architect Lockwood de Forest, Jr., reflects a remarkable continuity of architectural design and detail, a clear indication that the local architectural community embraced the idea of a common theme for the city. The trees on this block and surrounding blocks are Indian Laurel Fig (Ficus microcarpa var. nitida), an evergreen that was popular in the 1970s and 1980s before its problems as a street tree were known, causing upheavals in the sidewalk. **SBSM**

142.
Approx. 21-35 East Carrillo Street
Aguirre Adobe Site
1841

The Aguirre Adobe (1841-1884) was located on this site, making it of historical significance. José Antonio Aguirre, a wealthy merchant and landowner, constructed the palatial adobe for his bride, Francisca Estudillo. The quad-

rangle design, unique in California architecture, was centered around a courtyard with a 15' wooden-floored corridor onto which the 19 apartments opened. Although the family retained the property, the adobe was used as a residence for less than a year. From 1843 until 1880 the adobe met various needs of the city and county of Santa Barbara. It functioned as a military barracks, the county courthouse and jail, a school for the Sisters of Charity, the post office, and the meeting place for several church groups. It suffered from years of neglect and, unfortunately, was demolished in 1884.

143.
17-21 East Carrillo Street
Mihran Studio
1922; Robert W. Hyde

This Monterey Revival building with its projecting second story balcony is a worthy neighbor to the historic Hill-Carrillo Adobe next door to the west. So worthy, in fact, that it is often mistaken for an historic adobe itself. It is similar to the 1835 Pacific House in Monterey and resembles Santa Barbara's own Monterey style Ortega-Masini Adobe in Montecito. **SBSM**

144.
11-15 East Carrillo Street
Hill-Carrillo Adobe
1825-1826

Daniel Hill, an early Yankee immigrant to Santa Barbara, built this adobe for his Californiano bride, Rafaela Luisa Ortega. It is said to have had the first wooden floor in the pueblo. In addition, the first child of Anglo-American parents to be born in Santa Barbara was born here to Rachel Holmes and Thomas Oliver Larkin. The subsequent owner, Captain John D. Wilson, was in the fur trade, and evidently not a particularly literate man as can be seen in the following from a letter to Larkin in 1842: "I recevud your Litter before I laft St Barbara regarden the otter skins thair is now one hundred & four Skins in St Barbara all good Blak ones inded the beast lot that has been got. ..." Nonetheless, Wilson and his wife Ramona made their adobe one of the centers of social life in Mexican Santa Barbara. Later it served as a daguerreotype shop, a makeshift City Council meeting room, and the residence of Guillermo and Joaquin Carrillo. Mrs. Fiske Hammond repaired the house and remodeled the grounds in 1919. In 1928 the adobe was scheduled to be demolished for a motion picture theater. Max C. Fleischmann, one of Santa Barbara's premier philanthropists, saw the historic value of the adobe and stepped in to assure its preservation. **NR, CHL, SBL**

145.
10 East Carrillo Street
Gidney Building
ca. 1900
1925; Edwards and Plunkett

As with so many other buildings in the downtown area, this store is a post-earthquake remodeling of an older structure. The balconied window and arched entrance are characteristic of the Spanish style architecture prevalent in the 1920s. The westerly portion was demolished in 1963 to accommodate the construction of the large building at 936 State Street, but 10 East Carrillo Street still maintains its continuity with the rest of downtown architecture.

146.
12-14 East Carrillo Street
1926-1927; Associated Architects of Santa Barbara

The architectural style of this building is patterned after a 16th century Spanish townhouse. It relates nicely to its more impressive neighbor to the east, designed in a loose version of a 17th century Italian palazzo. This building is on the site of the city's first library, built in 1892 and designed by Peter J. Barber. The present structure is a sophisticated example of the Hispanic architec-

ture of the 1920s. Originally constructed for the Chamber of Commerce, it housed the iconic Hunt's China Shop for a number of years before reverting to office space. Note the medallion of Saint Barbara above the entrance.

147.
16 East Carrillo Street
Masonic Temple
1923-1924; Carl W. Werner

This building is a fine interpretation of late Northern Italian Renaissance architecture. The second and third floor loggia, with pointed voussoir and applied decoration patterned after the Masonic Order's emblem is particularly impressive. Although the first

floor has been altered on several occasions over the years, the building remains an excellent example of Mediterranean-style architecture, very much in harmony with Santa Barbara's Spanish tradition. **SBL**

148.
20 East Carrillo Street
El Castillo Building
1926; Wythe, Blaine and Olson

This two-story, post-earthquake Andalusian style building with its corner bay tower was constructed for E. J. Peterson and occupied originally by the Southern California Edison Company, which not only provided funds and equipment for the earthquake relief effort, but also strongly supported the community's effort to rebuild in a Spanish style. The tiled walk adjacent to the building, which now leads to a parking structure, was initially built as a continuation of Bernhard Hoffmann's "Street in Spain" paseo system, here called Paseo Carrillo or Callejon Carrillo.

149.
100 and 114 East Carrillo Street

Recreation Center
1914; J. Corbley Pool
1926 Gymnasium; Julia Morgan
2012 renovation; Kruger Bensen Ziemer Architects

Thomas Schmidt @ SBVintagePhoto.com

Although founded in 1907, the Recreation Center did not find permanent quarters until 1914, when this brick building was constructed. Responsible for this versatile structure were two women. Margaret Baylor, a Cincinnati social worker before coming to Santa Barbara, realized the need for a youth center as well as housing for unmarried women (See entry #140). She undertook a successful campaign to raise funds and construction began in 1913. The other force behind the Recreation Center was Bertha Rice, who was its dynamic director for many years, setting the tone that has carried the institution to the present. Architectural designer J. Corbley Pool executed the project in a Craftsman-Prairie School mode, which now stands in contrast with the city's Hispanic motif. The recent renovation cleaned and repainted the exterior to match the building's original appearance.

Julia Morgan, who designed Margaret Baylor's adjacent inn, was responsible for the gymnasium adjoining the Recreation Center at 114 East Carrillo Street. Opening in February 1927, it replaced a 1918 masonry gym damaged by the 1925 earthquake. The Morgan gymnasium represents one of the city's distinguished versions of the Hispanic tradition, one often missed because of its nearly hidden location. Julia Morgan posthumously received the AIA Gold Medal in 2014, the first woman to receive the honor. **SBL**

150.
222 East Carrillo Street
(1926; Mary Craig and Ralph Armitage)
1980-1981; Edwards-Pitman

The original building on this site, the Beard Motor Company's Dodge dealership, was the product of Mrs. J. A. Andrews, Mary Craig, and architect Ralph Armitage, the three who were responsible for many of the Plaza Rubio houses near the Mission (See entry #245), and was done in their typical Hispanic style. In 1973 the building was sold, and the original structure, to the dismay of many, was torn down. The present large office building was constructed in 1980-1981, and replicated the arcaded loggia and low-pitched shed roof of the original design, maintaining the city's Hispanic motif, even on a street that had gone more modern in the 1960s and 1970s.

151.
1034 Santa Barbara Street
Folk Mote Music Company Building
ca. 1887

This two-story Spanish Colonial Revival building, with its almost obligatory balcony, with wrought iron railing and scroll-like supports, came into being at 31 West Canon Perdido Street as a wood-sided, Italianate hotel. It remained a hotel under a variety of names until 1923, when it was acquired by the Jordano Brothers Grocery Company. A decade later, the Jordanos rebuilt, enlarged and modernized the structure, giving it a Spanish Colonial Revival face to conform to Santa Barbara's style. The building was sold in 1969, and became home to a number of commercial enterprises, the most longstanding of which was the Folk Mote Music Company. The city slated the building for demolition in the late 1980s in order to accommodate the Paseo Nuevo mall (See entry #213). The owners of Folk Mote asked the city if they could purchase the building, and the city agreed, providing the Folk Mote people found a suitable site on which to move the structure. They found a lot at 1034 Santa Barbara Street and the building was moved there in November of 1988. The building was also named a City Structure of Merit in that year. Since then, the Folk Mote Music Company building has added its complement to the Court House across the street, keeping the neighborhood in tune with Santa Barbara's general image. The store closed when its owners retired.   **SBSM**

152.
1112 Santa Barbara Street
District Attorney's Office Building
2004; Cearnal Architects, Inc.

Though rather massive in scale and urban in outlook, the District Attorney's Office Building nonetheless conforms beautifully to Santa Barbara's architectural style, with its roots in Hispanic design and details expressing its feel. It provides a fine complement to its iconic neighbor across the street, the Santa Barbara County Courthouse.

153.
1021 Anacapa Street
2001; Cearnal Architects, Inc.

On February 20, 1999, the original commercial building on this site, longtime home of the Paulson Furniture Company, and then remodeled to house the headquarters of Pacific Bancorp, parent of the local Santa Barbara Bank & Trust, burned to the ground. Committed to the city, and insistent upon keeping its offices in downtown Santa Barbara, Pacific Bancorp immediately announced its intention to rebuild, and engaged Cearnal Architects, Inc., to do the work. Dedicated to the Santa Barbara motif, and incorporating many Spanish Colonial Revival details into the design, the architects added this striking structure to the city's ambiance. When Union Bank absorbed Pacific Bancorp and Santa Barbara Bank & Trust into its orbit, it retained the building as its local headquarters.

154.
1036 Anacapa Street
1927; Edwards, Plunkett and Howell, and Marston, Van Pelt and Maybury
1990-1991 addition; David Bury and Brian Cearnal Associates

Another excellent example of the Spanish Colonial Revival style popularized after the 1925 earthquake, this building features a recessed arcade, wrought iron detailing, and deeply cut window openings. It was built as the Santa Barbara office of the Southern Counties Gas Company, a strong supporter of the city's move toward a unified, Hispanic architectural theme. After the city declined to approve demolition of the important 1927 building, the 1990s addition extended the original intent.

155.
10-18 East Figueroa Street

1925-1926; A. C. Sanders (10 East Figueroa)
1927-1928; Edwards, Plunkett and Howell (14-18 East Figueroa)

These two buildings were originally constructed as separate structures and were united in 1950. There are many architectural amenities exemplified here, including the recessed arcade, second story corbelling, and wrought iron detailing. These joined buildings demonstrate how historic structures can be altered to serve new needs without destroying their original architectural integrity. Notice the picturesque weathervane on the easterly building. The flowering trees brightening this block are New Zealand Christmas Trees (Metrosideros excelsa).

156.
224 East Figueroa Street
Brownsill House No. 1
ca. 1887

This Eastlake-Stick house presents a well preserved example of the Eastern architectural influence which began to enter Santa Barbara in company with a number of East Coast industrialists who came west in the 1870s. Built by Edwin Brownsill, the home's decorative patternwork, square bay windows with fixed transoms, fish scale shingle siding, and ornamental gable-end struts all suggest the affluence of the builder. He lived in this house only a short time before moving to 1116 Garden Street.

157.
1120 Anacapa Street
Santa Barbara County Courthouse
1927-1929; William Mooser and Company and J. Wilmer Hersey;
Ralph T. Stevens, landscape architecture
1988-91, 2013; Campbell and Campbell, landscape enhancements

Without doubt the most important 20th century building in Santa Barbara, and second only to the Mission in overall architectural significance, the Santa Barbara County Courthouse can rightly be considered the public monument to the Spanish Colonial Revival movement in the United States. The present courthouse is Santa Barbara's third. From 1850 to 1872 an adobe on this site was used. The adjoining jail was so porous, however, it was joked that the best way to get rid of a troublesome character was to imprison him there, from which he would promptly escape and leave town for good. The second courthouse was a classical centrally domed brick structure designed by Peter J. Barber. This building was badly damaged by the 1925 earthquake, necessitating yet another courthouse.

In 1919, prior to the earthquake, the County, anticipating the eventual need for a new courthouse partnered with the city to hold a competition for a new County Courthouse, City Hall, and Veteran's Memorial Building. This competition was won by Edgar Mathews of San Francisco; the second place design was by Mooser and Simpson, also of San Francisco. Due to financial constraints, no actual buildings resulted from this competition. After the earthquake of 1925, the County Supervisors turned to William Mooser and Company for the design of a new courthouse, and a scheme similar to that offered in the 1919 competition was proposed. This design was felt not to replicate the scale and informal Andalusian character of the city. The Architectural Advisory Committee, formed after the earthquake to promote the Hispanic character of Santa Barbara, and other interested individuals, prevailed upon the Supervisors to seek out a new approach to the design of the courthouse, one which would break the building up into separate units to be arranged around a central courtyard. J. Wilmer Hersey of the Community Drafting Room, in consultation with other Santa Barbara architects, then provided the sketches which informed the working drawings prepared by William Mooser and Company. There was serious disagreement among the Supervisors over whether the new courthouse should be what was termed an expensive showpiece or a less costly, ordinary building to meet County needs. The impasse was broken by city benefactor George Batchelder, who put up the funds to have a scale model of the proposed Mooser building made up. Once seen in three dimensions, there was little further debate, and the drive for the present courthouse went forward.

The building's most obvious feature is the Roman triumphal arch, which provides a dramatic view of the foothills of Santa Barbara and leads to the central courtyard and gardens. This "sunken garden" features the stone foundations of the 1873 courthouse. Other distinctive features include the many theatrical staircases, open loggia corridors, and, especially, Ettore Cadorin's fountain and statue adjacent to the great arch. The latter was lovingly reconstructed in 2012 by the Courthouse Legacy Foundation. The interior of the courthouse is equally ornate; the designers include Dan Sayre Grosbeck,

The original courthouse, built in 1873.

John MacQuarrie, J. B. Smeraldi, and George Hyde. Much of the extensive and colorful tile work was produced in Tunisia, North Africa, and the beautiful Mural Room, also recently brought back to its original condition, has become a favorite attraction for tourists. Floor tiles, stair risers, and special tiles were manufactured by Gladding, McBean and Co.

The landscaping of the building is equally typical of Southern California at its exotic best. It is so extensive and varied that only a few outstanding specimen trees can be noted here (A botanical guide is available inside). The Bunya-Bunya (Araucaria bidwilii) on the Anacapa Street side is notable for its unusual silhouette and huge pineapple-shaped cones, which can be a hazard, each of which can weigh up to ten pounds and can be a hazard to anyone standing under the trees. The carved sandstone entrances, retaining walls, and curbing outlining the entire block are now well past 100 years old.

Setting an example for the future, the courthouse is now ADA accessible, and it became a geothermal-heated building in 2014. There are several commemorative plaques at the Courthouse. **NHL, NR, CHL, SBL**

158.
40 East Anapamu Street
Santa Barbara Public Library
1916-1917; Henry Hornbostel, Francis W. Wilson
1925; Carleton M. Winslow
1930; Myron Hunt and H. C. Chambers
1979; Jerry Allen Zimmer

Santa Barbara's first lending library was established in 1870, and quickly outgrew a number of locations until a permanent structure, designed by Peter J. Barber, was built in 1892. That, too, proved incapable of keeping up with an expanding library, and in 1914 the City acquired a large parcel on the corner of Anacapa and Anapamu Streets for a new library structure. The Carnegie Corporation Library Grant Foundation contributed $50,000, which the City matched. The well-known Eastern architect Henry Hornbostel provided a modified Spanish Colonial Revival design, and local architect Francis W.

Wilson prepared the working drawings. He also supervised the construction of the new library, which opened in 1917. Like most of the downtown buildings in Santa Barbara, the library was severely damaged during the 1925 earthquake. Carleton M. Winslow, Sr., the designer of the beautiful sculpture surrounding the Anapamu Street entrance, was selected to do the rebuilding, which was completed a year later. Soon thereafter, local industrialist and library trustee Clarence A. Black donated the parcel of land adjacent to

the library to house an art gallery. With funds provided by Mary Faulkner Gould, architects Myron Hunt and H. C. Chambers were hired to design the new building. They did it in the then-popular Art Deco Egyptian style. The understated structure in its striking setting came to be known as the Faulkner Gallery.

No landscape plans for the gallery have been found, but Hunt & Chambers depicted numerous eucalyptus trees in their elevation drawings, and old photos confirm they were planted. These lemon-scented gum trees (Corymbia citriodora) have become dominant skyline elements in the city.

An extensive addition and remodeling took place in 1979 and 1980, changing the main entrances and adding library space. The new work, distinctive in itself, remained compatible with both structures. In 2012 the library, gallery, and five of the lemon gum trees became a City Landmark. The interior of the library was remodeled and the children's section was relocated in 2015. **SBL**

159.
24-28 East Victoria Street
Victoria Hotel and Shops
1925-1926; William A. Edwards

Although the corbelled course beneath the roofline appears to cover three buildings, the Victoria Hotel is a single structure built to accommodate a 31 room hotel on the second story and three shops on the first. Over the years the shop tenants have changed many times, but the Moorish-influenced Spanish Colonial Revival façade remains unaltered, contributing its special charm to the neighborhood.

160.
27 East Victoria Street
Normandy Hotel
1888
1980 remodel; Peter Walker Hunt

Its age and unusual architectural features, especially the two-story triangular side bays, make this one of Santa Barbara's noteworthy 19th century buildings. Until the mid-1890s it was the residence of Mrs. C. M. Prince and her two daughters, one an art and embroidery teacher, the other a music instructor. For the next 80 plus years it was used variously as a rooming house, apartment building, and hotel. A subsequent owner, Helen Reynolds, had the building's front extended in 1912. In 1980 the exterior was restored, decorative features were added, and the interior was converted into offices, putting a modern touch on an historic structure. **SBSM**

161.
21 East Sola Street
Our Lady of Sorrows Church
1928-1929; Edward A. Eames

The stately Our Lady of Sorrows Church, standing on the corner of Sola and Anacapa Streets, is the last in a series of Catholic church edifices which began with the Chapel at the Presidio. After its immediate predecessor, a large brick and adobe structure on the corner of State and Figueroa Streets, was destroyed in the earthquake of 1925, the parish set out to construct not only a beautiful building, employing a Romanesque Spanish design, but one impervious to earthquakes. Steel frame construction was utilized, as well as double walls and a floating foundation. The magnificent rose window above the altar is complemented by several other stained glass openings, giving the interior a wonderful glow. The church continues to serve its Catholic parishioners well, and despite the fact that after over 100 years of service, the Jesuit order left Our Lady of Sorrows in 2014, the congregation will persevere.   **SBL**

162.
116 East Sola Street
1924; Soule, Murphy and Hastings

This building is a relatively straightforward example of Spanish Colonial Revival style constructed by the original architects for use as their offices. The design combines an arched first-story entrance with a square-bayed and recessed second-story stairway and entrance. Prominent Santa Barbara landscape architects Lockwood de Forest and Ralph T. Stevens also had their offices here for several years.   **SBSM**

163.
City blocks bounded by Anacapa, East Micheltorena, Garden, and East Sola Streets

Alameda Plaza

1853

Shortly after Santa Barbara became an American town in 1850, the City set aside six blocks in this area for public use. Four of these blocks, one of which is the present Alice Keck Park Memorial Garden, were eventually lost, apparently because the City did not proceed with its intended park development and squatters claimed the land. During the 1870s and 1880s, these two remaining blocks were enclosed with picket fences, trees were planted, and a bandstand erected. Citizens in those decades, however, were more interested in developing, rather than beautifying, the city, and at times the park became overgrown and weed-infested. Finally, in 1902, a three-member Park Commission was created with Dr. A. B. Doremus, a dentist, as Park Superintendent. The Park Commission engaged Peter Poole in 1908 to construct the sandstone pedestal-flanked steps located on the corners facing Garden and Santa Barbara Streets. In 1912, Dr. Doremus traveled abroad and brought back rare plant specimens and seeds, then personally planted them in the park. Doremus also laid out the walkways that meander diagonally through each block. There is a plaque honoring him in the east plaza. The wooden bandstand, now a City Landmark, dates back to 1888.

Among the many specimen trees to be noted here are the three redwoods planted as a group in 1919 by King Albert of Belgium, his wife, Queen Elisabeth, and their son, Prince Leopold. The seeds of the East African Fern Pines (Podocarpus gracilior) were literally shot down by Stewart Edward White, a Santa Barbara novelist and big game hunter, and given to Dr. Franceschi by Mrs. White to propagate. The one in the eastern block is female, the other to the west is male.

Alameda Plaza received an infusion of interest and usage when the city created Kids' World in 1994. Designed by Robert Leathers and Associates of Ithaca, New York, Kids' World became an instant success, and has been a delight to children of all ages since. **SBL (bandstand)**

164.
City Block Bounded by East Micheltorena, Garden, East Arrellaga, and Santa Barbara Streets
Albert and Mary Herter House site
El Mirasol Hotel site
(Alice Keck Park Memorial Garden)
1905; Delano and Aldrich 1914
1976; Grant Castleberg and Elizabeth de Forest, landscape architecture

ca. 1912

This block, like those that constitute Alameda Plaza, was part of a six-block area set aside in 1853 for eventual city park development. Unlike the two blocks to the south, however, this one was privately developed. In 1905, noted artist Albert Herter and his second wife, Mary, built their vacation home here. Albert Herter was the father of Christian A. Herter, who once served as Governor of Massachusetts and, later, as Secretary of State during a portion of the administration of President Dwight Eisenhower. Their extraordinary house was done in Mission Revival style by the New York office of Delano and Aldrich. Later the house was converted into what became the internationally famous El Mirasol Hotel. The completed hotel complex consisted of a U-shaped building enclosing a luxurious flower garden with several cottages scattered alongside the main structure. The hotel's principal building was badly damaged by fire in 1966 and, eventually, all the buildings were demolished.

At this point Santa Barbara's commitment to its Spanish Colonial Revival style was put to the test. The owner of the property appealed to the city for a change in zoning, and, with it, a height variance to permit construction of a nine-story hotel, a proposal that was denied by the Planning Commission. Undaunted, the petitioner then made application for an 11-story condominium project, which was also denied. As these applications were being made, the public was becoming increasingly aware of what was going on, and finally a "Citizen's Committee" was put together by Pearl Chase and others to deal with the subject of high rise buildings in Santa Barbara. Their call was for the creation of a city policy on high rises. Each time a new proposal for a height variance was put forth by the developers, the last for two 9-story condominiums, the Planning Commission rejected it until, in March of 1969, the City Council overrode the last Planning Commission denial, apparently giving permission for the developers to go ahead. Three citizens then filed a lawsuit to stop any building, and a judge agreed, issuing a stay order prohibiting construction. Those same three citizens, acting on behalf of a rapidly growing chorus of opposition to the project, then filed a petition to have the City Council decision set aside.

A Superior Court judge agreed, and so ordered. In the wake of that decision, a three-meeting forum was organized to allow direct public input into the discussion. The result was that the City Council placed on the November 1972 election ballot "a Charter Amendment to incorporate the current building height limits into the City Charter." After serious campaigning by both sides, the measure passed by an overwhelming vote of 26,499 to 8,048. The opening lines of the Charter Amendment state it best, "It is hereby declared the policy of the City that high buildings are inimical to the basic residential and historical character of the City." And so it remains.

For a few years, an urban farm was operated on the property. In December 1975 philanthropist Alice Keck Park presented the land to the City of Santa Barbara, and in 1980 the Garden, with its magnificent layout and plantings, was opened as a memorial to her. Yet even in the development of the new garden, the landscape architects drew upon Santa Barbara's past horticulture. Some tall Canary Island Date Palms (Phoenix canariensis) were retained from the hotel garden, as was the sprawling old Australian Tea Tree (Leptospermum laevigatum) at the corner of Garden and Micheltorena Streets. There have been numerous revisions to the 1976 plan, both in design and planting, but the emphasis is still on flowering trees. In addition to its ever-blooming palette, notable features include the artificial stream and koi pond full of turtles and ducks, the spiral path that leads up a small hill to a dedication plaque and sundial, the Butterfly Garden, and the Sensory Garden. A Plant Directory is located in the center of the park. Alice Keck Park Memorial Garden constitutes a wonderful oasis of peace and quiet in the middle of the city.

165.
220 East Sola Street
Alameda Court
1916-1917

This bungalow court was originally constructed as a winter retreat
for eastern visitors to the city. It
provided such amenities as small
apartments above the garage at
the rear for the chauffeurs of these
families. It was later converted to
housing. This is one of the best
preserved of the bungalow courts,
so popular in the 1910s and 1920s.

166.
1332 Santa Barbara Street
University Club
1880
1922; Soule, Murphy and Hastings

Originally built as a residence
for J. W. Calkins, vice-president of Mortimer Cook's
First National Gold Bank,
this building was described
at the time as "unsurpassed
for beauty by any residence
in this city," and built "after
the Elizabethan style of architecture … with pleasant
peculiarities of the style." It
was, in fact, simply peculiar, with battlements, towers, buttresses, drip lintels,
multiple gables and everything else the architect could pile on the structure to
make it appear Elizabethan. By 1922, "Calkins' Castle" was considered a Victorian
"horror," and the exterior was remodeled in a suitably genteel Spanish style. The
interior retains much of its earlier appearance, including massive redwood beams,
oak paneling, and stairway. University Club first occupied the remodeled mansion
in 1923. Previously, per a 1922 listing, the club was located at 25 E. Micheltorena

Street, and in that year the occupant of the mansion was "Ye Castle Inn." The club was founded in 1919 by a group of eleven men, each representing a different alma mater, as a place to meet, enjoy a good meal, discuss the news of the day, shoot a game of billiards, or play a game of bridge.

167.
1301 Santa Barbara Street
1931; Edwards and Plunkett
1999; Cearnal Architects, Inc.

From its construction to 1973, this was the site of the Automobile Club of Southern California office. The architecture, with its peaked chimney hoods, deeply cut and arcaded façade, and stout corner buttresses, is an excellent example of the Spanish Colonial Revival style.

168.
32 East Micheltorena Street
1922; Alfred Jensen, builder

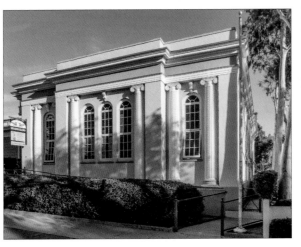

Initially a part of the First Church of Christ, Scientist, this striking structure, with its Classical Revival style, Ionic columns, and un-usual color scheme quickly became, and remains, a distinc-tive part of the Santa Barbara scene. Since its construction, the building has served variety of religious and commercial enterprises over the years and its vitality remains undiminished.

169.
33 East Micheltorena Street
Dolores School
Santa Barbara Catholic School
(Notre Dame School)
1926; I. E. Loveless

This basic Spanish design structure, with its Churrigueresque appointments, opened in 1926 as the Dolores Elementary School. It so remained until 1941, when the Santa Barbara Catholic High School took over and the elementary school was moved to a different building. In 1959, Bishop Garcia Diego High School was established in another area of the city and incorporated all Catholic high school students, permitting the elementary school to return to its original building. In 1974, Dolores School merged with the closing Our Lady of Guadalupe School and became Norte Dame School, a name it retains to the present. **SBL**

170.
1435 Anacapa Street
1885
1910; moved and enlarged

Thomas Schmidt @ SBVintagePhoto.com

This attractive colonial revival structure was originally located at 1228 State Street. In 1902 it was purchased by the two-year-old congregation of First Church of Christ, Scientist and, in 1910, moved to the corner of Micheltorena and Anacapa Streets. The building was enlarged at a cost of $4,000 and used by the church until it relocated to the larger East Valerio Street site in 1932. The Anacapa property was sold in 1941. For many years various church groups used the building, and the City Club had its headquarters there for over twenty years. In early 1964 the architectural firm of Arendt, Mosher and Grant began its lengthy occupancy of the structure. It is now used for commercial offices. The viewer's eye is drawn to the building's temple front façade with its pediment and four columns.

171.
1126 Santa Barbara Street
Schauer Building
1930; Edwards and Plunkett
1975-1976; Edwards-Pitman

The Schauer Building was constructed for the Schauer Printing Company, which then occupied it for the next 45 years. Its architects were among the most prominent exponents of Santa Barbara's Spanish renaissance during the 1920s, and this is a fine example of their work. It stands as an appropriate foil to the monumental Courthouse across the street. In 1975-1976 Edwards-Pitman sensitively remodeled the structure for offices for owner Michael Towbes, along with the adjacent Storke Building on Anapamu Street.

The eleven blocks from 1000-2100 Santa Barbara Street are planted with Queen Palms (Arecastrum romanzoffianum), a Brazilian tree. The portion from Victoria Street to Mission Street was planted in 1929 by the man who did so much to promote horticulture in Santa Barbara, Dr. A. B. Doremus.

172.
914 Santa Barbara Street
Alhecama Center
1925; Soule, Murphy and Hastings

This complex of buildings was established in 1925 by the Santa Barbara School of the Arts, a part of the Community Arts Association. It had been founded in 1920 to "give instructions in the arts that beautify and enrich life," and "to develop especially the different forms of community festivals, which feature dancing, singing and drama in its many branches." The Community Arts Association, led by such prominent Santa Barbarans as Pearl Chase and Bernhard Hoffmann, played an important role in the Spanish revival of the 1920s, not only in the arts but also in architecture, city planning and landscaping. Though its expansive building plan was never achieved (with the notable exception of entry #136) the school persisted until 1938, when it closed. Alice Schott bought the property and began to make improvements. She eventually deeded the complex, including the Alhecama Theatre (See entry #173), to the Adult Education Program of Santa Barbara City College in the mid-1940s. The Santa Barbara Trust for Historic Preservation, aware of the fact that a portion of the original Presidio was located on the front corner of the property, purchased it from Santa Barbara City College in 1980, and the State of California then purchased it from the Trust, adding it to El Presidio de Santa Barbara State Historic Park. The Trust immediately began the process of rebuilding the Northeast Corner of the old Presidio on its original foundations at the junction of Santa Barbara and Canon Perdido Streets, with architect Milford Wayne Donaldson providing the plans. In 2008 the Trust, in partnership with the Santa Barbara Contractors Association, undertook the rehabilitation of the old wooden Alhecama Studio building on the property, and making it one of the first "green" buildings in the State Park system. **NRD**

173.
914 Santa Barbara Street
Alhecama Theatre
1925; Soule, Murphy and Hastings

Located in the former Festival Arts School of Santa Barbara, the theater was built as a dance and acting studio. Known until 1940 as the Little Theatre or the Pueblo Theatre, it was purchased in that year by Alice Schott, who changed the name to Alhecama, a name derived from the first two letters of her daughters' names – Alice, Helen, Catherine and Mary Lou. The Alhecama property was given by Mrs. Schott to Santa Barbara City College for use as an adult education center in the mid-1940s. The Santa Barbara Trust for Historic Preservation acquired the property in 1980, as part of the footprint of the old Presidio covers a corner of it. The property was then acquired by the State of California in 1982 and became a part of EI Presidio de Santa Barbara State Historic Park. Under the supervision of the Trust, the Alhecama Theatre has undergone a restoration to its original condition, with the addition of such facilities as ADA compliant restrooms and other modern requirements. The restoration will include a rehabilitation of the striking mural on the back wall of the auditorium. It was painted in 1928 by Ross Dickinson, an artist who, at the time, was both a student and teacher at the Festival Arts School. He later went on to have a distinguished career. Although the restoration is ongoing, the Alhecama Theatre is already a functioning part of the Park and once again serves the public. **NRD**

174.
915 Santa Barbara Street
Bonilla House
1887

Visible just in front of this modest late 19th century cottage are the foundations for the outer defense wall of the Presidio. The house was built over the underpinnings of the old fort by Florentino Bonilla. He was a descendant of Presidio soldiers, a stagecoach driver, and member of José Lobero's orchestra. The house originally had a small front porch and crowning widow's walk. It is presently a part of El Presidio de Santa Barbara State Historic Park and houses offices of the Santa Barbara Trust for Historic Preservation. As reconstruction of the Presidio continues, the Trust has plans to move the Bonilla House to the area next to the Pico Adobe, where it will become a part of the Trust's education complex. **NRD**

175.
834 Santa Barbara Street
Moullet House
1896
1955; Jack Boydston

Built on a portion of the Presidio site by J. F. Moullet for his bride, this brick house, unusual in Santa Barbara, was used first as a residence and then a tamale parlor before becoming the rented headquarters for a branch of the Chinese Nationalist Party in the 1930s. The house was remodeled for commercial purposes in 1955, making changes which included replacement of a pair of arched windows with display windows, and the removal of the chimney. It was acquired by the Santa Barbara Trust for Historic Preservation from the

Moullet family in 1977, and sold to the State of California in 1984. It is now part of El Presidio de Santa Barbara State Historic Park, and will eventually be restored to its original configuration. It will thus remain a poignant reminder of an earlier day in Santa Barbara.   **NRD**

176.
820 Santa Barbara Street
Rochin Adobe
1856

Although this adobe was constructed relatively late, in fact after Mexican rule had passed, its history can be traced back to the city's very founding. It was built by a descendant of Captain Francisco Ortega, first Comandante of the Presidio, using adobe bricks salvaged from the almost destroyed fort. Around 1900 the adobe was sheathed in clapboard and the west porch was remodeled. The Native Daughters of the Golden West placed a plaque, noting its historical value, on the property in 1972. It is presently part of El Presidio de Santa Barbara State Historic Park.   **NRD, SBL**

177.
814 Santa Barbara Street
Sloyd School Site
1893

On this site stood Anna Sophia Blake's Sloyd School building. It was a typically fanciful Queen Anne design dominated by a large round tower and dome. Sloyd School, the forerunner of the present day University of California, Santa Barbara, was a public school with classes in manual, applied and household arts, patterned after the Scandinavian method. The school quickly outgrew the building and, in 1907, moved to a new location at the corner of Chapala and Victoria Streets, taking the tongue-twisting name of the Anna S. C. Blake Normal School of Manual Arts and Home Economics. The original Sloyd building was badly damaged in the 1925 earthquake and demolished in 1930. It is located within El Presidio State Historic Park. A plaque now marks the location. **NRD**

178.
223 East De la Guerra Street
Site of the Arrellanes Adobe
De la Guerra Court
1927; Soule and Murphy

The original adobe on this site is believed to have been the first house of significance to have been constructed outside the Presidio walls. It was built in 1795 and was later used as a residence and merchandise store. The Neighborhood House Association pur-chased it in 1910 and restored and remodeled it, one of the first restorations of an historic adobe in Santa Barbara. Unfortunately, the adobe was heavily damaged in the 1925 earthquake and was demolished shortly thereafter. The present structure was built in its place by Alexander MacKellar for Associated Charities, and now houses offices. The wooden columns along the front porch were originally part of the Aguirre Adobe on East Carrillo Street (See entry #142). They are among the most unusual in the city.

179.
724 Santa Barbara Street
1929; Soule, Murphy and Hastings

This is one of the many Spanish Colonial Revival buildings designed by one of Santa Barbara's premier architectural firms following the 1925 earthquake. It is now the maintenance and operations building for Santa Barbara City Schools. The structure is noted for its general proportions and detailing.

180.
715 Santa Barbara Street
Covarrubias Adobe
1817
1940; J. J. Plunkett
Malo, or "Historic Adobe"
ca. 1825

The Covarrubias Adobe was built in 1817 by Domingo Carrillo for his bride, Concepcíon Pico, sister of Alta California Governor Pío Pico. José María Covarrubias acquired it in 1853, the year after he had gone east to deliver California's first electoral vote for Franklin Pierce. The structure is a California Historic Landmark. Interesting architectural features of this L-shaped adobe include, on the interior, a 55' long "sala," or main hall, and, on the exterior, massive adobe buttresses and a chimney, which were added in 1940 by the Rancheros Visitadores and give the adobe a monumental appearance. This, with the adjacent Malo, or "Historic" adobe and the main museum building facing De la Guerra Street (See entry #125), form the Santa

Barbara Historical Museum complex. John Southworth moved the "Historic Adobe" from the 900 block of Anacapa Street in 1921. It was first used as a studio and then as the headquarters of the Rancheros Visitadores for a number of years. Remodels of the old courtyard landscape design include entry gates, fountain, paving, new arbor and numerous California Pepper Trees (Schinus molle). **CHL, SBL**

181.
228 East De la Guerra Street
Gonzales-Castro House 1883

The Gonzales family owned portions of several blocks in this area, and Ramon Gonzales built this typical wood frame home next to an old adobe which extended partially into the De la Guerra Street right-of-way. A red tile roof was applied to the structure in about 1930. Members of the Castro family, long active in Santa Barbara's Old Spanish Days Fiestas, still live here.

182.
214 East De la Guerra Street
Ygnacio House
ca. 1875

This modest one-story house is a survivor of a popular residential area that grew up around the Spanish Presidio. In the 1880s the property was owned by one of the Dominguez families, who had lived in an adobe house on the same block. In 1908 Louisa Ygnacio, widow of J. M. Ygnacio, purchased the house after she sold the family ranch in the Goleta area. She and her husband were full-blooded Chumash of the coastal peoples. In 1912 Alfred Kroeber, renowned anthropologist and scholar of California Indians, interviewed Mrs. Ygnacio at the house. Two years later John Peabody Harrington visited her and made recordings of Mrs. Ygnacio speaking the Barbareño Chumash language. The family remained in contact with Harrington, a famed ethnographer who had grown up in Santa Barbara, until his death.

The house is Italianate in style, with wide shiplap siding. An Ygnacio family photograph shows a multi-pronged ornamental finial at the center of the roof ridge. The main building has been little altered. Walter F. Cota, a plaster contractor, and his wife Beatrice Goux Cota, acquired the property in about 1944. In that year he built an apartment over the garage, enlarging it in 1949; Richard Pitman was the designer. The Cota family lived on the property until about 1987. The Ygnacio house is now an office.

183.
317 East De la Guerra Street
Senior Center of Santa Barbara
1952; Louise Murphy Vhay
1964; 1973; Edwards-Pitman
2004; Thompson-Naylor

American Women's Voluntary Service planned these Spanish Colonial Revival cottages as apartments for the low-income elderly. Their designer was Louise Murphy Vhay, who was responsible for much of the development on this block (See entries #184, #185, #188). Since its construction the Senior Center has been a model for low-cost housing, giving occupants privacy in a garden setting near the downtown business district. The units added by Edwards-Pitman, and the most recent by Thompson-Naylor, have continued the Hispanic image of the complex, though the resultant crowding has severely lessened the original expansive garden setting designed by landscape architect Elizabeth de Forest.

184.
835 Laguna Street
Gonzales-Ramirez Adobe
ca. 1825
1923; Louise Murphy Vhay
1956

When this adobe was constructed in the 1820s by Rafael Gonzales for his Italian bride, this area of the old pueblo was known as "Las Isletas" due to the many small areas of high ground which were surrounded by swamp, part of the lagoon for which the street is named. Gonzales was the alcalde, or mayor, of Santa Barbara in 1829. The adobe remained in the Gonzales family until 1923, when Louise Murphy Vhay, who did so much work in the neighborhood, restored and enlarged it. Considered a classical example of California's adobe tradition, the Gonzales-Ramirez house was one of six selected in 1937 by the Historic American Buildings Survey as typifying that tradition. In 1969 the Native Daughters of the Golden West placed a plaque on the property noting its history. **NHL, NR, SBL**

185.
322 East Canon Perdido Street
Pedotti House
1926; Louise Murphy Vhay
1956; Lutah Maria Riggs
2013 remodel; Peter Becker

The main portion of this residence, which had two buildings separated by a patio, was built by Louise Murphy Vhay, who also built the house to the west. It is said that the bricks and doors of the buildings came from the second Arlington Hotel when it was demolished after the 1925 earthquake. In 1956 an addition extended the house to the street line, and, in 2013, another remodel combined the separate parts and created a new entrance. Even with the changes this dwelling represents a delightful Californiano-style urban oasis, and its charm adds to the general ambience distinguishing Santa Barbara from anywhere else.

186.
312 East Canon Perdido Street
Vhay-Hyde House
1932-1933; Robert W. Hyde
1952; Barbara Parker Ray

A portion of this authentic appearing apartment was originally constructed as a storage building by Louise Murphy Vhay, owner of much of the block. She was also a writer on Mexican Colonial architecture, member of the Community Arts Plans and Planting Committee, creator of the art colony between De la Guerra and Canon Perdido Streets, and creator of the "El Caserio" complex nearby. In 1933 Robert Hyde constructed a dwelling to the rear, and in 1952 another owner connected the two buildings. Architecturally, this house continues Santa Barbara's adobe tradition.

187.
301 East Canon Perdido Street
Grocery Store
ca. 1898

Originally constructed a block to the west, this wooden building with its semi-circular false front is a rare remaining example of a neighborhood grocery store of the turn of the 20th century. While this area is now almost entirely commercial, it was originally an Hispanic residential area with this building serving as the social and commercial center. It has undergone a variety of uses since dispensing groceries, including being a dance hall, a gift shop, and a restaurant, as well as offices. The lush landscaping in the private garden extending toward the Cordero Adobe recaptures much of the almost rural atmosphere of this area in the 19th century. There is a fine Jacaranda tree in front of the building (Jacaranda mimosifolia),

and the trees that line the 200-500 blocks of Canon Perdido Street are Snowy Fleece trees (Melaleuca decora) and Prickly-leaved Paperbark trees (Melaleuca styphelioides). The latter are unusual for their white, sponge-like bark. **SBSM**

188.
820 Garden Street
Tiers-Peake-Schott House
1953-1954; Louise Murphy Vhay

This secluded late Spanish Colonial Revival house was designed by Louise Murphy Vhay. Built for Alex Tiers, a designer, it was later occupied by the noted artist Channing Peake, and owned by the important Santa Barbara benefactor, Alice F. Schott.

189.
908 Garden Street
Cordero Adobe
ca. 1855
1969; Paul Soderburg

This adobe, the only one remaining of several owned by the large Cordero family, is sheathed with board and batten siding, and hidden by a garden screening it from the street. Members of the José Cordero family resided here until about 1940. Mrs. Lyla Harcoff restored the house, and the next owners re-landscaped the grounds. The adobe and garage were converted into offices in 1959, and the siding, designed to protect the adobe, was applied ten years later. **SBL**

190.
924 Garden Street
El Caserío
1936-1937; Louise Murphy Vhay, J. J. Plunkett, Lutah Maria Riggs
(various remodels)

This picturesque grouping of nine Spanish Colonial Revival studios and bungalows has sometimes been called the Greenwich Village of Santa Barbara. Since its construction, it has been associated with such artists as John Gamble, Don Freeman, and William Hesthal, as well as designer J. J. Plunkett, furniture designer Paul Tuttle, and descendants of Col. W. W. Hollister, the latter using two of the studios as townhouses in the 1950s. **SBL**

191.
1027 Garden Street
1983-1984: Lenvik & Minor Architects

This modern interpretation of Hispanic design includes a ground-level garage, offices on the second level, and a residence on the top floor. It demonstrates how the Santa Barbara Hispanic motif can be adapted to modern automobile culture.

192.
1028 Garden Street
Spiritualist Association Church of the Comforter 1921
1932; J. H. Weston

This interesting structure, noted for its vintage sign (since removed) and asymmetrical false front, began life as a print shop and grocery store. It was remodeled in 1932 into a synagogue by the B'nai B'rith Congregation. A group of Spiritualists, descendants of a movement that was quite popular in the 1870s, purchased the building in 1950 and turned it into what one newspaper reporter called "a quaint sanctuary at 1028 Garden Street." And so it remains.

193.
1116 Garden Street
Brownsill House No. 2
1889

Although the first story of this wooden structure has been extensively altered, the second still features the fish scale siding and decorated bargeboard on the front gable, characteristic of the Eastlake and Queen Anne styles of the 1880s, providing contrast to Santa Barbara's Hispanic motif, and recalling the days of the Americanization of the city.

194.
307 Lloyd Avenue
Holland Cottage
1883

This is a modest example of the Italianate style with brackets and lintels reduced to a minimum, an L-shaped plan, and a corner porch. The raised floor level makes it somewhat unusual in that area. The house was built by Arthur Holland, listed as a "capitalist" in the city directory.

195.
1122-1126 Garden Street
Maguire Bungalows
1916

These three Craftsman bungalows are relatively unaltered examples of the speculative housing of the 1910s. Hundreds of similar modest houses were constructed throughout Southern California and Santa Barbara during that decade. This trio of bungalows was built by Henry F. Maguire, who lived around the corner in the Italianate house at 307 Lloyd Avenue.

196.
305 East Anapamu Street
First United Methodist Church
1926; Thomas P. Barber

The Romanesque style of this church blends nicely into the Santa Barbara idiom, with its campanile and large rose window over the central entrance. The work of prominent Los Angeles architect, Thomas P. Barber, the church was constructed in 1926, after the 1925 earthquake had destroyed its predecessor. Note the huge redwood tree located in the churchyard and dedicated to Dr. Charles Stoddard.

197.
328 East Anapamu Street
Wood-Lockhart Cottage
1888

This is a relatively late example of an Italianate cottage. Typical features include the square bay window, the paired brackets, and shiplap siding. Very well maintained, this house has an especially attractive façade. It was built by Mary C. F. Wood, who purchased the lot from Clio Lloyd. Mrs. Wood published a guidebook, "Santa Barbara As It Is," in 1884.

The magnificent rows of Italian Stone Pine trees (Pinus pinea) in the 300-800 blocks of East Anapamu Street were planted in 1908 by Dr. Doremus from seed grown by Dr. Franceschi, and in 1929 by landscape architect Ralph Stevens. The entire allee is a City of Santa Barbara Historic Landmark. **SBL**

198.
1219 Laguna Street
Dutton Cottage
1878

This house, built for carpenter J. R. Dutton in 1878, is similar to many artisan cottages erected by and for working class families in the 1880s and 1890s. The delicate turned-work on the porch columns and supports is of particular interest, and indicates the builder's desire to decorate and individualize this modest house.

199.
1236 Garden Street
1899
2012-2013 remodel; Thompson-Naylor

Unusual architectural features of this early Colonial Revival cottage include the off-center bay and tiny Palladian window above the pedimented gable. It recalls, almost with nostalgia, an earlier, less hurried time. The recent remodel added the dormers to the second floor.

Presidio and Pueblo ~ West of State

No.	Property Address/Location	Property Name
200	12 West Haley Street	Virginia Hotel
201	33 and 35 West Haley Street	Salvation Army Building
202	317 Chapala Street	Santa Barbara Tobacco Building
203A	350 Chapala Street	(Chapala Lofts)
203B	401 Chapala Street	(Sevilla)
203C	523-531 Chapala Street	(El Andaluz)
203D	721-791 Chapala Street	(Paseo Chapala)
204	Brinkerhoff Avenue	Brinkerhoff Avenue Landmark District
205	136 West Cota Street	Hernster House
206	501 Chapala Street	Frank B. Smith House
207	506 Chapala Street	Fred Whaley Tire Company
208	505 and 509 Chapala Street	Levy House and Dancaster House
209	530 Chapala Street	
210	614 Chapala Street	C&H Chevrolet
211	623 Chapala Street	Sherman House
212	17-21 West Ortega Street	Elkhorn Creamery
213	651 Paseo Nuevo	Paseo Nuevo Shopping Center
214	101 West Canon Perdido Street	Telephone Company Building
215	911 Chapala St	Hollister Estate Building
216	919 Chapala Street	Crawford Building
217A	110 West Carrillo Street	Site of Old YMCA (Ralphs Supermarket)
217B	110 West Carrillo Street	Tree of Light
218	125 West Carrillo Street	De Riviera Hotel
219	925 De la Vina Street	Saint Vincent's School and Orphanage
220	232 West Carrillo Street	Poor Richard's Pub
221	1023 Bath Street	Botiller Adobe
222	222 West Carrillo Street	
223	31 West Carrillo Street	Carrillo Hotel (Canary Hotel)
224	15 West Carrillo Street	
225	1025 Chapala Street	
226	1105 Chapala Street	Santa Barbara Club Building
227	1111 Chapala Street	

Presidio and Pueblo – West

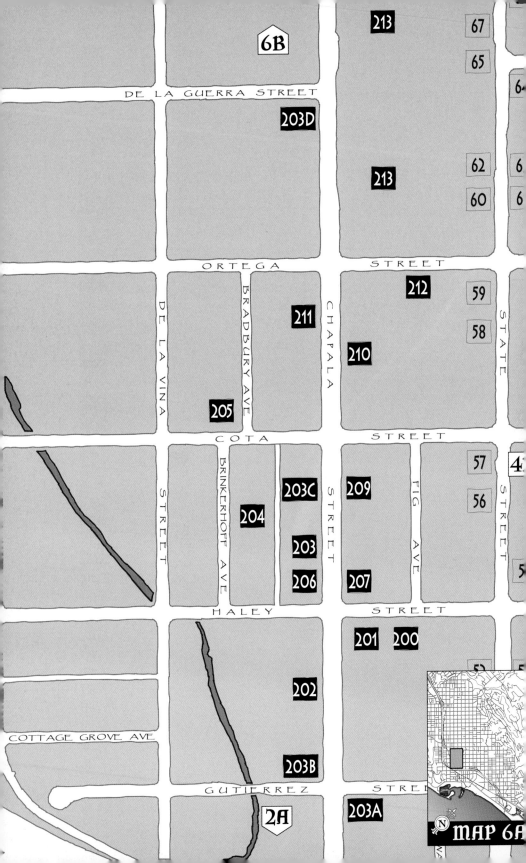

DE LA GUERRA STREET

213

67

65

203D

213

62

60

ORTEGA STREET

212

59

58

211

210

DE LA VINA STREET

BRADBURY AVE

CHAPALA STREET

205

COTA STREET

STATE STREET

BRINKERHOFF AVE

204

203C

209

57

56

FIG AVE

203

206

207

HALEY STREET

201

200

202

COTTAGE GROVE AVE

203B

GUTIERREZ STREET

203A

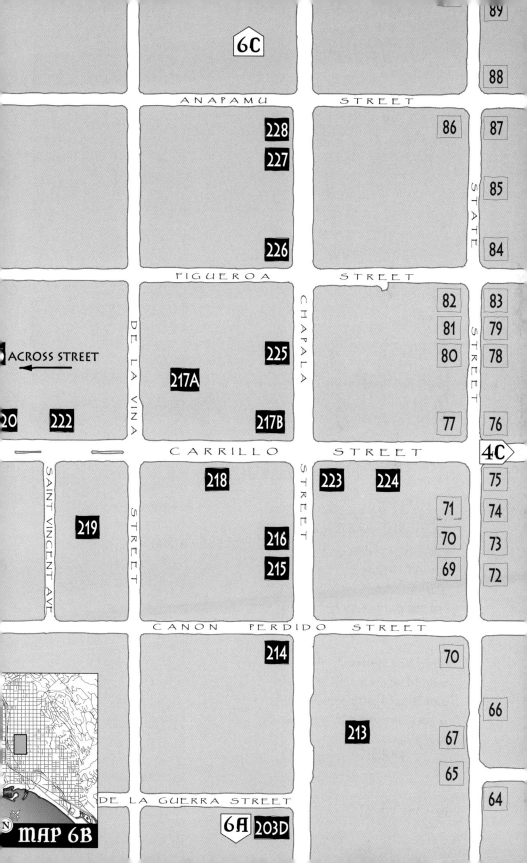

6C

A N A P A M U   S T R E E T

228

227

226

FIGUEROA   STREET

CHAPALA

DE LA VINA

ACROSS STREET

225

217A

220   222

217B

CARRILLO   STREET   4C

218

STREET

219

SAINT VINCENT AVE

216

215

223   224

CANON   PERDIDO   STREET

214

213

DE LA GUERRA STREET

MAP 6B   6A 203D

89

88

86   87

STATE   85

84

82   83

81   79

80   78

77   76

75

71   74

70   73

69   72

70

66

67

65

64

N

6D

ARRELLAGA   STREET

107

106

236

MICHELTORENA   STREET

235

234

233

237

103

102

SOLA   STREET

232

99
98
97
96
95
94
93
92

231

VICTORIA   STREET

229   230

ANAPAMU   STREET

6B   228

227

DE LA VINA   STREET

CHAPALA   STREET

STATE   STREET

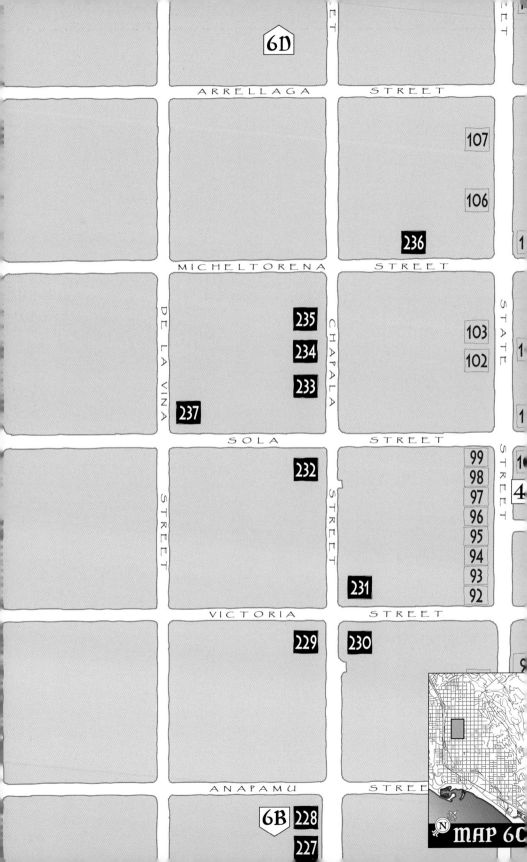

MAP 6C

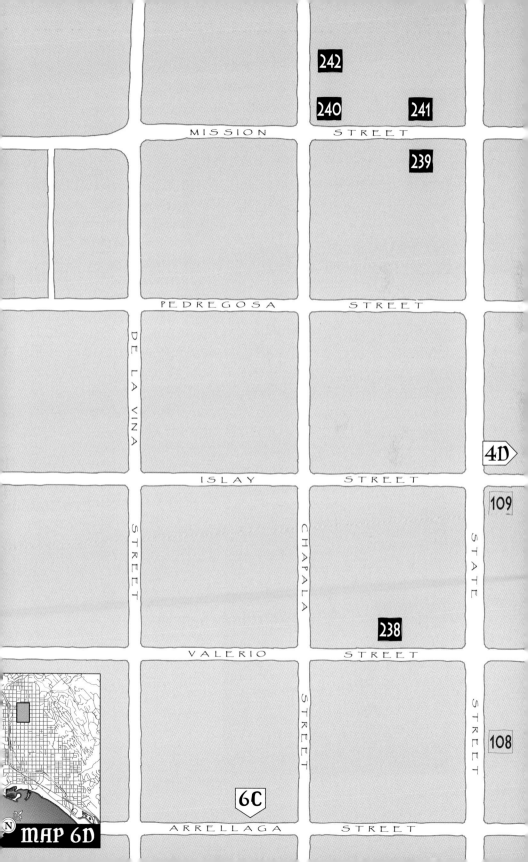

242

240   241

MISSION   STREET

239

PEDREGOSA   STREET

DE LA VINA

ISLAY   STREET

4D

CHAPALA

STREET

109

STATE

238

VALERIO   STREET

STREET

STREET

108

6C

N   MAP 6D   ARRELLAGA   STREET

200.
17 West Haley Street
Virginia Hotel
1916
1922
1926; C. K. Denman

The original Virginia Hotel was a two-story structure constructed in 1916, with Charles Maas as proprietor. A three-story building was erected in 1922. The latter was advertised in that year's city directory as the "Headquarters for Commercial Men. Newly Built, Fire Proof, Modern in Every Respect." Although the hotel might have been fireproof, it was not earthquake proof, as was demonstrated in 1925. Both the east and west walls fell, as well as the cornice. The building was rebuilt in 1926 in the prevailing Spanish Colonial Revival style. Unusual features include the twisted columns on the third story and the flanking arched windows. In keeping with modern times, the building now houses a chain hotel. **NR**

201.
33 and 35 West Haley Street
Salvation Army Building
1926; Soule, Murphy and Hastings

These post-earthquake two-story buildings have many typical Spanish Colonial Revival features of the 1920s, including arched windows, wrought iron detailing, round bull's-eye windows, and a low-pitched, hipped roof. They complete a streetscape of substantial commercial buildings illustrating the style. The

Salvation Army originally built these structures as an auditorium on the corner and gymnasium next door. The buildings are now devoted to commercial use.

202.
317 Chapala Street
Santa Barbara Tobacco Company Building
1926; Soule, Murphy and Hastings

Unusual details of this shoebox-like building include the double arched façade with engaged Ionic columns and scalloped corbelling decoration above. It shows how, in the hands of a creative architect, and with minimal effort, a basically ordinary building type can be made visually interesting.

203A.
350 Chapala Street
Chapala Lofts
2001; Berkus Design Studios

203B.
401 Chapala Street
Sevilla
2006; DesignArc

203C.
523-531 Chapala Street
El Andaluz
2008; Jeff Shelton

203D.
721-791 Chapala Street
Paseo Chapala
2006; Peikert Group Architects

These four major structures sited along Chapala, Santa Barbara's secondary commercial street, combine the perceived need for urban density in housing with the community's desire for historical continuity in architecture. These relatively massive buildings house commercial enterprises on the ground floor, a means of utilizing the entire building lot, with housing, some low-cost, on the floors above. Controversial from the beginning, and protested for their mass and height, the projects were, nonetheless, allowed to go forward. The architects were made aware that they were covering up history, and made the attempt to preserve at least some of it. For example, the 700 block of Chapala Street project was built atop the site of a building, erected in 1921, that served the Pacific Produce Company until it was demolished in 2004. The architects salvaged the beautiful sliding wooden entrance doors from the old structure and incorporated them into the new. The project at 401 Chapala, built over the rubble that once was the headquarters of the Santa Barbara Building Trades Union, commemorates that fact with a tile plaque on the new structure. More importantly, perhaps, was the fact that the architects were sensitive to the Santa Barbara idiom, and to their locations within El Pueblo Viejo, and incorporated elements of Spanish Colonial Revival architecture into their designs, allowing them to conform, as well as possible, to the style of the city.

203A. ~ Chapala Lofts

*The architect evoked Mexican Colonial architecture design details and
a reference to the purplish volcanic stone and yellow cantera stone, most
notably used in Mexico City's Palacio Nacional.*

203B. ~ Sevilla

*The architecture suggests a modern mixed-use interpretation of an
Andalusian Village in southern Spain, incorporating north African
Moorish influence with the simple direct minimalism of the Spanish
Colonial Revival style so characteristic of Santa Barbara.*

203C. ~ El Andaluz

The architect considered the major boulevard aspect of Chapala Street and strove to make Chapala feel narrower and more pedestrian. The broken mass of the front façade with the bridge connecting the two sides provides a window to the courtyard. The mystery of spaces you can see and can't approach is a small seduction point, key to this architecture.

203D. ~ Paseo Chapala

Formerly the site of the Pacific Produce Company, the architects salvaged the beautiful sliding wooden entrance doors from the old structure and incorporated them into the new.

204.
Brinkerhoff Avenue Landmark District

The houses at 501, 505, and 509 Chapala Street are located in the Brinkerhoff Avenue Landmark District, centered on Brinkerhoff Avenue. This second landmark district was established in 1982; its earliest houses were constructed in 1887. All of the antique and gift shops, galleries, and homes share a turn-of-the-century ambience. Major architectural styles found in the Brinkerhoff District are Italianate, Eastlake (Stick), Colonial Revival, and Queen Anne. **SBSM**

205.
136 West Cota Street
Hernster House
1883-1884; Peter J. Barber

This elegant Italianate structure was built as a residence for the George Hernster family, the patriarch of which was associated with a local liquor dealer. Peter Barber, who not only became the City's major Victorian-period architect, but also served as mayor, was an Ohio-born cabinet maker who studied with San Francisco architects before plying his trade in Santa Barbara. Miss Barbara Hernster remained in the family home until the late 1940s. In 1957 Elmer Whittaker bought the property and restored the house. For several decades a beauty salon had occupied the building.

Hernster House lies within the Brinkerhoff Avenue Landmark District, an architectural control district established by the City in 1982. **SBSM**

206.
501 Chapala Street
Frank B. Smith House
1895-1896

The obviously ornate house, typical of those included in the Brinkerhoff Avenue Landmark District, was built in the 19th century by Frank B. Smith, agent for the Pacific Coast Steamship Company. Although it has been used for a variety of purposes over the years, the house is relatively unaltered on the exterior and the interior first floor. The octagonal tower, with its "Witch's Cap," and the corner square bay are particularly good examples of the Queen Anne style. **SBSM**

207.
506 Chapala Street
Fred Whaley Tire Company
1930; The Austin Company
1998; John Watson

The automobile in-
fluenced the design
of commercial build-
ings in the 1920s, and
led to a variety of
examples of drive-
in architecture. One
of the most popular
forms was the L-shaped building, placed on a street corner with parking
provided between the two arms of the building. In Southern California, drive-
in markets and auto stores of one kind or another frequently used the form.
This building is a characteristic example, and in addition, is one of the few
examples of Art Deco Moderne in downtown Santa Barbara. Fred Whaley
was the Firestone Tire distributor in the early 1930s. **SBSM**

208.
505 and 509 Chapala Street
Levy House and Dancaster House
1887; 1888

These houses were constructed
during a building boom in Santa
Barbara which occurred after the
railroad reached the city from
Los Angeles. Mrs. Sarah Levy
was the original owner of 505,
while F. H. Dancaster owned
509. Both houses, which were
joined in the 1960s, display the typical Italianate style of architecture: 505
has a particularly characteristic off-center bay window; 509 has the more
usual cubical massing and low hipped roof associated with that style. New
House rehabilitation services for men occupied the joint structure for a
number of years. It is now partially residential and partly commercial, but
retains the feel of its origins. **SBSM**

209.
530 Chapala Street
1930; Roland J. Sauter

By 1930, when this building was constructed, Chapala Street was evolving from residential to commercial, especially auto related, uses. The architect, Roland J. Sauter, designed the building in stripped-down Spanish Colonial Revival style in keeping with the Santa Barbara idiom. Decorative Spanish details include the octagonal tower and the scalloped relief molding. Although essentially Hispanic in design, there is a touch of the 1920s Art Deco Moderne in this L-shaped corner building, originally occupied by Freeze & Freeze, 'Everything For the Automobile.' The firm remained here until 1942 when Joe Dal Pozzo succeeded the company, and his auto service and supply business was a familiar sight for many years.

210.
614 Chapala Street
C & H Chevrolet
1946; A. Godfrey Bailey; Soule & Murphy (associate architects)
2005; DesignArc
2014; Shubin-Donaldson Architects; John Beauchamp

This Streamline Moderne building was constructed after World War II as a public garage and salesroom for local Chevrolet dealer, George C. Young. It continued in that function into the new century, when the auto dealership moved to a new location. Remodeled twice since for new commercial tenants, the building remains a rare example of an architectural style that never quite caught on. Yet even in the Streamline Moderne, vestiges of the Spanish Colonial Revival architecture appear, in this case the red tile roof, tying the style and the building to the Santa Barbara motif. **SBSM**

211.
623 Chapala Street
Sherman House
1877

Charles F. Sherman, the original owner and builder of this striking house, was a wholesale and retail butcher with a meat market a block away at 646 State Street. Later, in the 1880s, he was Sheriff of Santa Barbara County. His house is a typical L-shaped story-and-a-half Italianate structure of the mid-1870s. It has been converted to office uses and thus preserves a peek into a bygone era in Santa Barbara. **SBSM**

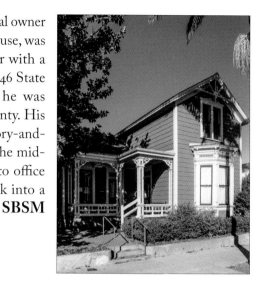

212.
17-21 West Ortega Street
Elkhorn Creamery
1905-1906

One of Santa Barbara's remaining Mission Revival style commercial buildings, this small gem was erected for the owner of the Fithian Building at the corner of State and Ortega Streets. In the same year, R. Barrett Fithian constructed a two-story building to the east, with Francis W. Wilson as architect. It was demolished following the 1925 earthquake, but the creamery building survived. Over the years a variety of commercial entities have occupied this simple Mission Revival building, preserving a bit of pre-earthquake Santa Barbara.

213.
651 Paseo Nuevo

Paseo Nuevo Shopping Center
1990; Field Paoli Architects, Callison Architecture,
Associated Architects & Planners

The ordinary shopping mall does not, as a rule, conform to established local architecture, but Paseo Nuevo, a two square block facility bounded by State, West Ortega, Chapala, and West Canon Perdido Streets, is an exception. Perhaps that is because it was dreamed about and thought about for a number of years as Santa Barbara, like so many small cities, struggled to find ways to rejuvenate its downtown. Paseo Nuevo, amid much controversy, eventually evolved into a City Redevelopment Agency project, with the city in partnership with the developer, the Reininga Corporation of San Francisco. That partnership practically guaranteed conformation to Santa Barbara's Spanish Colonial Revival architectural theme. The anchor stores, Broadway (now Macy's) and Nordstrom, each had its own architect and, in the eyes of one contemporary observer, better reflected the local style by utilizing towers, balconies, and other Spanish Colonial features in their structures. But with meandering walkways, Spanish tiles, and wrought-iron work, certainly, it complements the city style while accomplishing its purpose of stimulating the downtown economy.

214.
101 West Canon Perdido Street

Telephone Company Building
1928; Russel Ray
1957 remodel; Chester Carjola

Built originally for the General Telephone Company, this large structure was initially two stories and faced with textured concrete veneer, the facing in response to the growing Hispanicization of the downtown. A third floor and small fourth floor were added in 1957. The designer of the latter was Chester Carjola, who enhanced the Spanish Colonial Revival aspects of the building with inspiration taken from Spanish medieval architecture. The building exhibits what one observer called "rich Churrigueresque" fea-

tures surrounding the windows, prominent ironwork, balconies, and even a touch of Classical, with Corinthian columns on the top two floors. The structure remains a communications center, and a massive tribute to Santa Barbara's Spanish Colonial theme. In 1928, the original building won an award from the Plans and Planting Committee.

215.
911 Chapala Street
Hollister Estate Building
1931; Edwards and Plunkett

This California adobe-style building was built by the descendants of Col W. W. Hollister in 1930, utilizing the services of one of Santa Barbara's premier architectural firms. Although Col. Hollister died in 1886, his family continued to exert considerable influence in Santa Barbara throughout the 20th century. The building has since hosted a variety of enterprises, but continues to exude its special charm.

216.
919 Chapala Street
Crawford Building
1936; Soule and Murphy

This miniscule office building boasts two squat Doric columns and a tiny red tiled roof, in accord with the architect's intent to keep the structure within Santa Barbara's general style. It was originally constructed for James D. Crawford, a realtor.

217A.
110 West Carrillo Street
Site of Old YMCA
(Ralphs Market)
1913; Winsor Soule and Russel Ray
2000; Lenvik & Minor Architects

In 1910 the family of Col. W. W. Hollister donated this site to the nascent YMCA. From a city that then boasted about 11,659 people, a fund-raising campaign netted some $87,567 to construct a proper building. The prominent firm of Soule and Ray developed an interesting combination of Mission Revival style with elements of Tuscan architecture to produce this striking structure, complete with basement, in 1913. For the next 47 years the YMCA served the city from this building. When, in 1960, the building could no longer support the YMCA's growing activities, the organization vacated it for a new site on Hitchcock Way. Thereafter, the building housed a variety of tenants, including two popular restaurants in the basement, Chez Paul and Casa Madrid. Others included the Bachelor Club Lodgings, the Alano Club, a health studio, a short-lived hotel, and several offices, among others. Lack of proper maintenance led to the deterioration of the structure and it was finally demolished in 1986. At that time several projects were proposed for this prime property, including a large, four-story office building. The final approval was given to a Ralphs Grocery Supermarket. The architectural firm of Lenvik & Minor Architects, acutely aware of Santa Barbara's downtown motif, produced a wonderfully compatible building, addressed at 100 West Carrillo Street, with underground parking. An expansive outdoor patio encourages shoppers to take time out to enjoy the shade of the Tree of Light, and the rest of the extensive landscaping on the north end of the site. Even supermarkets, in the hands of sensitive architects, can add to the general aura of Santa Barbara's downtown.

Presidio and Pueblo – West

Thomas Schmidt @ SBVintagePhoto.com

# 217B.
110 West Carrillo Street
Tree of Light
1878

Standing tall at the corner of West Carrillo and Chapala Streets, this magnificent example of a Norfolk Island Pine (Auraucaria heterophylla) is an official City Landmark. It was planted in 1878 by Dr. Robert Winchester, who was then living on the property in an adobe built by José Lobero, founder of the Lobero Theater (See entry #129). The adobe had also been used by Col W. W. Hollister as his city residence. Now anchoring a new public patio which includes a fountain, Olive trees, 'Iceberg' roses, and a pergola covered with 'Climbing Cecile Brunner' roses, the Tree of Light is decorated annually as the city's Christmas Tree, thus the name. **SBL**

218.
125 West Carrillo Street
De Riviera Hotel
1915

This charming old Craftsman style building, with its wood frame construction, deep stained clapboard siding, low profile, and unique pole sign, gives the appearance of a European type cottage hotel, and contrasts pleasantly with the cityscape surrounding it. Built in 1915 as a "Norwegian Hotel for Norwegians," for owners Millie Bern and Carl L. Holstrum, the De Riviera has remained essentially unaltered over time. One of its more famous tenants was the renowned anthropologist, Dr. John P. Harrington, who maintained an apartment here while gathering ethnographic materials locally. While no longer a hotel, the De Riviera now serves as housing for those with special needs. In 1979 the City Landmarks Committee included it on a list of sites sent to Sacramento to be put on the State of California Inventory of Historic Resources. **SBSM**

219.
925 De la Vina Street
St. Vincent's School and Orphanage
Knights of Columbus Hall
1874-1875; A. Marquis
1983; Rolly Pulaski and Associates

The Knights of Columbus Hall is generally considered to be Santa Barbara's finest surviving Anglo-American building of the 19th century. It was constructed in 1874-1875 by the Catholic Daughters of Charity of St. Vincent de Paul as a girls' school. The sisters had arrived in Santa Barbara from their Provincial House in Emmitsburg, Maryland, in 1858 and were originally housed in the Aguirre Adobe (See entry #141). There the predominantly Catholic-Irish Sisters ran a day and boarding school for the predominantly Catholic-Hispanic children of the town. In the 1860s the

Thomas Schmidt @ SBVintagePhoto.com

school acquired the Cieneguitas Ranch, then beyond the edge of town. The tuition at the school was $150 per year, payable half-yearly in advance. In 1869-1870 a school building was constructed on this site, only to burn down in 1874. Funds raised from the motherhouse in Maryland allowed construction of a new building to begin immediately. This structure was originally three stories high and of Italianate design. The third story was removed after the 1925 earthquake. Fortunately the children had been moved the previous year to a new school on the Ranch. The local Knights of Columbus lodge occupied the building from 1924 to 1980. The building has undergone extensive internal renovation, and has become a desirable office location, assuring its preservation. Architecturally, this edifice is a good example of the Italianate style popular in the 1860s and 1870s, with emphasis on the vertical, recessed windows beneath segmental and flat hoods, a prominent cornice, and a projecting and pedimented entrance porch. There are two large sandstone hitching blocks on the De la Vina Street frontage, a prominent reminder of the days before automobiles. **NR, SBL**

220.
232 West Carrillo Street
Poor Richard's Pub
1971; Richard Headley; Paul Unander

This unusual building is a close copy of an early 16th century English farmhouse. Although somewhat out of place in Hispanic Santa Barbara, its fidelity to history and original construction methods, shipwrights erected the building without the use of metal fasteners, makes it an interesting architectural anomaly, a monument to the aesthetics of its designer. **SBSM**

221.
1023 Bath Street
Botiller Adobe
1843

Santa Barbara's last two-story reminder of its origins, the Botiller Adobe, was the handiwork of vintner Pascual Botiller, who purchased the property in 1843 and immediately constructed the adobe as a home for himself and his family. He also planted a vineyard on the property, in an area which had hosted grape vines since 1802. Botiller's descendants resided in the adobe until 1969, when the last of them passed. The lot was put up for sale, and there were fears that the adobe might be razed. In an effort to give it a modicum of protection, the City landmarked the structure in 1970, and the Native Daughters of the Golden West attempted to raise the money to purchase it. A private buyer, Henry Perkins, finally came forward in 1971 and saved the adobe. He further did a major restoration of the structure. The Native Daughters provided an historical plaque on the property in 1971. Since then, the adobe has gone through both residential and museum uses, but remains a solid connection to Santa Barbara's adobe past.   **SBL**

222.
222 West Carrillo Street
1927; G. H. Jacobs

This is an exceptionally late example of the Mission Revival Style which flourished in Santa Barbara from the late 1890s through the early 1910s. One of the distinguishing features of this Revival was the use of Mission-style towers, well exemplified in this building. It was originally constructed for the Knights of Pythias lodge and later became the Carrillo Auditorium. It continues to house retail establishments, and maintains its vitality along busy Carrillo Street.

223.
31 West Carrillo Street

Carrillo Hotel
(Canary Hotel)
2004; Cearnal Architects Inc. with Mark Shields, J G Johnson Architects

On Christmas Day, 1923, the 200 room Carrillo Hotel opened for business. The massive though rather plain structure was praised at the time as having "nothing garish, nothing ornate...no ledges laden with gingerbread, no meaningless ornaments, no grinning faces or posing chiseled figures. It's just plain beauty." This was partially because the Pasadena architects "worked in harmony with suggestions outlined by the Community Arts." The building's concrete construction enabled it to survive the 1925 earthquake with only minimal damage. As the years wore on, the hotel gradually

deteriorated and was finally turned into a retirement hotel. In 1996, developers came before the City Council with a proposal to demolish the old hotel and build a new one in its place. The proposal was controversial because it exceeded Santa Barbara's building height limits, and because it would displace the elderly residents. Nonetheless, demolition of the old structure took place. The developers ran into financing problems, and the site became a hole-in-the-ground eyesore for several years before construction on the present building began in 2003, causing chaos in one of the city's major intersections. It opened as the Andalucia Hotel in 2004, morphed into the Canary in 2008, and was taken over by Kimpton Hotels in 2012. It remains what it was in the beginning, a fine hotel in the heart of the downtown area.

224.
15 West Carrillo Street
1930; Edwards and Plunkett

The architects of this building, who did so much to transform Santa Barbara after the 1925 earthquake, chose to break up the relatively long façade of this building through the use of an off-center entry and irregular arch window placement. Attorneys have occupied offices here since the building's construction. **SBSM**

225.
1025 Chapala Street
1926; Edwards, Plunkett and Howell
1987; Brian Cearnal

Although the first story of this post-earthquake building has been considerably altered, the second story and red tile roof are typical of the 1920s architecture in Santa Barbara. Once home to a Piggly Wiggly supermarket and to Elmer's Restaurant, it has hosted a variety of retail outlets over the years, while maintaining its tie to the Santa Barbara motif.

226.
1105 Chapala Street
Santa Barbara Club Building
1903-1904; Francis W. Wilson

The Santa Barbara Club, a private organization, originally for men only, was founded in 1892 by such prominent community leaders as Col W. W. Hollister, Dixey W. Thompson, and Joel Fithian. The club quickly outgrew its first facility and the present structure, designed by club member and prominent architect, Francis W. Wilson, was built. It is a Neo-classical design, with cornice, egg and dart moldings, pilasters, and lintels over the windows. This style, derived from Italian Renaissance palazzos, was popularized by the New York firm of McKim, Mead and White, and soon became the norm for establishments such as this. The original formal entrance was removed to provide for the widening of Chapala Street in the summer of 1925, but the unusual arched entrance with its Palladian-style side windows remains. In 2013 the windows were replaced with new ones meticulously matched to the originals. **SBL**

227.
1111 Chapala Street
1986-1987; Lenvik & Minor Architects

The west side of the 1100 block of Chapala Street, anchored by the Santa Barbara Club Landmark, has evolved from small residences to large handsome Spanish Revival office buildings. This three story modern Hispanic office building maintains a moderate scale at the street by providing below grade parking. The automobile entrance is set back substantially from the street allowing for a ground floor arcade and second floor balcony along both the side and front elevations. These features add interest and scale to the exterior façade while offering natural light and air for the tenants. Santa Barbara Capital was the owner/developer and original tenant of the building.

228.
1123 Chapala Street
1984; Sharpe, Mahan and Associates

A really grand tiled dome tower looks down on the raised terrace entrance of this handsome Hispanic building. The architects have done an admirable job of blending the Santa Barbara Hispanic tradition with modern needs as they placed an essential parking garage on the ground level with two floors of offices above.

229.
1235 Chapala Street
1922; H. C. Weeks

Although this building is of some interest architecturally due to its yellowish brick and general Mediterranean styling, its main significance is historical. The building was constructed as the administrative office for the Santa Barbara Schools, and was sited between the Anna S. C. Blake building and both the Santa Barbara Junior High and High Schools which occupied the rest of the block. The earthquake of 1925 destroyed the high school, but this building, and a similar structure to the rear survived. In the mid-1960s the property was acquired by the City of Santa Barbara and later served as the City Land Use Controls Office. More recently, the building has moved closer to its roots, becoming the Twelve35 Teen Center.

230.
1236 Chapala Street and 33 West Victoria Street
First Baptist Church and office building
(New Victoria Street Theatre)
1910, 1921; Norman F. Marsh
2013; Phillips, Metsch, Sweeney (33 West Victoria)

This Tudor Revival church complex was originally constructed in two stages. The rear portion, initially the chapel and kindergarten, exhibits such Tudor elements as half-timbering and steeply pitched roofs. The main portion is dominated by a squat three-story tower with buttresses, lancet windows, and stained glass in a Gothic Revival style. Since the church relocated, the complex has undergone a number of owners and uses. From 1981 to 1988 the main auditorium was the Victoria Street Theatre. In 1988, three local charities, CALM, RSVP, and the Unity Shoppe purchased the venue and moved their offices to the site. After some twenty years, there was a falling out among the charities, and the 33 West Victoria portion was eventually sold to the Ensemble Theatre Company. The Ensemble had the main auditorium modernized for theatrical productions and re-opened it as the New Victoria Street Theatre in 2013. The essential complex remains, however, adding to the architectural diversity of the city. **SBSM (theater)**

231.
Chapala Street Between Victoria and Sola Streets
Joseph Knowles Mural
1958; Joseph Knowles
2014; Cearnal Andrulaitis LLP

When the Safeway Corporation built a new store in Santa Barbara in the late 1950s, it was designed in the "industrial modernism" style, but Safeway made two concessions to the city. First, it utilized local sandstone for planters, walls, and some building cladding, and second, it commissioned a mural to face the Victoria Street side of the store. To create the mural, which was designed to extend almost 120 feet along the building, local talent Joseph Knowles was chosen. A noted artist with numerous commissions, exhibitions, and honors, Knowles had deep ties to Santa Barbara, where he had first arrived in 1927. He was a graduate of the Santa Barbara School of the Arts, taught extensively in a variety of Santa Barbara schools, helped create the Santa Barbara Art Association, and was the first education director of the Santa Barbara Museum of Art, among other things. His creation was a polychromatic mosaic in six panels, separated by the vertical piers of the building. Each panel depicted an historical era in Santa Barbara history – the Chumash; the Spanish explorers; Mission Santa Barbara; the Californio Rancho; the American settler; and finally the modern era. It was the largest public art piece in the city at the time. Not only was it strikingly beautiful, but the mosaic quickly became embedded in the city's aura. Thus when the store building was demolished to provide for a new mixed-used development, the mural was carefully removed, cleaned, and re-installed in its present location on the west wall of the new structure, where it will continue to delight residents and visitors for a long time to come.

232.
105 West Sola Street
The Edgerly Court Apartments
1913; Arthur B. Benton

The Edgerly is one of Santa Barbara's oldest and largest residential hotels. It sits on the site of an earlier three-story hostelry known as Harrison House, which was developed in the mid-1880s. When the Edgerly opened, it housed many employees and actors of the American Film Company (See entry #240). Architecturally, the hotel is representative of the late 19th and early 20th century interest in wooden structures expressed as skeletons. That effect is achieved on this Craftsman style building chiefly through the half-timbering on the massive overhanging two-story balcony. According to Davis' Commercial Encyclopedia of the Pacific Southwest, Nelson Millett made suggestions to the architect which formed the basis for this design. Mr. Millett was an officer of the West Coast Apartments Company of Los Angeles who served as manager of Edgerly Court. An actor named Arthur Nelson Millett appeared in some of the Flying A company's films and resided at the court briefly. Were they one and the same?

233.
1407 Chapala Street
Mortimer Cook House
1872; Peter J. Barber

The Cook house, one of Santa Barbara's finest remaining examples of the Italianate style, has a history that reflects, in microcosm, the flamboyant Victorian era. As with many of the larger Italianate houses Barber designed, the Cook house boasts a splendid central cupola. Mortimer Cook, a native of Ohio, lived in Santa Barbara for only about a decade, but in that short time managed to build and lose a fortune. Shortly after he arrived in 1871 by boat from San Francisco, and floated his considerable wealth ashore in a massive safe, he opened a private bank. A year later he established the First National Gold Bank in partnership with Amasa Lincoln, owner of the Lincoln House (still standing as the Upham Hotel at 1404 De la Vina Street; see entry #237). In 1874, banker Cook entered politics and was elected city mayor. That same year, the First National Gold Bank purchased land on the northwest corner of State and Canon Perdido Streets and began construction of a three-story Italianate brick bank and office building, completed in 1876. By that time Cook was more interested in real estate development than in banking, and in 1876 he undertook the construction of the town's largest building at the corner of State and Carrillo Streets (the Upper Clock Building). Cook, however, was about to meet his nemesis. Financially overextended, he suffered heavy losses in the 1877 panic. Shortly thereafter he sold his remaining assets and moved to Washington state, intent on building another fortune.

The house has had a number of subsequent owners, none of whom impacted the city like the original, and Cook's story seems destined to remain as impressive as the house, a City Landmark. **SBL**

234.
1415 Chapala Street
Thompson House
1906

This two-story American Colonial Revival house was constructed for Nancy P. Thompson, widow of prominent 19th century businessman, Dixey W. Thompson. Except for the first-story window alterations and the added exterior stairway, the house is a good example of its style, which was quite popular at the turn of the 20th century. Mrs. Thompson lived here until 1927, and since then, the house has had but two owners: the Foursquare Gospel Church (1929-1955), and the Santa Barbara Association of Realtors (1956 to the present), which accounts for the structure's integrity and longevity.

235.
1421 Chapala Street
Medical Arts Building
1926; Edwards and Plunkett

The handsome tripartite arched arcade and formal landscape of this Spanish Colonial Revival building suggest an elegant residence. The building, however, was designed by one of Santa Barbara's premier architectural firms for use as medical offices for the original owner, Dr. Horace F. Pierce. Several additions have been made to the rear since it was built in 1926, but the impressive façade remains unaltered.

236.
22 West Micheltorena Street
1926; George Washington Smith; Snook and Kenyon, builders
1948; Lutah Maria Riggs

In 1926, Dr. Samuel Robinson commissioned prominent architect George Washington Smith to create a medical office building to house his practice, but as a commercial structure it was not to intrude on the residential character of the neighborhood. The result was a wood frame and stucco building, done in the standard Spanish Colonial Revival style, with its obligatory red tile roof, designed to look like a residence. It served Dr. Robinson well, and was gradually expanded with the addition of other rooms to the rear. In 1948 the growing complex was remodeled, and the Robinson estate chose Lutah Riggs for the task, probably because of her direct connection to original architect Smith. Further additions were made in 1951 and 1959, but the building still retains its original character.

237.
1404 De la Vina Street
Upham Hotel
1871; Peter J. Barber

Standing on the corner of De la Vina and Sola Streets is Southern California's oldest continuously operating hotel, The Upham. First called the Lincoln House, it was built by Amasa Lincoln, a native of Massachusetts who had come west with a flood of other easterners searching for a more healthful climate. On the advice of Santa Barbara's most prominent citizen, Col. W. W. Hollister, Lincoln purchased the Tajiguas Ranch, west of town along the coast. But after a year in the lonely, quasi-wilderness of the ranch, Lincoln moved to Santa Barbara, hired architect Peter Barber, and built what he called a proper New England boarding house on the lot where it still stands. The ten room, three bath building was constructed of redwood lumber cut in Santa Cruz, shipped down the coast, and floated ashore on the beach, as Santa Barbara had no wharf. Built in the New England style, with a "widow's walk" on the top, it sported one of Peter Barber's signatures, the ornate, hand-sawn brackets on the porch and the walk. The hotel was purchased in 1898 by Cyrus Upham, who renamed it for himself, and that name has remained. The numerous owners since, some of them descendants of the original, recognized the unique nature of the hotel, and wisely preserved it. On its hundredth anniversary in 1971, the Native Daughters of the Golden West gave it a landmark plaque, the city designated it a Landmark in 1980, and, in a celebration of the hotel's 125th year in 1996, the featured speaker was 92 year old Anna Lincoln Ellis, the granddaughter of the first owner, Amasa Lyman Lincoln, keeping a personal connection over all the years. While the hotel has been expanded and modernized over time, the original building still graces the city, and reminds locals and visitors of a long past, more gracious time. **SBL**

238.
20, 30, 32, and 36 West Valerio Street
Turn-Of-The-Century streetscape
1887-1903

West of State Street along this
block stand four two-story
houses that present passersby
with a glimpse of one of Santa
Barbara's middle-class residential neighborhoods much as it
appeared at the turn of the 20th
century. A stately and tastefully
ornamented Italianate/Eastlake
(20 West Valerio) is followed by

two restrained Colonial Revival style houses (30 and 32 West Valerio), and a
Queen Anne/Eastlake which stands sentry-like on the west corner (36 West
Valerio) and has a fanciful pagoda-influenced front porch.

For many years the 1887 Lunt House at 20 West was the home of J. J. Callahan,
former city councilman and county supervisor. The Herbert House at 30 West
was erected in 1902. The two houses closest to Chapala Street were built for the
Eberle family, the house at 36 West in 1889-1890, and the one at 32 West in 1903.

239.
11 West Mission Street
Modoc Substation
1930; Russel Ray

This electrical power
substation was specif-
ically designed by the
architect, Russel Ray,
to project a residen-
tial or bungalow im-
age. In doing so, Ray

combined two architectural fashions of the 1920s, the
Spanish Colonial Revival and Art Deco Moderne. Particularly noteworthy
Moderne details are the repeated lightning bolt motif on the building and
on the wrought iron gates. **SBSM**

240.
00 Block West Mission Street
American Film Manufacturing Company Site
1913; J. Corbley Pool

The Mission Revival building at 34 West Mission Street stands as a reminder of Santa Barbara's leading role in the early days of the film industry, as well as exemplifying the Santa Barbara architectural motif. In 1912, the American Film Manufacturing Company, popularly known as the Flying A Studio, purchased this block and built an indoor studio and darkroom. Other buildings were added until the complex spread over the entire block and half the adjacent one to the north. The surviving corner building was used as actors' waiting and dressing rooms. Behind the corner building sits another of the Flying A structures, which the company originally used as a garage.

Flying A's production schedule was tight – two films per week. Its first production was shot on July 10, 1912, at the old Dixey Thompson ranch west of the city. Three days later the film crew set a record by shooting a 1,000 foot finished film in two hours and fifteen minutes. The film "Stranger at Coyote" was shot at Oak Park (Alamar Avenue along Mission Creek) and was described as a "real lurid western drama." American Film producer-director-manager-writer Alan Dwan kept churning out westerns and thrillers for the next decade, but by the 1920s the industry had centralized in Hollywood and Flying A was in decline.

Most of the film company's buildings were demolished in the early 1940s, and gradually replaced. The Spanish Colonial Revival shops and offices at 2001-2007 State Street and 2-4 West Mission Street were built in 1950. In keeping with the rest of the city, the Mission Street shops and offices are intimate in scale and gently step up and down the slopes of Mission and State Streets. **SBL**

241.
22 West Mission Street
1934; Henry W. Howell
1982; Stan Riffle

This imposing structure gives every impression of being a church which, actually, it once was. Though built in 1934, the building preserves a bit of earlier history by incorporating, in the rear section, a one story brick and concrete structure dating back to 1913 and the Flying A studio. Originally constructed in 1934 as a mortuary chapel, and utilized as such for a number of years, the building subsequently housed several different churches over the years before being remodeled in 1982 to become the Northwestern Preparatory School. Since then it has housed other commercial and office enterprises. Exuding the Santa Barbara architectural idiom in its own unique way, 22 West Mission Street adds both dignity and interest to its neighborhood.

Presidio and Pueblo – West

242.
2020 Chapala Street
St. Mark's Episcopal Church
ca. 1875; attributed to Peter J. Barber

This steeply gabled, board and batten church is Santa Barbara's best remaining example of early Gothic Revival architecture. It is also the city's second oldest extant church building, outdated only by Mission Santa Barbara. A particularly noteworthy detail is the stylized cross design of the bargeboards, especially along the façade, where, at the apex, a simple quatrefoil is flanked by two circles. At one time a tall spire rose from the belfry. Presumably it was lost in one of the building's several moves, for, in its century plus existence, it has served four different congregations in three separate locations. In the early 1970s the church was converted to commercial uses, but one can hardly tell from the remarkably preserved exterior and the beautifully landscaped setting. The building is a City Landmark. **SBL**

Mission Area

In *Two Years Before the Mast*, published in 1835, Richard Henry Dana described Mission Santa Barbara, which he had seen a few years earlier, as standing, "a little back of the town...a large building, or rather collection of buildings, in the center of which is a high tower with a belfry of five bells. The whole being plastered, makes quite a show at distance, and is the mark by which vessels come to anchor."

With little change, although by 1835 the Mission had two bell towers, the same view met the eyes of all nineteenth-century travelers who arrived at Santa Barbara on seagoing vessels. "The town," Dana continued, "is composed of one-story houses, built of sun-baked clay, or adobe, some of them whitewashed, with red tiles on the roofs. I should judge that there were about a hundred of them; and in the midst of them stands the presidio, or fort, built of the same material and apparently but little stronger. The town is finely situated, with a bay in front and amphitheater of hills beyond."

This is, without doubt, the image of past idyllic beauty that captivated those who first sought to guide Santa Barbara's twentieth-century architectural and spatial development. The focal points of this image, the Presidio and the Mission, are, of course, symbols of the California lifestyle and culture that made the Southwest regionally distinct.

From 1786 until the mid-nineteenth century, the Mission complex stood alone overlooking the Presidio and dusty pueblo. Fr. Fermin Lasuen, OFM, chose this particular site for the Mission not because of its natural beauty but because it was a sufficient distance from the Presidio to mitigate the corrupting influence of the soldiers yet close enough to enjoy the benefits of their protective sphere. The Mission is located on the former site of a Chumash rancheria, Xana'yan; and the Christianized Chumash, who provided the labor necessary to build the religious compound, continued to live in a small village of adobe shelters located west of the Mission entrance. Orchards of fruit and olive trees grew in the area which is now the southern part of Mission Historical Park (entry #244). Workers tended a large garden planted south of the Chumash village, occupying an area now roughly bounded by Mission, Garden, East Los Olivos, and Santa Barbara Streets. And grain fields, mostly wheat, stretched west and north of the Mission.

The orchards and garden were irrigated with water supplied by the Mission water system, a portion of which is now incorporated into Mission Historical Park. A native sandstone dam built in Mission Canyon in 1806 is still standing; it is now a part of the Botanic Garden, located one mile north of the Museum of Natural History. Water from the Mission Canyon dam ran through an aqueduct to a filter house, also still standing, east of the Mission, near the juncture of East Los Olivos Street and Mountain Drive. The filtered water ran into a reservoir located near the same intersection, and the reservoir stored water for the city water system. Fragments of aqueducts that traversed the Mission property remain in several places. Legend has it that women, including the Cota sisters, did laundry in the aqueduct just outside the cemetery wall, so two Sycamore trees (Platanus racemosa) were planted ca. 1866-70 to shade them as they worked. Historians attribute the planting to either Father O'Keefe or Juan de Dios Juarez. It is also likely that the trees occurred naturally because Sycamores are abundant in Mission Canyon. One of the "Cota Sycamores" still stands.

After the Mexican government secularized the missions in the 1830s, the Santa Barbara complex ceased to function as a self-sustaining communal society. Mission lands were confiscated and divided up, eventually passing into private ownership. Without land, the Mission community could not carry on its agricultural and related cottage-industry pursuits, but the friars were allowed to continue their religious duties.

In 1874, Messrs. Van Vactor and Myers began to subdivide the area, but the first private residence did not appear until 1880 when Don Gaspar Oreña built a mansion southeast of the Mission, where Roosevelt School is now located. A few years later Lucy Noyes Brinkerhoff, widow of Dr. Samuel Brinkerhoff, built "The Olives" on part of the Mission's former garden site. These elegant dwellings were both demolished many years ago, but their appearance seems to have set the residential character for the area. During the next five decades many of Santa Barbara's socially prominent citizens built homes, and in some cases second or summer homes, in this neighborhood. Between 1890 and 1930 much of the land near the Mission was privately developed. Two of the most architecturally distinguished developments, Crocker Row (entry #261) and Plaza Rubio (entry #245), were undertaken with the Mission setting in mind. Several Mission-related buildings are also located in this area: St. Anthony's

Seminary (entry #257), the Monastery of Poor Clares (entry #260), and Junípero Serra Hall (entry #256).

Another group of architecturally notable buildings, the Museum of Natural History complex (entry #249) and Mt. Calvary Retreat (entry #247), are historically linked. The museum began in 1916 as the dream of ornithologist William Leon Dawson, who spent his lifetime collecting and studying birds' eggs. Dawson housed his sizable collection in a small cottage north of St. Anthony's Seminary and near Mission Creek. In 1917, he and several other Santa Barbara nature lovers formally associated for the purpose of establishing a natural history museum. Dawson's dream became reality in 1922 when his neighbor, Caroline Hazard, who also sat on the fledgling museum's board, decided that the family estate would be a fitting site. She and her sister-in-law not only donated a portion of the Hazard estate to the cause, but they financed construction of the museum's first buildings as well. The museum is considered to be one of the finest small natural history museums in the United States.

In 1926, Caroline Hazard once again involved herself in an effort to preserve local history when she joined Mrs. Joseph Andrews and several other women to purchase land east of and across from the Mission. Their purpose was to see the spot turned into a park before it could be claimed for residential development. In the same year Anna Blaksley Bliss purchased a parcel of canyon land located further up Mission Canyon in order to prevent developers from proceeding with plans to build houses in that area. She donated the parcel to the public for use as a botanic garden, originally placing it under the aegis of the Museum of Natural History. Thus, through the timely efforts of several Santa Barbara women who had the financial means to demonstrate their civic concerns, Santa Barbara has preserved much of the natural setting and natural history that complement the architecture and cultural history of the Mission.

While the overall character of the Mission area has changed very little since the turn of the century, some older residences have been demolished. Population and building densities remain low here, and many buildings in this neighborhood enhance the city's Hispanic image. Some of the city's most beautiful examples of stonemasonry are also found in this area, including the stone arch bridge over Mission Creek (entry #248) and the Junípero Plaza gates (entry #250).

The Mission area, 1896.
The Crocker Row houses (entry #261) can be seen to the right of the Mission.

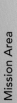

Mission Area

No.	Property Address/Location	Property Name
243	2201 Laguna Street at East Los Olivos Street	Mission Santa Barbara
244	East and North of Mission Santa Barbara	Mission Historical Park
245	East of Mission Historical Park	400 Block of Plaza Rubio
246	530 Plaza Rubio	Dardi-Patterson House
247	505 East Los Olivos Street	St. Mary's Retreat House (Mount Calvary Monastery)
248	East Los Olivos Street/ Mission Canyon Road at Mountain Drive	Mission Creek Bridge
249	2559 Puesta Del Sol Road	Santa Barbara Museum of Natural History
250	2100 Block of Laguna and Garden Streets (Mid-Block)	Junipero Plaza Gate Posts
251	340 East Los Olivos Street	Edwards House
252	333 Junípero Plaza (Formerly 326 East Los Olivos Street)	Dibblee House
253	316 East Los Olivos Street	Vaughn House
254	306 East Los Olivos Street	Dennison House
255	232 East Los Olivos Street	Frothingham House
256	2210 Garden Street	Junípero Serra Hall
257	2300 Garden Street	Saint Anthony's Seminary
258	2420 Garden Street	Hoffmann House
259	2401 Garden Street	Boyd House
260	215 East Los Olivos Street	Monastery of Poor Clares
261	2010-2050 Garden Street	Crocker Row

Not on map

No.	Property Address/Location	Property Name
262	500 James Fowler Road	Santa Barbara Municipal Airport, Earle Ovington Terminal

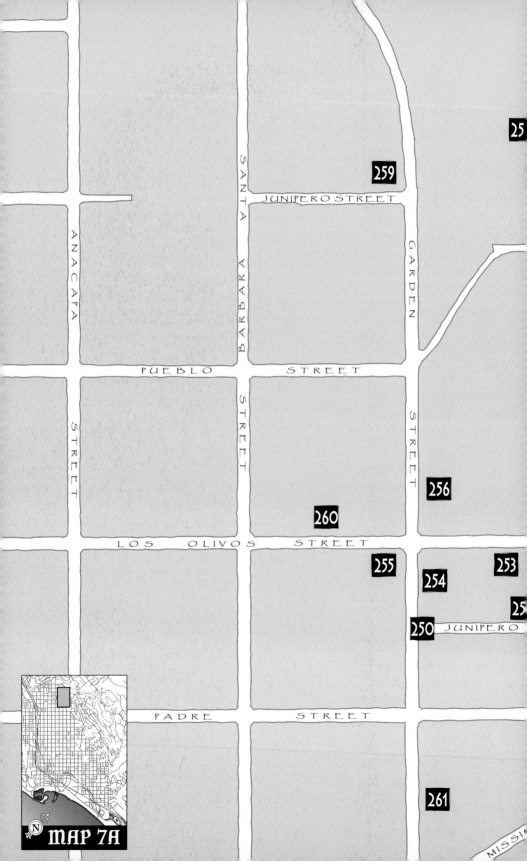

ANACAPA STREET

SANTA BARBARA STREET

JUNIPERO STREET

GARDEN STREET

259

25

PUEBLO STREET

256

260

LOS OLIVOS STREET

255

253

254

250 JUNIPERO

25

PADRE STREET

261

MISSI

MAP 7A

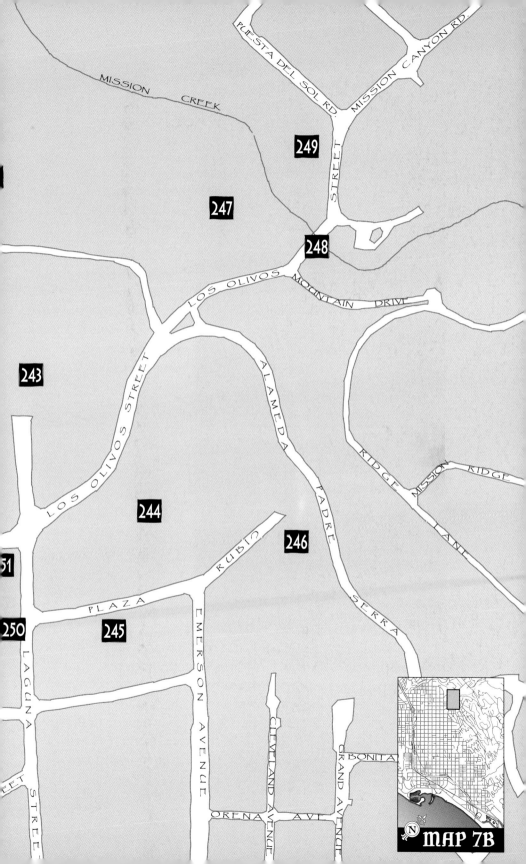

MISSION CREEK

FIESTA DEL SOL RD.

MISSION CANYON RD.

STREET

249

247

MISSION

248

LOS OLIVOS

MOUNTAIN DRIVE

243

LOS OLIVOS STREET

ALAMEDA

PADRE

RIDGE

MISSION RIDGE

LANE

244

RUBIO

246

SERRA

51

PLAZA

250

245

LAGUNA

EMERSON AVENUE

CLEVELAND AVENUE

GRAND AVENUE

BONITA

STREET

ORENA AVE

243.
2201 Laguna Street at East Los Olivos Street
Mission Santa Barbara
1796 (back row of rooms of the south convento and
east wall of west convento wing)
1809-11 (front row of convento, front portico and pillars)
1815-20 (present church); Fr. Antonio Ripoll and Jose Antonio Ramirez
1952-53; Oswald Da Ros (façade and tower reconstruction)
1956-58; Howell, Arendt, Mosher, Grant (quadrangles in rear)
1967-68; Kruger-Bensen-Ziemer (Archive-Library wing added to front portico)

Established in 1786, four years after the Royal Presidio of Santa Barbara, by Father Junipero Serra's successor, Fermin de Lasuen, Mission Santa Barbara was located near the Chumash village of Xana'yan in Mission Canyon some distance from the Presidio fort. The mission complex was constructed over a period of 47 years, and the physical development may be divided into 3 stages: wood/brush (wattle) construction, adobe, and stone buildings. The original compound consisted of wattle-and-daub wood-frame buildings surrounded by a wooden stockade. These buildings accommodated the missionaries' needs in the early years, but the construction of permanent quarters began as soon as the wooden structures were in place. The first adobe quadrangle was built between 1787-1794, the second quadrangle to the north of the first, between 1797-1811. No sooner had the adobe complex been completed when Santa Barbara was wracked by a severe earthquake in 1812. The Mission suffered serious damage, requiring another cycle of building. While the quadrangle remained, the church had to be completely rebuilt. This third church was constructed of native sandstone and was built between 1815 and 1820. Father Antonio Ripoll supervised the construction.

A second bell tower was added in 1833, the final piece that gave the Mission its present appearance. Its façade, with engaged Ionic columns, a dentilated cornice and frieze, and a crowning pediment, is based upon a plate in an 18th Century Spanish edition of *The Ten Books of Architecture by Vitruvius*, a Roman architect in the 1st Century B.C. Jose Antonio Ramirez, master mason of Mission San Luis Rey, is believed to have been in charge of the carpentry and

masonry. The labor and artistry of the stone carvings and wall décor were provided by the Chumash craftsmen who lived at the Mission village. The Mission received a facelift to its crumbling facade in 1952-53 by a team of local master masons under the direction of Oswald Da Ros, and though the two towers were rebuilt of poured concrete with grout lines painted on, the Mission façade retains the look of the original and the rest of the 1820 church remains intact. Earthquake retrofit work by Nels Roselund Engineering, including the addition of steel reinforcements to walls and attics of the church and convento was completed in 1997. Mission Santa Barbara finished another rehabilitation in 2015 funded by a grant from the National Park Service's "Save America's Treasures" program, administered by the California Missions Foundation, and by private donations. The projects included the drilling of hydrology wells to measure water intrusion, restoration of the "solstice" window, seismically retrofitting the historic crypt, and repairing the façade and convento wing.

While the Mission water system, whose remains dot the landscape, is original, the Mission's ornamental gardens are not. Paths and plantings in both cemetery and "sacred garden" enclosure are characteristic of the 19th Century.

Mission Area

A plaque on the side of the north tower notes that the Lone Woman of San Nicolas Island, whose rescue and death were in 1853, is buried beneath the plaque at the foot of the tower. Her story was inspiration for the book *Island of the Blue Dolphins*. The "sacred garden" in the cloister quadrangle today features flowerbeds and California fan palms (Washingtonia filifera) and is not typical of original mission era gardens, which were entirely utilitarian. An extensive olive orchard was once located in front of the Mission and east of Los Olivos Street. The street is named for the orchard. Original trees dot the southwest corner of the Mission property and adjacent private homes on Garden Street. Near the 1808 fountain and lavanderia an original mission grape was planted on the fence which protects the laundry pool basin from damage from climbing and wheeled sports. Both the fountain and the lavanderia were fed by an underground clay pipe system of aqueducts that came from nearby reservoirs, part of an extensive system that stretched into Mission and Rattlesnake Canyons.

The Mission huerta, or food gardens, were also once irrigated with water from the nearby reservoirs. The original Indian pueblo, or village, to the south of the Mission was located in the vicinity of the Stations of the Cross olive grove and extended to the southwest across Garden Street. Adobe buildings had decayed in the 19th Century after abandonment in the Mexican era. Only footings were visible in the mid-20th Century and were covered by parking areas. The northwestern portion of the original Chumash Mission-era village is now the location of La Huerta, a living museum of California Mission-era plants (open by appointment). There is also a small Chumash Ethnobotanical Garden near the front convento steps that displays native plants traditionally utilized by the local Native Americans.

Mission Santa Barbara, the only one of the California Missions that has been in continuous use as a house of worship, continues to play a prominent role in the life of the city. The Mission hosts such major public events as La Fiesta Pequena, the opening of Santa Barbara's annual Fiesta celebration,

and I Madonnari, an annual street painting festival which draws partic-
ipants from all parts of the community and thousands of visitors to the
Mission's grounds. This magnificent structure, so carefully preserved by
generations of caring Santa Barbarans, truly deserves its title "Queen of
the Missions." It is a City Landmark, a State Historical Landmark, and a
National Historic Landmark. There are several commemorative plaques at
the Mission. **NHL, NR, CHL, SBL**

244.
East and North of Mission Santa Barbara
Mission Historical Park
acquired by the city, 1928-1939, 1948

After the earthquake in
1925, the Franciscan fathers
were forced to sell land in
order to pay for needed
Mission repairs. Mrs. J.
A. Andrews, for whom
Plaza Rubio was designed,
joined with several other
socially prominent women
to raise money in order to
aid the city in its efforts
to acquire the open land
between the Mission and
Plaza Rubio. Their purpose
was to keep residential development from obscuring
the view of the Mission's
impressive eastern eleva-
tion. This section contains
an aqueduct, a large lawn
area, and the A. C. Postel
Memorial Rose Garden.

Aqueduct

The smaller portion above Alameda Padre Serra was given to the city by
the padres in 1948. This portion of the park contains most of the mission era
ruins: the aqueduct and upper reservoir (ca. 1807), grist mill (1807), filter house
(1806), and pottery (1808). A tannery (1802) was located in the "rustic" portion

Grist mill

of the park below Alameda Padre Serra. A lower reservoir, built in 1806 and situated next to the intersection of Los Olivos Street and Mountain Drive, continued to serve the city water system into the 20th century. The entire mission water system was designated an Historic Civil Engineering Landmark by the American Society of Civil Engineers in 1976 and a commemorative plaque was placed by the Society in 2001. There are other plaques in the park. **CHL, SBL**

245.
East of Mission Historical Park
400 Block of Plaza Rubio
1925-1926; Mary Craig (except 412)

Architecturally and conceptually this group of Spanish Colonial Revival homes, combined with Mission Historical Park, represent a notable early achievement in design and urban planning in Santa Barbara. Mrs. J. A. Andrews commissioned Mary Craig to design most of the group, giving special attention to the relationship of the individual houses to one another and to the Mission. A publicly owned paseo, which was incorporated into the original subdivision design, links Plaza Rubio to Padre Street.

Plaza Rubio is named after Father José Gonzales Rubio, the last of the California missionaries to come to Santa Barbara. Parishioners so admired the distinguished Franciscan that they kidnapped him in 1856 in hopes that their aggressive display of affection would dissuade him from leaving the Mission. They succeeded, and he lived out his life in Santa Barbara. An 1883 account described Father Rubio as an "accomplished linguist and genial gentleman."

246.
530 Plaza Rubio
Dardi-Patterson House
1927; George Washington Smith

Sandstone and brick steps lead gracefully to the oversized arched entryway which opens into the courtyard of this two-story Spanish Colonial Revival residence. Sited to overlook the village-like grouping of the houses below, this hillside home was designed for Mrs. J. A. Andrews, the creator of Plaza Rubio. It was the last of the group to be built and, along with the others, was constructed by local contractors, Davidson and Maitland. Beautiful as her creation was, Mrs. Andrews own home was on Mission Ridge. She also developed property on Plaza Bonita.

247.
505 East Los Olivos Street
"Mission Hill" 1885
"Dial House" 1916
St. Mary's Retreat House
(Mount Calvary Monastery)

The one and two-story gabled house, called Mission Hill, as was the estate on which it stands, was constructed in 1885 for Rowland Hazard, a transplanted Rhode Islander, after he purchased the property from Dr. S. B. P. Knox. Hazard, knowledgeable in the art of stonemasonry, noted the skilled work of Joe Dover as the latter erected the large stone wall for the Mission fronting Los Olivos Street, and engaged him in 1891 to extend that wall across his own property, and construct the entryway to Mission Hill. In 1916, Hazard's son, Rowland G. Hazard, built the large Tudor Revival house. It was called Dial House because it was situated close to a sundial which Hazard Sr. had mounted on an aqueduct wall on his property. The Hazards' daughter, Caroline, retired to Santa Barbara after serving as President of Wellesley College from 1899 to 1910. She took a personal interest in community affairs, especially during the 1920s, acting as one of a group of women who assisted the city in purchasing the land that is now part of Mission Historical Park, and in initiating construction of the Museum of Natural History.

During World War II, Dial House was leased to American Women's Voluntary Services, which used it as a shelter for the wives of wounded soldiers and a residence for war brides. For a short time in the 1950s both houses were utilized by the University of California, Santa Barbara, sororities. In 1955 the complex became a convent and retreat house for the Anglican Sisters of the Holy Nativity. Just recently, after more than fifty years in residence, the Sisters left, and the complex is now the Mount Calvary Monastery of the Holy Cross Benedictines of the Episcopal Church.

248.
East Los Olivos Street/Mission Canyon Road at Mountain Drive
Mission Creek Bridge
1891; Dover and Woods

This magnificent sandstone arch, easily visible from Rocky Nook Park, is the oldest extant bridge in Santa Barbara County, and one of the oldest in the state. Joe Dover, the chief builder, learned to cut stone during his brief naval career in the late 1870s and early 1880s. He told an interviewer in 1922 that "he had studied the fine stonework of naval docks," and later 'tried to achieve [a similar] strength and symmetry in his own work." When Dover returned to Santa Barbara in the mid-1880s, he took up stonemasonry and it became

his occupation until his death in 1930. This bridge is an enduring testament to his skill and artistry. Built at a cost of $2250, the bridge opened in October, 1891. On October 21st, 1891, the *Daily Independent* reported "The new bridge over Mission Creek is completed, and is certainly an ornamental as well as substantial piece of work."

The nearby water trough at the corner of Mountain Drive and East Los Olivos Street was commissioned by Mrs. G. S. J. Oliver in 1910 in memory of her husband. George Robson was the stonemason. **SBL**

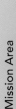

249.
2559 Puesta Del Sol Road
Santa Barbara Museum of Natural History
1922-23, 1926; Floyd E. Brewster
1927-1928, 1932-33, 1934; Carleton M. Winslow
1938; 1953, 1956-57; Chester Carjola
1960; Chester Carjola and Frank Greer
1962; Arendt, Mosher and Grant
1989; Edwards-Pitman

The birth of what has become Santa Barbara's magnificent Museum of Natural History came with the founding of the rather esoteric Museum of Comparative Oology (the study of bird eggs) in 1916. Six years later, Caroline Hazard and her sister-in-law, Mary P. Hazard (See entry #247) gave a portion of their estate, Caroline donating the land and Mary providing funding, to the fledgling museum in memory of Rowland G. Hazard, who had died in 1918. Construction began that same year on the original building, which consisted of a central patio surrounded by a square of single rooms, and the path to a broader based, more significant institution was open. A tile tablet frame and a fountain, crafted by Gladding, McBean and Co. in 1922, memorializes Mr. Hazard. The first large wing to be added was the Indian Hall in 1926, designed by architect Floyd Brewster. Later additions to the rapidly expanding museum included Botany Hall, Mammal Hall, and the Library, constructed in 1927-1928, the Junior Nature Center, 1932-33, and Bird Hall and laboratories in 1934. This group constitutes one of Carleton Winslow's largest and most successful projects in Santa Barbara. The Fleischmann Lecture Hall, designed by Chester Carjola, was built in 1938 with a bequest from Santa Barbara benefactor, Max C. Fleischmann. Carjola also designed the original Geology and Marine Halls in 1953, and the Gladwin Planetarium in 1956-1957. The whole cluster is a beautiful example of the Spanish Colonial Revival style of the 1920s. The Chase-Coggeshall Bird Habitat Hall, designed by Carjola and Greer, was added in 1960. Two years later the Hale-Rett building was added, and, in 1989, a major addition to that structure was designed by Edwards-Pitman.

Throughout all of this building and adding to what was becoming a major local asset, as well as a nationally prominent institution, the architecture remained generally true to the Santa Barbara ideal.

The unusual sandstone wall with the sawtooth top which fronts the Museum entrance and runs along the west side of Mission Canyon Road was constructed by master mason Joe Dover in 1891 (See entry #248). Dover once remarked that he considered this to have been his best work. Drawing upon English antecedents, and utilizing a variety of tricks to "antique" the wall, Dover created an appropriate outline for the property that would eventually house the museum.

Time takes its toll on everything, including the best of the past, and the museum is now engaged in a program designed to restore the sense of the original Museum, rehabilitating the initial structures to bring them up to modern standards and needs, including seismic retrofit, removing some of the structural add-ons stylistically incompatible with the originals, and returning the natural setting closer to its origins. In keeping with Santa Barbara's Hispanic style, the Museum of Natural History is modernizing without sacrificing its past. **SBSM**

250.
2100 Block of Laguna and Garden Streets (Mid-Block)
Junípero Plaza Gate Posts

1904-1905

This pair of beautiful sandstone entryways, together with a similar, but lesser pair at the other end of this small street, bookend an exclusive residential area near Mission Santa Barbara. The Junípero Plaza tract was subdivided in early 1905 by T. D. Wood and Edward F. R. Vail, and the fashionable homes in the tract, along Junípero Plaza and the 300 block of East Los Olivos Street, were built in the decade that followed. The master stonemason who designed and built these entrances is unknown, but many people practiced the craft in Santa Barbara in the late 19th and early 20th Centuries. It may have been a masonry contractor of Scottish or English background. The superior workmanship and massive size of these extraordinary structures make them particularly noteworthy, even in an area where sandstone walls, hitching posts, and curbs are abundant.

The Windmill Palms (Trachycarpus fortunei) on Junípero Plaza are native to China and are characterized by a thick mat of hair-like fiber on their slender trunks.

251.
340 East Los Olivos Street
Edwards House
1911; Bliss and Faville

Although built in the same decade as the other houses along this block of East Los Olivos Street, this gambrel-roofed Colonial Revival dwelling stands in direct contrast to the Hispanic designs of the others. It was built as a honeymoon cottage for John S. Edwards and his wife, Ruth. John Edwards, his father, and his brothers were all prominent bankers in Santa Barbara.

252.
333 Junípero Plaza (Formerly 326 East Los Olivos Street)
Dibblee House
1909; Francis T. Underhill

Partially screened from view by a high wall along Los Olivos Street, the Dibblee House is noteworthy as an early Spanish design by Francis T. Underhill, who, for a period of a decade, practiced architecture and landscape design in Santa Barbara. Underhill, who designed this U-plan house for his mother-in-law, Francisca de la Guerra Dibblee, successfully combined Classical and Spanish elements to create a stately and elegantly simple mansion. **SBL**

253.
316 East Los Olivos Street
Vaughn House
1914; Russel Ray and Winsor Soule

In 1914, original owners Reginald and Miriam Vaughn engaged Ray and Soule to design this large Hispanic brick and stucco home. Soule was highly accomplished in the style, and this house reflects his proficiency as well as his sensitivity to the area around the Mission.

254.
306 East Los Olivos Street
Dennison House
1916; Russel Ray and Winsor Soule

The Dennison House was the last of these three impressively large Hispanic houses to be built along this block. The original owners, Mary and Charles Dennison, were prominent Bostonians who owned the Dennison Paper Company. The high stucco walls and wrought iron gates shield the house from view, but they also combine with the luxuriously landscaped surroundings to create a villa-like setting in an urban situation.

255.
232 East Los Olivos Street
Frothingham House
1922; George Washington Smith

George Washington Smith, Santa Barbara's premier practitioner of the Spanish Colonial Revival style, designed this home for original owner Brooks Frothingham, thus contributing his insight into the generally Hispanic neighborhood below the Mission. A terraced garden is located in the back, between the two wings of the L-shaped house. **SBL**

256.
2210 Garden Street
Junípero Serra Hall
1929-1930; Ross Montgomery

This Spanish Colonial Revival meeting hall was designed by Los Angeles church architect Ross Montgomery. He received the second honor award from the Santa Barbara Plans and Planting Committee's 1929 design jury for civic and commercial architecture. Its rectangular plan and low-pitched roof suggest an earlier tradition of adobe construction, a design that befits the hall's namesake. It is titled, of course, for Father Junípero Serra, the Franciscan padre who was placed in charge of all the Alta California missions from the late 1760s until his death in 1784, and who was present at the founding of Santa Barbara's Presidio in 1782.

The three large olive trees in the garden of Junípero Serra Hall are remnants of the original olive orchard which once occupied this area and from which the name of Los Olivos Street is derived.

257.
2300 Garden Street
St. Anthony's Seminary
1899-1901; Brother Adrian Wewer, OFM
1926 Chapel and tower; Ross Montgomery
2009-2010; Machin and Mead

The former St. Anthony's Seminary is a complex of several elaborately detailed buildings. In keeping with Santa Barbara, the dominant architectural style is Spanish Colonial Revival, and the buildings offer a variety of construction techniques:

sandstone, stucco over wood frame, and poured concrete. Ornate towers, arches, pillars, engaged columns and quoins dress the buildings, which are linked together by covered passageways, while gatepost studded sandstone walls define and enhance the perimeter. Although the Seminary was founded in 1896, its first permanent home was a magnificent three-story sandstone structure which opened in 1901. It was enlarged in 1923 by the addition of a study hall, classrooms and a dormitory. The earthquake of 1925 severely damaged the building,

and, during the reconstruction, it was deemed safer to rebuild the upper two stories with wood frame and stucco. In 1926 another wing was added, as well as a new chapel and tower, the latter designed by Ross Montgomery. Gladding, McBean and Co. manufactured the architectural terra cotta. A number of other changes have been made over the years, including a new dormitory (1939-1940), and a swimming pool in 1945. The east kitchen wing was added in 1949.

The Seminary was closed in 1987. The complex was eventually sold in 2006 to the San Roque Charitable Trust, which took on the task of retrofitting the buildings to meet modern earthquake standards. The classic structures, currently used for several schools, still dominate the hill beside the Mission. **SBL**

258.
2420 Garden Street
Hoffmann House
1922; James Osborne Craig; Florence Yoch and Lucile Council,
landscape architects

James Osborne Craig designed "Casa Santa Cruz" for Bernhard and Irene Hoffmann, leaders in the 1920s movement to encourage the creation of an Hispanic image for Santa Barbara's streetscapes. The house is one of the city's grandest versions of the Rural Andalusian Tradition. It opens onto south and north terraces, the latter of which is perched on the brink of the hill with an expansive view of Santa Barbara's backdrop of mountains. A fragment of the Spanish gardens laid out by Pasadena landscape architects Florence Yoch and Lucile Council can still be seen west of the house.

Hoffmann, a native of Massachusetts, was trained as an engineer at Cornell University, after which he held a position with the New York Telephone Company until 1916. He first came to Santa Barbara in 1920, and he and his wife soon established a winter residence here. Like many professional engineers of his generation, Hoffmann had a keen interest in the burgeoning city planning movement, and, in the 1920s, he joined with others to institute Santa Barbara's first attempts to control building and development. Among the Hoffmanns' many projects were the partial restoration of the De la Guerra adobe and the construction of El Paseo which surrounds it, also designed by Craig. Hoffmann's civic leadership earned him the respect and admiration of many Santa Barbarans. He continued to spend part of each year in the city he helped redesign until his death in 1949 at his summer home in Stockbridge, Massachusetts. Casa Santa Cruz, the Hoffmanns' winter home for many years, was acquired by St. Anthony's Seminary in 1940 and was turned into its library. With the closing of the Seminary in 1987, and the subsequent liquidation of its assets, Hoffmann House once again became a private residence. It has been restored by its devoted owners, Tanny and Kent Hodgetts. **SBSM**

259.
2401 Garden Street
Boyd House
1929; George Washington Smith
2003 addition; Ferguson-Ettinger

While George Washington Smith is usually associated with Santa Barbara's Hispanic tradition, he, like his contemporaries, could work as well in a variety of historic modes. The Boyd House, built for Scott Lee Boyd, is a story-and-a-half French Norman cottage, similar to others Smith designed in Montecito. All of the elements of French Norman imagery are present, but, as in the case with all of his buildings, they have been simplified and highly abstracted. From 1943 until his death in 1968, Dwight Murphy, a city park commissioner, famous palomino breeder, and Fiesta El Presidente, resided here. A large addition was attached to the home in 2003.

260.
215 East Los Olivos Street
Monastery of Poor Clares
1904; two houses
1929-1930; Brother Leonard, designer
1935; addition
1956 additions and remodel; Howell, Arendt, Mosher & Grant
1986 additions; Ernest A. Watson
1999 mausoleum; Ernest A. Watson

Completing the set of Mission related buildings in the neighborhood is the Monastery of Poor Clares. The Order of Sisters of Poor Clare came to Santa Barbara from Oakland in 1928. They purchased two houses at this location, the Stewart Edward White house and the Wingate-Culley house, both built in 1904. White, a well-known writer of Western stories, had lived on and off in Santa Barbara since the 1880s, and he and his wife occupied the house from 1904 to 1916. Undaunted by the Depression, the small delegation of six Sisters undertook the building of a chapel and monastery in 1929. Brother Leonard, who designed the building, chose the Mission Revival style, presumably to complement the Mission up the street. The scalloped parapet and the deeply recessed quatrefoil and stained glass windows are particularly noteworthy details. The complex was enlarged in 1935 when a one-story convent residence was added, and in 1956 some major changes were made. The Wingate-Culley house, which had been used as refectory, kitchen and workrooms since 1930, was demolished, and replaced by a large addition to the chapel. The cloister was also substantially altered at that time, and a mausoleum was added in 1999. But the Los Olivos Street front still reflects the original, and continues to grace the city with its formal façade.

261.
2010-2050 Garden Street
Crocker Row
1894-1895; Arthur Page Brown

In the late 19th century, when few homes were located near the Mission, William H. Crocker of San Francisco, in November of 1893, commissioned the office of Arthur Page Brown to design these five houses. Brown, a prominent San Francisco architect, had earlier designed Crocker's Nob Hill mansion. Before construction of the entire group was complete, a San Francisco newspaper advertisement listed them as "exclusive rentals for affluent winter visitors." The five houses were among the first in Santa Barbara to be designed as a group, and architect Brown stepped up each of the houses along the street so that all of them could have a clear ocean view. Architecturally, they are

early and excellent examples of the Mission Revival style, made popular by the California Building at the 1893 Chicago World's Columbian Exposition, and at the San Francisco Mid-Winter Exposition held in Golden Gate Park in 1894. In addition to the familiar scalloped parapet, typical of the Mission Revival style, window details further distinguish these residences: a quatrefoil (at 2010 Garden), a sunburst patterned bullseye (at 2014 Garden), and pointed arch windows in four of the houses.

The 300 pound bronze dog statue on the front lawn of 2010 Garden Street has been poised there since 1904, when the Warren Willits family moved it with them from Three Rivers, Michigan. The lifelike, but larger than life-size, canine sentry was sculpted in memory of a family pet whose birthday coincided with that of a Willits daughter. The memorialized pet, contrary to local legend, is not buried beneath the sculpture. Occasionally costumed for special holidays, the dog has become a familiar and beloved part of the Santa Barbara scene.

Original, now old, trees still grace the row including a Deodar Cedar (*Cedrus deodara*) and many fine Palm trees. Perhaps most notable is the pair of Chilean Wine Palms (*Jubaea chilensis*) which were introduced into the area by nurseryman Kinton Stevens.

262.
500 James Fowler Road
Santa Barbara Municipal Airport, Earle Ovington Terminal
1942; Edwards and Plunkett

The beginnings of the Santa Barbara airport date back to the heyday of aviation, when Gordon Sackett and Royce Stetson opened the Goleta airport in a swampy cow pasture near the corner of Hollister and Fairview Avenues in 1928. A couple of years later the General Western Aero Corporation moved to Goleta, giving the nascent facility some stability. Two airstrips in the city of Santa Barbara were closed, and it was apparent that Goleta was an excellent site for the local airport, being far enough outside the city to have room to expand without disturbing a large population, yet close enough to be convenient. During the Depression, Santa Barbara received a large federal grant to build an airport on the site. The prominent Santa Barbara architectural firm of Edwards and Plunkett was hired, and as the leading practitioners of the Spanish Colonial Revival style, showcased its talent in the new terminal structure, investing it with arched entrances, a tower, with an outdoor circular stairway, balcony, timbered ceilings, and a host of other appropriate details, creating a unique and charming entrance to the city for air travelers.

The United States Marine Corps took over the airport for the duration of World War II, training fighter pilots for the Pacific Theater, and making major improvements to the site. Postwar, the property was deeded back to the public, with UCSB receiving the high ground, and Santa Barbara get-

One of two remaining original hangars

ting the airport proper. Since Santa Barbara County was not interested in operating the site, the city was left with the problem of how to run an airport which was not on connected city property. In the 1950s, with a series of machinations worthy of Machiavelli, Santa Barbara City annexed a strip of ocean 300 feet wide and 37,000 feet long from downtown to the airport, making the site a proper part of the city. In 1969, the city named the terminal in honor of Earle Ovington, pioneer aviator.

As the 21st century dawned, it was deemed necessary to expand the Santa Barbara airport terminal to accommodate the ever increasing passenger load being serviced. The architectural firm of Phillips, Metsch, Sweeney and Moore utilized Spanish Colonial designs in the new terminal, and the old one, beloved by the whole community for its charm, was incorporated into the new building design. It was moved to the new terminal site, and in keeping with Santa Barbara's tradition, its placement was based on, in the words of architect Fred Sweeney, "the spatial relationship of the patio at the beautiful and historic El Paseo designed by James Osborne Craig in 1922." Now a museum housing the history of Santa Barbara's numerous aeronautic pioneers, the Ovington Terminal still serves the citizens of Santa Barbara as well as its traveling public.

Mission Area

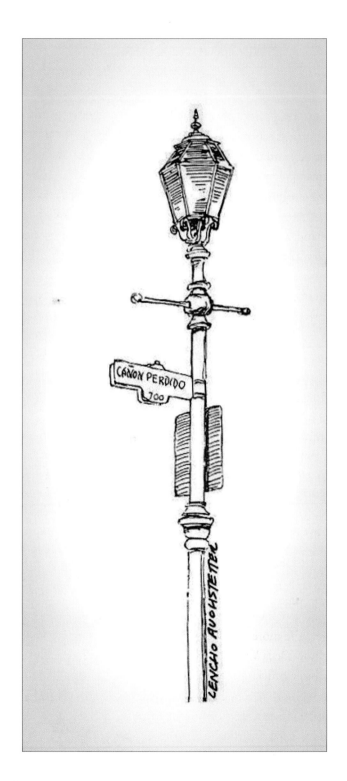

Street Name Glossary

Mary Louise Days

Santa Barbara's street names are among her most fascinating assets. Most of the earliest named streets commemorate events or persons important to the heritage of the city and the state. A subsequent effort to follow the common Anglo-American policy of numbering streets was nullified. The development of residential subdivisions after both world wars led to a need for many more streets, and a significant number of these subdivisions perpetuated the Spanish-language street names found on the city's first official maps.

In January, 1851, the mayor and Common Council contracted with Salisbury Haley to make a survey of the city. On February 1, a three- member committee on streets was appointed; its report was presented and accepted the following week. Two weeks later three men, Eugene Lies, Antonio Maria de la Guerra and Joaquin Carrillo, were appointed "a committee to name the streets about to be laid down on the map of Salisbury Haley." Haley presented his map of boundaries on April 7, 1851. The street names proposed by the committee were apparently accepted, as the August 16 minutes refer to State Street.

The Common Council then saw the necessity for an official map of the Haley survey, and in October, 1852, Vitus Wackenreuder, the county surveyor, proposed to perform the work. After delays caused by "want of a drawing board" and by complicated and unclear property ownership titles, Wackenreuder presented his maps in April, 1853. His written title report refers to "the difficult and tiresome task entrusted to me." In return for his efforts, Vitus Wackenreuder was deeded a waterfront corner property as well as City Block 287, bounded by State, Montecito, Yanonali and Anacapa Streets.

Haley-Wackenreuder Map No. 1 encompasses the area between Mission Street and San Buenaventura Street, and between Robbins Street and Canada Street. The more detailed Map No. 2 includes the area surrounded by Vineyard (now De la Vina), Gutierrez, Laguna and Victoria Streets. These are the city's basic official maps, so declared by Ordinance No. 7.

On July, 29, 1854, the Council appointed a committee of two to "correct the orthography of the names of certain streets as laid down on city maps." This could have been the result of confused spelling of some names and difficult pronunciation of others, such as "Enecapap" (Anacapa).

By the 1860s some of the Spanish words had been translated to English in official documents and maps. In 1873 a newspaper editor demanded that the Indian and Spanish names be abandoned in favor of numbers and letters of the alphabet to aid in direction-finding.

This was not done; however, in 1873 and 1874 the Van Vactor and Myers subdivisions designated their streets above Mission Street as First, Second, Third, Fourth and Fifth Avenues or Streets. In late 1927 the City Council changed these street names to Padre, Los Olivos, Pueblo, Junipero and Quinto, to match the portions east of State Street. A strong effort was also made at that time to return to the use of "Estado" for State Street.

In 1900 a group of citizens had petitioned the County Board of Supervisors to name the roads leading westward from the city. These included Ontare Road, Hope Avenue, Cieneguitas Road and Modoc Road, and most of this land is now in the city.

Post-World-War II subdivisions frequently used saints' names in Spanish, or Spanish words coupled with "calle" (street) or "paseo" (walkway). On Memorial Day 1948, streets at the airport were dedicated to the memory of members of the United States Army Air Force who were killed in World War II. Nine years later the municipal airport area was annexed to the city.

For many years the Planning Commission recommended approval of street names to the City Council. In the late 1960s a street name committee made up of city staff and post office representatives assumed this duty. Attempts were made to establish a policy to prevent mixed Spanish-English street names and to assure correct usage. Since the late 1970s naming of public facilities and streets has been handled by the city administrator and the appropriate departments.

The following street name glossary applies only to streets included in this book. An asterisk indicates an 1851 street.

Anacapa* — The end of the street points to Anacapa Island, one of the Channel Islands, named for the Chumash Indian term for mirage or deception, "Eneapah." Wackenreuder's Map No. 1 spells it "Enecapap" and a later map listed "Enecapa." One of the oldest buildings on the street is the Valdéz House at 1010 Anacapa Street. The wood-frame house was built for Concepción Valdéz ca. 1871. It remained in the family for over 40 years.

Anapamu* — In the Chumash tongue, "anapamu" means "rising place," a high location possessing intense supernatural power.

Arrellaga* —Jose Joaquin de Arrillaga, a Basque native of Spain, was twice interim governor of the Californias during the Spanish period. He was constitutional governor of Alta California from 1804 to 1814. A dedicated patriot, Arrillaga is buried at Mission Soledad in Monterey County.

Bath* — This street name was anglicized from the Spanish "Baños" shown on the 1853 map. The street led directly to the bathing beach at what is now West Beach. At the turn of the twentieth century the first of a series of public bathhouses or swimming pools named "Los Baños del Mar" was constructed at the end of West Cabrillo Boulevard.

Brinkerhoff Avenue — Dr. Samuel Brinkerhoff, a New York native, arrived in Santa Barbara in 1852 and became the community's first Anglo-American doctor. In 1857 he and Lewis Burton bought Blocks 230 and 231 from the city for twenty dollars in gold. After the doctor died in 1880, Block 231 was sold to Henry Tallant and Edward Harper, who divided it. On the official 1886 subdivision map, Brinkerhoff Avenue was the name given the street bisecting the block in memory of the popular physician.

Cabrillo Boulevard —The beach boulevard is named for João Rodrigues Cabrilho, a Portuguese explorer, seaman and navigator. While in the employ of Spain, his two ships discovered Alta California and Santa Barbara Channel in 1542. West Cabrillo Boulevard. was developed first, in the 1890s; the eastern extension came a decade later. The two sections became known as the East and West Boulevard, although for a time in the early 1900s the westerly portion in front of the Potter Hotel was called "Esplanade del Mar." The name "Cabrillo Boulevard" with Spanish spelling became official in 1919.

Calle Puerto Vallarta — Formerly the southerly two blocks of Punta Gorda Street, an 1851 street name, this portion was renamed in honor of one of the city's Sister Cities, Puerto Vallarta, Mexico.

Canon Perdido* —In the Spring of 1848, the American commanding officer of the Presidio discovered that a cannon was missing from the beach. Suspecting an insurrection, Governor Mason fined the town five hundred dollars. A fiesta held on July 4 raised the money, which was to be returned to the town later. The "lost cannon," spirited away by five boys, reappeared during an 1858 storm, but it was later sold for scrap.

Carrillo* — This intersecting main street is named for the prominent early California family which intermarried with most of the other well-known California families. Its members include a Comandante of the Santa Barbara Presidio, Mexican governmental deputies, mayors of Santa Barbara, and the mother of an American governor of California, Romualdo Pacheco.

Castillo* — Another of the streets laid out in 1851, Castillo begins below the hill on which was situated the Presidio's castillo, or defensive gun battery. At other times in its history the high point of land has been the site of Mispu, a Chumash village, and of "Punta del Castillo," the Dibblee family's masonry mansion. Santa Barbara City College is now located on the hill.

Chapala* — This street could be named for Lake Chapala in Mexico, or for the prison from which Governor Micheltorena recruited some of his unruly troops in the late Mexican period.

Coronel — This short street at the northeasterly edge of the Mesa is named for Antonio Franco Coronel who was born in 1817 in Mexico and came to California in 1834 with the Hijar-Padres expedition. His father Ignacio was a schoolteacher and rancher. Antonio Coronel held several public positions in Los Angeles, including mayor in 1853. The Spanish word coronel means colonel.

Cota* — A crosstown street, it is named for the Cota family, descendants of some of the earliest Spanish Colonial residents in the area. Sargento Pablo Antonio Cota and Soldado Mariano Cota traveled from Mission San Gabriel with Father Serra and Governor Felipe de Neve to found Mission San Buenaventura and the Presidio of Santa Barbara in 1782. Pablo Antonio Cota remained in charge of the escolta at San Buenaventura when the presidio was founded three weeks later. Both men were from Loreto, Baja California, Mexico.

De la Guerra* — The second prominent California family for whom a street was named was that of de la Guerra ("of the war"). Captain Don Jose de la Guerra y Noriega was born in Spain and became the fifth Comandante of the Santa Barbara Presidio. His son Pablo was a signer of the California State Constitution, a state senator and a judge. Several family members were Santa Barbara mayors or council presidents. De la Guerra Street passes in front of Casa de la Guerra. The former family home faces Plaza de la Guerra.

De la Vina* — Earlier called Vineyard, the lengthy street traversed a vineyard said to have been planted by Comandante Felipe de Goicoechea during presidio times. For a number of years, the uppermost portion of the street was named Hollister Avenue.

Equestrian Avenue — This short street commemorates a livery stable, "The Saddle Horse Parlors," at 225-27 Equestrian Avenue, in operation during the 1890s and 1900s. The building still exists. The oldest residence on the avenue is the Calder House at 206-208 Equestrian Avenue. Built on the corner of Santa Barbara Street in 1876, it was moved eastward in 1924. It is a Santa Barbara landmark.

Figueroa* — Jose Figueroa was governor of Mexican Alta California from 1833 to 1835. A native Mexican, he had earlier served as comandante-general of the Sonora-Baja California district. He was sympathetic to the Indians and encouraged establishment of schools. Figueroa is buried at Santa Barbara Mission.

Garden* — Wackenreuder's Map No. 1 shows this street name in both Spanish and English, "Jardines" and "Garden." The street passes through the site of the Presidio's vegetable and fruit gardens, also called de la Guerra gardens, which were in the vicinity of Ortega and Cota Streets.

Haley* — In deference to the sea captain who surveyed the town in 1851, Santa Barbara's street naming committee named Haley Street for Salisbury Haley. Problems with the survey led to later legal and political quarrels, but the central city was developed in accordance with it.

James Fowler Road — The street at the municipal airport upon which the John T. Rickard terminal faces is named for U.S. Marine Lieutenant James L. Fowler, a pilot who, in 1944, was lost in action in the Pacific.

Junípero Plaza — This charming block-long street was developed as the centerpiece of the Junípero Tract at the beginning of the twentieth century. It is distinguished by two sets of ornate stone gate posts and metal gates, one at each end of the avenue. The words "Plaza Junípero" are incised into the upper area of the stone structures. The name commemorates the religious name given to Saint Junípero Serra when he became a member of the Franciscan order.

Laguna* — On the 1852 Coast Survey map a "Laguna" or "lagoon, pond" is shown in the vicinity of Laguna and Ortega Streets. Maps of the 1870s also recorded the lagoon extending from the "estero" or "estuary" to the southeast.

Lloyd Avenue — This block-long street is named for the Lloyd family, which owned property in the block. Its most prominent member was Clio Lloyd, who became mayor in 1909. He held other public positions as well.

Los Olivos — This street, called Second Avenue for many years, was renamed for the graceful olive trees in the vicinity of the Mission. The first olive trees were brought to California by the Franciscans who founded the missions.

Los Patos Way — "Pato" means "duck," and this portion of the historic Old Coast Highway, the former Highway 101, was named in 1968 for the ducks in the nearby Andrée Clark Bird Refuge.

Mason* — Richard B. Mason, military governor of California from 1847 to 1849, was the official who assessed the $500 fine for the "lost cannon," so the 1851 street-naming committee christened this street in his honor.

Micheltorena* — Manuel Micheltorena (a Basque name), was Mexican governor of California from 1842 to 1845. He was faced with the unrest prevalent during the period prior to the American takeover. Micheltorena tried to get along with the Californios and to save some of the missions, but events were moving too quickly.

Milpas* — This word is Central American and Mexican usage for a maize field or vegetable garden. In 1851 the street-naming committee recognized the rich soil of the east side, suitable for farms and orchards.

Mission* — Mission Santa Barbara was founded December 4, 1786, by Father Fermin de Lasuen, who succeeded Father Junipero Serra as father president of the missions and is credited with California's major period of mission expansion. The street closest to Mission Santa Barbara on Haley's survey is named for it, although spelled in English, not the Spanish "mision."

Mission Canyon Road — The "Queen of the Missions" sits at the mouth of a beautiful wooded canyon with a rushing creek, originally called

Arroyo Pedregoso for its stony terrain. Later the canyon became a popular excursion area, known as "Mission Cañon" or "Mission Canyon"

Montecito* — Another 1851 street, this one points in the direction of Montecito, or "little woods," the suburb to the east. Father Serra had hopes of founding the Mission at Montecito in 1782; this did not happen, but a village of Presidio soldiers' families grew up in the area.

Mountain Drive — Named for the Santa Ynez Mountains, whose foothills and southerly flanks it ascends, Mountain Drive, which begins at the Mission, has been a favorite excursion route since the late 19th century.

Natoma Avenue — This street in the 1924 Ambassador Tract commemorates a Chumash princess in "Natoma," a Victor Herbert opera first performed in Philadelphia in 1911.

Niños Drive — In 1965 the street next to Sycamore Creek, at East Beach, was named "Niños" or "children" to commemorate the city park called A Child's Estate, to which it leads. The park land was previously the John and Lillian Child estate.

Olive — The original name of this street was Canal, Spanish for channel, because it led to the Santa Barbara Channel, avoiding the nearby estero. In the 1920s the name was changed to Olive Street and olive trees were planted in the parkway. Later in the century many of the trees were removed.

Ortega* — Jose Francisco de Ortega, a native of Mexico, was a founder of the city in 1782 and the first Comandante of the Spanish Royal Presidio. Prior to this Ortega had explored Alta California with the 1769 Portola expedition. This is one of a series of streets named in 1851 for well-known California families.

Plaza Rubio — This charming street, part of the 1925 subdivision of the same name, honors Father Jose Gonzales Rubio, beloved Franciscan missionary of the late Mexican and early American eras.

Por la Mar Drive — In the early 1920s the Cabrillo Park Tract was developed near East Beach, and this street, meaning "by the sea," was included in it.

Puesta del Sol Road — Located partly in the city and partly in unincorporated county area, this road leads to the west where the sun rests; hence the name "sunset."

Punta Gorda* — This 1851 street points toward a promontory or "fat point." It is one of the most easterly of the Haley Survey streets.

Santa Barbara*—The channel, the Presidio, the Mission, and the city are all named for Saint Barbara, patroness of sailors, artillerymen, and protectress against explosion or lightning. This naming sequence began when the sea expedition of Sebastian Viscaino entered the channel waters on December 3, 1602, the eve of Saint Barbara's feastday. In 1851 the city fathers continued the tradition in a street which was aligned with the Presidio.

Shoreline Drive—A blufftop road with an unobstructed view of the Pacific Ocean was developed on the Mesa with the Marine Terrace Subdivisions of the 1950s. Within fifteen years the most southwesterly portion of Cabrillo Boulevard, near the site of Fossil Hill and Punta del Castillo, had been renamed "Shoreline Drive" to join a newly constructed road climbing from Leadbetter Beach to the original blufftop Shoreline Drive.

Sola*—Pablo Vicente Sola served as the last Spanish governor of California, from 1815 to early 1822. Although an opponent of revolution, the haughty Basque native swore allegiance to Mexico in April, 1822, and served as Mexican governor until November.

State*—The city's main street received two names on the 1853 Wackenreuder maps, "Estado" and its English version "State." On the No. 1 map the first four blocks are called "Estado" and the blocks on the other side of the cluster of downtown adobe houses are called "State." The No. 2 map calls the entire main street "State Street," honoring the new State of California. Apparently the latter name was common then, as the council minutes for late 1851 refer to it. In the 1870s parts of the central area of State Street were graded and opened. The street was paved with asphalt in 1887. Official maps used the name "State Street," as did early guidebooks. After the 1925 earthquake, when Hispanic architectural themes were being widely promoted, the City was urged to change the name to "Estado" or "Calle Estado." The old maps were reviewed, and for a time "Estado" received wide usage. Newspaper articles in late 1927 praised the resumption of the name, and business addresses used "Estado" for the next few years. By the 1930s, however, "State" was again appearing in advertisements. The 1924 Olmsted-Cheney plan for the street and park system used "State," but architectural design articles such as the 1926 "New Santa Barbara" used the Spanish version. The 1941 WPA guidebook to Santa Barbara comments "State Street (Calle del Estado) is the main business thoroughfare." A "Paseo Estado" is proposed in the city's General Plan, adopted in 1964: "Particular and special treatment...so that...the principal street in Santa Barbara reflects the character of the town." At one time, the Landmarks Committee recommended that downtown street signs carry the double appellation "Calle del Estado/State Street."

Valerio*—This 1851 street, according to different sources, is named either for an Indian who may have been a mountain cave dweller, living off the land, or for a robber.

Victoria*—Manuel Victoria was a Spanish/Native American military figure who served as Mexican governor of California from 1831 to 1832. He disapproved of secularization of the Missions and took stern measures against wrongdoers. Californio insurgents drove Victoria out of office. This is the final street in our 1851 series named for California governors.

Yanonali*—The great Chumash, Yanonali, was chief of the large village of Syuxtun at West Beach, and leader of the South Coast rancherias. He cooperated in the establishment of the Presidio, and was baptized a Christian several years later. Yanonali (Yanonalit, Yanunali) was memorialized in one of the city's original streets, a street which passes the site of Syuxtun.

* **An asterisk indicates an 1851 street**

Biographies

REBECCA CONARD, Ph.D. is Professor Emerita of History and former Director of Public History at Middle Tennessee State University. She received her Ph.D. from the University of California, Santa Barbara, and her M.A. from U.C.L.A. In the course of her career, she has co-founded two historical research firms and worked extensively with national, state, and local-level agencies. She is a past president of the National Council on Public History. In addition to co-authoring the original edition of *Santa Barbara ~ A Guide to El Pueblo Viejo*, she has published widely on the history of parks and protected areas, historical/cultural landscapes, and the history of public history. Major publications include *Places of Quiet Beauty: Parks, Preserves and Environmentalism* (1997), *Benjamin Shambaugh and the Intellectual Foundations of Public History* (2002), and *"All Men and Women are Created Equal": An Administrative History of Women's Rights National Historical Park* (2012).

MARY LOUISE DAYS is a native Santa Barbaran and fifth generation Californian. She was employed by the City of Santa Barbara's Planning office from 1961 to the end of 1996. She was staff to the Historic Landmarks Commission for thirty years, as well as the Planning Commission. Miss Days earned degrees in history from Santa Barbara City College and the University of California, Santa Barbara. For many years she has served on the board of the Santa Barbara Trust for Historic Preservation and is a past president. A member of several other boards, she holds positions with the Native Daughters of the Golden West. Miss Days has written numerous chapters and articles of historic interest, the book *Park Histories, City of Santa Barbara*, and an architectural highlights brochure. She supervised production and wrote portions of the 1986 first edition of *Santa Barbara ~ A Guide to El Pueblo Viejo*.

RICHARD E. OGLESBY, Ph.D. is a retired Professor of Western American and California History at the University of California, Santa Barbara, and has nurtured his long term interest in historic preservation as a longtime Board Member of the Santa Barbara Trust for Historic Preservation and The Santa Barbara Conservancy. He participated in the production of the Conservancy's first publication, *Stone Architecture in Santa Barbara*.

CHRISTOPHER H. NELSON, Ph.D. is a 1985 recipient of the Ph.D. degree in history at the University of California, Santa Barbara. He has performed services for the U.S. Department of the Interior, the State of Maryland, the City of Santa Barbara, and U.C.S.B., specializing in cultural history. In addition to co-authoring the original edition of *Santa Barbara ~ A Guide to El Pueblo Viejo*, he is the author of "Pre-Earthquake Santa Barbara" in *Environmental Hazards and Community Response*, published by the U.C.S.B. Public Historical Studies program, he has also written articles on architecture in Santa Barbara and the West.

DAVID GEBHARD, Ph.D. (1927-1996) was an internationally-known architectural historian, professor, and author. He served for many years as a member of the City of Santa Barbara Historic Landmarks Commission. Dr. Gebhard was educated at the University of Minnesota and taught at the University of California, Santa Barbara. He directed the university's art museum and founded its architectural drawing collection. The facility is now called the U.C.S.B. Art, Design and Architecture Museum. An expert on the works of George Washington Smith and Lutah Maria Riggs, Dr. Gebhard was the author or co-author of books, guides, articles, and exhibition catalogs. He was a past president of the national Society of Architectural Historians and of the Citizens Planning Association of Santa Barbara County.

Aerial view of the Arlington Hotel block soon after the June 29, 1925 earthquake. The former I. Magnin building at 1315 State Street can be seen in the center foreground. The still-existing arched gateway can be seen at the far right corner of the block, between two junipers. (entry #95)

Photography and Artwork Credits

Color Photographs
All color photography by David Jones except for the following:

Credit	Entry No. (Page No.)
Julie and Adam Ross	1
Michael H. Imwalle	7, 40, 41, 116, 132, 134
Bill Dewey	(pp. 18, 19), 130
Jim Bartsch	199
Wayne McCall	203C

Black and White Historical Photographs

Art, Design, & Architecture Museum, University of California at Santa Barbara	Inside front cover and title page, 59, 86
Bancroft Library, UC Berkeley	(pp. 121, 122 [modified by Michael H. Imwalle])
Collection of Mary Louise Days	257 (p. 280)
Collinge Collection, Thomas Schmidt @ SBVintagePhoto.com	3, 7, 28, 29, 36, 40, 50, 55, 87, 116, 121, 149, 158, 158, 170, 187, 217, 219, 243, 251
Gledhill Library, Santa Barbara Historical Museum	6, 8, 32, 39, 64–68, 86, 95, 117-119, 129, 135, 138, 140–143, 157, 164, 177, 178, 223, 239, 248 and (pp. 10, 24, 68, 69, 244)
Hal Boucher Photography	(p. *v*)
Santa Barbara Trust for Historic Preservation	(p. *v*)

Artwork

Steve Hausz	Cover Design and Maps
Lencho Auchstetter	(p. 268)

Index

B

Bachelor Club Lodgings 221
Bagley, J. W. 78
Bailey, A. Godfrey 216
Bandini, Josefa 131
Barbara, Saint 276–277
Barbareño Chumash. *See* Chumash
Barber, Peter J.
  Oceanfront properties 32, 55
  Presidio and Pueblo properties
    East 162, 170, 172
    West 214, 233, 236, 240
  State Street Plaza properties 80, 106, 109
Barber, Thomas P. 200
Barry, Gilbert 53
Batchelder, George 171
Bates, Mrs. West 82
Bathhouses 22, 24, 35, 271
Bath Street 271. *See also* specific properties
Bayer, Herbert 58
Baylor, Margaret 164
Beale, John 62
Beard Motor Company 165
Beauchamp, John 216
Becker, Peter 193
Beittel, Will 47
Bellosguardo 64
Belvedere Apartments 43
Belvedere Hotel 41
Benton, Arthur B. 108, 109
Berkus Design Studios 210
Bern, Millie 222
Biltmore Hotel 57
Bishop Garcia Diego High School 181
Black, Clarence A. 173
Black, David 78
Blake, Anna Sophia 187
Blatter, Hochhauser 78
Bliss and Faville 258
Bliss, Anna Blaksley 243
B'nai B'rith Congregation 198
Bonilla, Florentino 186
Bonilla House 186
Borein, Edward 140
Bothin Building 93
Bothin Helping Fund 79, 81, 88, 93
Bothin, Henry 79, 81
Botiller Adobe 224–225
Botiller, Pascual 224
Boyd House 263
Boyd, Scott Lee 263
Boydston, Jack 186
Bradley Race Track 63

Breakwater and Harbor 36–37
Bregante, Lisa 98
Brewster, Floyd E. 256
Brian Cearnal Associates 167
Brinkerhoff Avenue 271
Brinkerhoff Avenue Landmark District
    213–214. *See also* specific properties
Brinkerhoff, Lucy Noyes 242
Brinkerhoff, Samuel 242, 271
Brinks Grocery 115
Brooks, Clayton 154
Brown, Arthur Page 265
Brownsill, Edwin 169
Brownsill House No. 1 169
Brownsill House No. 2 198
Buenaventura Pico adobe 121, 156
Burton Adobe 40, 121
Burton, Lewis T. 40
Burton Mound 21, 40–41
Bury, David 167

C

Cabrilho, João Rodrigues 271
Cabrillo Ball Field 58
Cabrillo Boulevard 271. *See also* specific
    properties
Cabrillo Pavilion 59
Cadorin, Ettore 143, 171
Calder House 273
California: A Book for Travelers and Settlers
    (book) 21
California Department of Motor Vehicles
    Building 65
California Highway Patrol 65
Calkins, J. W. 179
Callahan, J. J. 237
Callahan, Neal 78, 83
Callejon Carrillo 163
Calle Puerto Vallarta 271. *See also* specific
    properties
Callison Architecture 218
Campbell and Campbell 170
Canary Hotel 226
Cañedo Adobe 151
Cañedo, José María 151
Canon Perdido Street 271–272. *See also* specific
    properties
Carberry, James F. 59
Carjola, Chester L.
  Mission Area properties 256
  Oceanfront properties 65
  Presidio and Pueblo properties 157–158, 219
  State Street Plaza properties 81, 103